Vintage LA

also by

JENNIFER BRANDT TAYLOR

Life Is a Movie Starring You

Vintage  LA

by

JENNIFER BRANDT TAYLOR

photography by

JEANEEN LUND

Collins

An Imprint of HarperCollinsPublishers

FOR

Mrs. Moira and Miss Lizzie

THE ORIGINAL VINTAGE VAMPS

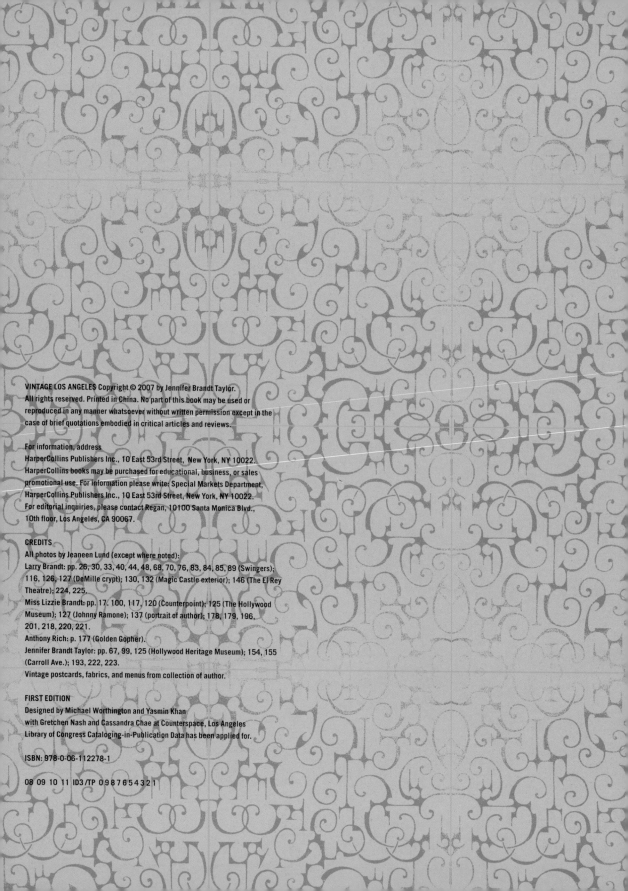

For information, address
HarperCollins Publishers Inc., 10 East 53rd Street, New York, NY 10022.
HarperCollins books may be purchased for educational, business, or sales
promotional use. For information please write: Special Markets Department,
HarperCollins Publishers Inc., 10 East 53rd Street, New York, NY 10022.
For editorial inquiries, please contact Regan, 10100 Santa Monica Blvd.,
10th floor, Los Angeles, CA 90067.

CREDITS
All photos by Jeaneen Lund (except where noted):
Larry Brandt: pp. 26, 30, 33, 40, 44, 48, 68, 70, 76, 83, 84, 85, 89 (Swingers);
116, 126, 127 (DeMille crypt); 130, 132 (Magic Castle exterior); 146 (The El Rey
Theatre); 224, 225.
Miss Lizzie Brandt: pp. 17, 100, 117, 120 (Counterpoint); 125 (The Hollywood
Museum); 127 (Johnny Ramone); 137 (portrait of author); 178, 179, 196,
201, 218, 220, 221.
Anthony Rich: p. 177 (Golden Gopher).
Jennifer Brandt Taylor: pp. 67, 99, 125 (Hollywood Heritage Museum); 154, 155
(Carroll Ave.); 193, 222, 223.
Vintage postcards, fabrics, and menus from collection of author.

FIRST EDITION
Designed by Michael Worthington and Yasmin Khan
with Gretchen Nash and Cassandra Chae at Counterspace, Los Angeles
Library of Congress Cataloging-in-Publication Data has been applied for.

ISBN: 978-0-06-112278-1

08 09 10 11 ID3/TP 0 9 8 7 6 5 4 3 2 1

Gee, Thanks!

Old-Fashioned Silver Screen Kisses to

Judith Regan, for recognizing my passion for vintage and inspiring me to write this book; my sweet and diligent editor Alison Stoltzfus; Jeaneen Lund for your friendship and gorgeous photography; Moira Brandt for your love and set design brilliance; Larry Brandt for always setting my dreams in motion (love you, Dad!); my sister and best friend Miss Lizzie for living her life in Technicolor; everyone at HarperCollins, especially Cassie Jones, Cal Morgan, Richard Ljoenes, Chase Bodine, Kristy Silvernail, Suzanne Wickham, and all the fabulous publicity and production peeps; the mystical muse Jade Gordon; the glamorous Miss Caruso; Brandon Holley; Bob and Julia Stein (I'm keeping my racquet back!); Jessica DiBiase; Cameron Silver; Alix Sloan; Daniel Tures; Marcella Ruble; Donelle Dadigan; Ramesh and Ellen at The Icon for fab photo processing; Denise at Nadine Johnson; The Chateau Marmont; Kenya of Greta Garbage; Alison Zero; Elizabeth Mason; Joe McFate; Douglas Kirkland; Cassandra Kegler; Justin Champion; Ricky Byrd; Eve Babitz for "Slow Days, Fast Company;" and to my supernaturally cool husband, Nic Taylor, for capturing my heart with his thunderwings and beard of stars.

Also, to my star-studded cast: Bob Mackie, Dominick Dunne, Giddle Partridge, The Heartstring Symphony, Irving, Fawn Gehweiler, Janet Klein, Johnny Grant, Kime Buzzelli, Liz Goldwyn, the Denman family, Marion Peck, Mark Ryden, Miss Kimme Aaberg, My Barbarian, Rodney Bingenheimer, Samantha Shelton, and Theadora Van Runkle.

Special thanks to all the proprietors who graciously allowed us to photograph their spaces.

This book has been a lifetime in the making, and in my thirty-plus years of living in Los Angeles, I've met countless colorful individuals who have further inspired my great love for this city. It would be impossible to thank all of you on this page, but rest assured that my memory is long and you will be forever remembered in my nostalgic heart.

Finis.

Jennifer Brandt Taylor

"A town that has to be seen to be disbelieved."
——*Walter Winchell*

INTRODUCTION

Where else in the world can you actually stand in Clark Gable's footprints, attend a séance to meet Houdini's spirit in a haunted castle, drink whiskey while sitting on Bukowski's favorite barstool, watch *Casablanca* under the stars in a historic cemetery, meditate at George Harrison's favorite beachside temple, and ride horses into the sunset under the Hollywood sign?

Every day in L.A. is filled with its own unique cinematic magic, cast with ghosts of glamorous eras gone by—silent movie cowboys, film noir detectives, decadent lotharios, and tragically beautiful bombshells.

Los Angeles is a collage. It's a Technicolor mélange of people, cultures, styles, images, history, and myths. And if L.A. is indeed "the dream factory" or "Tinseltown" or "the glamour capital," or any of the other grandiose names people dub this "LaLaLand," then just imagine the dazzling items that its famous residents discard—that feed its hungry hunters and collectors. This is a city where debonair playboys run their Aston Martin's into trees after too much Veuve Clicquot, and have their houseboy hock their vintage Hermès watch to pay the bail (lucky you). This is a town where Oscar winners and rock 'n' roll divas have nervous breakdowns, move to an ashram, and drop all their Diors off at the Salvation Army (lucky *us*). It's a town full of buried treasure. Thereby, I proclaim Los Angeles the official vintage capital of the world!

Over the years, I've heard many people (mostly New Yorkers and San Franciscans actually) dismiss L.A. for lacking a rich architectural history, but I beg to differ.

This is a town where architecture has flourished, and its vast open spaces and idyllic climate have inspired many of the world's most innovative builders of the last century. It was not only the weather that lured these architects to Los Angeles, but they were practically snake-charmed by the glamorous elite who resided here, and the fact that these entertainment industry characters would undoubtably be in need of their services. L.A. is accessorized with magnificent structures like diamonds on an Oscar nominee. Around the city you will see joints built by Frank Lloyd Wright, John Lautner, Richard Neutra, Paul Williams, Rudolf Schindler, Charles and Ray Eames, Richard Meier, Frank Gehry, and many more. Not to forget the fantastical interior decorators, like Billy Baldwin and Tony Duquette, who decked out the insides of these shrines to design sense, or the visionary men who built our city's historic movie palaces, like Sid Grauman and S. Charles Lee.

Vintage L.A. is an all-encompassing guide for the connoisseur of the used. It's a tome where you'll find no reproductions—all places covered are purely for the true-blue, old-school history seekers and collectors of secondhand coolness. As I was re-exploring my hometown for this book, including places I've been frequenting since birth, my mantra became "give 'em the best of the best." And that's what I've done. I am giving you a tour of Los Angeles' best—the places where you'll have the best experiences, find the best stuff, see the best movies, eat the best food, hear the best music, and all is happening within the best architecture from the best eras. I am an L.A. native who has lived in this town for the past thirty years (since birth), and with this book, I am revealing hundreds of locations—from Anaheim to Venice—and clueing you in to secret spots it's taken me a lifetime to discover.

Vintage is always unique. If you're wearing something vintage, you know the chances are slim to none that anybody else in the room will be wearing the same thing as you. The vintage lifestyle is based on the desire for something well-made and rare. Another upside to being a "vintager" is that if someone happens to recognize what you are wearing, driving, or the hidden old place you are patronizing, then it becomes a unifying experience. Those who love vintage are entered into a secret club—one that naturally finds individualism through a love of history.

You will also meet some of Los Angeles' best vintage lovers and artists, both famous and non, who share an unbridled adoration for this city's glittering history. These people are Los Angeles, and they will give you a list of their own favorite historic haunts, secondhand shops, and personal vintage stories. These are the people who embody the lifestyle of vintage Old Hollywood—they make up this city and keep it glamorous and rich.

I have been a secondhand soul since birth. My parents were both native New Yorkers and were in the women's fashion business throughout the '60s and '70s. They met in L.A. while having a meeting in Downtown's California Apparel Mart. My dad, Larry Brandt, repped a line of mod dresses called Young Edwardian (which I now collect), and he had an appointment to show them to my mom, Moira Hollmen, who was head buyer for Contempo Casuals (back in the '70s, when it catered to a cool, Stevie Nicks-type clientele). She reminded my dad of Diane Keaton in *Annie Hall*, she knew he would always make her laugh, and that's where I come in.

Being raised by a bohemian, one-time antiques dealer and an old-school New York City garmento, I was a vintage-obsessed little girl. I've been collecting vintage all my life and was raised watching black-and-white movies. I have been enamored by the golden age of Hollywood ever since I can remember. Even the hospital I was born in, Cedars of Lebanon in Hollywood, must have had the ghosts of glamour's past watching over me (at least I'd like to think they were). It was the same hospital where Marilyn Monroe would check into whenever she had a breakdown, where Elvis was admitted when he swallowed a tooth cap, and where Liza Minnelli was born.

As kids, my little sister Lizzie and I were obsessed with Vivien Leigh, and we'd watch our videotapes of *Gone with the Wind* until we finally wore them out. We would spend hours in our Studio City home playing dress-up in my mom's collection of 1920s embroidered Art Deco piano shawls, emerald flapper jewelry, floppy straw hats, and gauzy Zandra Rhodes dresses. My first real vintage obsession was a 1950s faux leopard fur, glamour-girl coat that was handed down to me by my mom at the age of fourteen. Let's just say, that at fourteen I couldn't really do this coat justice—especially with my braces. It would've been better suited to Kim Novak, but my vintage collecting mom knew the timing was perfect. It was very formal, entirely innapropriate for my age, and I completely fell in love with it. I wore it with jeans, I wore it with bikinis, I wore it with Chinese pajamas, and I wear it to this day, with black cocktail dresses. It was my introduction into the world of collecting secondhand treasures—and to the unique lifestyle and perspective you can achieve by having them inhabit your world.

My parents took us along to flea markets, art museums, haunted hotels, fancy dinners at stuffy old speakeasies like Musso & Frank's, and hippie picnics on the beach in Malibu. I grew up with the entire spectrum of L.A. at my fingertips, and the city was my first playground. We went to 1950s coffee shops before they were knocked down to make way for mini-malls. We'd go for late-night milkshakes at Tiny Naylor's carhop (just like in *American Graffiti*), and Ben Franks on Sunset Boulevard, where I'd stare in fascination at all the rockers with their teased platinum hair while we had family dinners. The vintage neon signs that accessorized L.A. dazzled my eyes from the backseat window of my dad's vintage Caddy Coupe. As I grew up in this town, my heart would break each time we'd see a favorite spot vanish (sometimes overnight), and even as a little girl, I never understood why anyone would want to tear down places that were *just so cool*. I wanted to save them, but was born too late.

I now write this book to celebrate the best vintage structures that still grace this dreamy metropolis. I hope that visiting vintage lovers will swoon at their beauty and that immune Angelenos will see them as if they've never seen them before. *Vintage Los Angeles* is for those who are hoping to reclaim LaLaLand from it's flip-flop-shod, terry cloth sweats-wearing, peroxided stigma. Our new regime goes to see classic films at Hollywood Forever Cemetery, eats old-school McCarthy salads at the Beverly Hills Hotel, and delights in going to the Magic Castle to be mystified—as Cary Grant did before them. They buy vintage Ossie Clark at Decades, they live in minimalist Neutra houses overlooking the Silver Lake, and wink at Robert Evans when they see him eating at Dan Tana's. They are Vintage Los Angeles.

So I say, out with the new, and in with the old!

INSIDE SCOOP

L.A. is *not* a pedestrian town. Even though they built a subway, it will only take you short distances, so if you really wanna get around, rent a convertible, hire a driver, or have your friends chauffeur you around, then buy them dinner at the Ivy as a gift (they'll adore you forever).

Contents

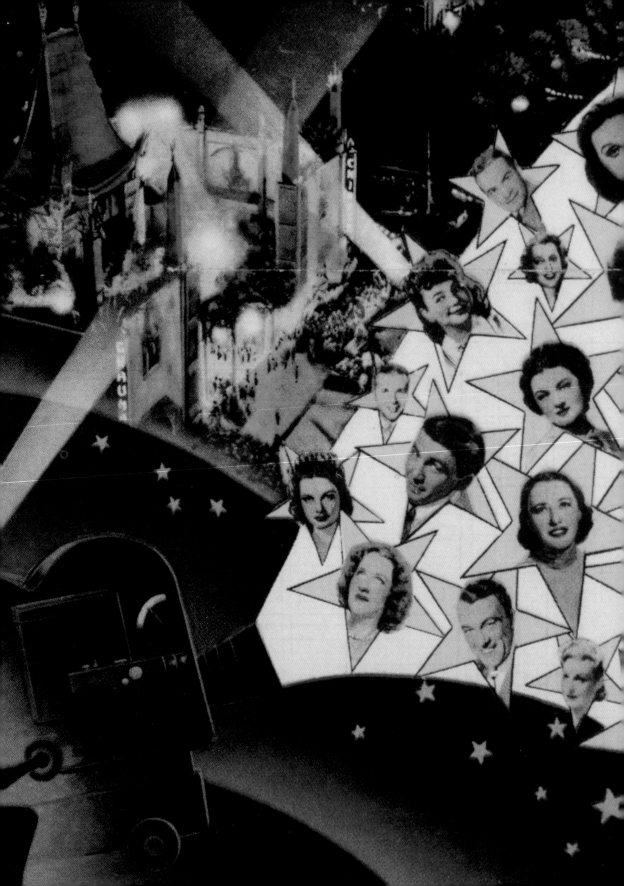

CHAPTER ONE
YOU HAVE ARRIVED
Burbank ✦ *LAX* ✦ *Long Beach Airport*

Chances are, if you're reading this book, you are the kind of person who doesn't dash through an airport without noticing and delighting in all the cool, vintage, 007-worthy architectural details.

These are things nonvintage lovers would never even see. You may even be one of those very special aestheticians who not only *enjoys* being delayed so you can sit longer on the waxed leather tandem chairs at the gate, but knows that they were manufactured by Herman Miller in 1962. And if you are indeed one of these readers, I salute you!

Each of L.A.'s three major airports happens to hark back to past eras and enables you to arrive in L.A. swathed in architectural integrity, landing on the very same tarmacs as Brigitte Bardot, the Rolling Stones, Lana Turner, and Marlon Brando did before you.

BURBANK AIRPORT (AKA BOB HOPE AIRPORT)

This has always been my favorite place to take off or arrive. The Burbank Airport opened in 1930 and is a quaint Art Deco-style airport without the stress or fuss of LAX. As you walk through the terminal, enjoy the New Wave tunes that pump through the speakers. Not Muzak—that could make you sick too early in the morning—New Wave! So if your flight is delayed and you've forgotten your iPod, you will be relaxed by the Ramones, Siouxsie and the Banshees, and Blondie. It's the perfect location for any rock 'n' roller take off or landing.

2627 N. Hollywood Way, Burbank
(818) 840-8840
bobhopeairport.com

BOB'S BIG BOY

Built in 1949 by innovative architect Wayne McAllister, this is the oldest surviving Big Boy in the United States, and it's also the most popular; one of Cali's finest examples of free-form, Googie-style coffeehouse architecture. It's a historic landmark, and has been fully restored to its Naugahyde-style perfection with the signature Bob statue (remember to take a photo with him!), actual carhop service on weekends (just like in *American Graffiti!*), and a vintage hot rod show on Friday nights in the parking lot. Jay Leno likes to stop by and show off his many tricked-out rides.

4211 Riverside Dr., Burbank
(818) 843-9334
bobs.net

TIP

When deplaning in Los Angeles, always wear a pair of very large, dark sunglasses—even at night. It helps start off your trip on the right rock 'n' roll foot.

INSIDE SCOOP

The Beatles visited this Bob's Big Boy during their first American tour in 1964. Check out the permanent plaque on the booth in back, commemorating where they actually sat.

LOS ANGELES "JET - AGE" AIRPORT

LAX

(LOS ANGELES INTERNATIONAL AIRPORT)

If you're a fan of tabloids and relish paparazzi pics of disheveled starlets emerging from flights wearing oversized Chanel sunglasses, then you may prefer to schedule your flight to arrive here, in true old-school, jet-setting style.

LAX is more bombastic than the smaller airports, but if your flight is delayed, at least there's a chance you'll be sitting next to an icon at the gate. I've shared the drama of a canceled flight with Yoko Ono, smelled Elvis Costello's intoxicating cologne wafting through the United Airlines lounge, and had the honor of staring at Liza Minnelli for over an hour. It's essentially always an exciting scene.

I World Way, Los Angeles
(310) 646-5252
lawa.org/lax

THE BUGGY WHIP

This has been a popular post-flight watering hole since 1952. It's heaven for old-school foodies. It has red leather booths, a great bar, signed photos of Liberace, beehived waitresses, and a piano man who takes requests (a little "Love on the Rocks" by Neil Diamond with your whiskey sour perhaps?). The food is all about iceberg lettuce, baked potatoes, crab legs, roast beef, and some very potent cocktails for nervous fliers like me.

7420 La Tijera Blvd., Los Angeles
(310) 645-7131
thebuggywhip.com

TIP

Fourth Street is a fabulous vintage district with dozens of great stores to explore. You'll find unique apparel, furniture, and collectibles that focus mostly on midcentury styles, but they also sell many antiques. It's best to make a day of it since there's so much to see.

ENCOUNTER (AT LAX AIRPORT)

Designed in 1961, this trendy restaurant was formerly the LAX Theme Building. The Theme Building was the most recognizable landmark at LAX and one of the most famous edifices in L.A. It's a 70-foot-high monster that looms like a giant futuristic spider over the parking lot at the nation's third busiest airport. For many years, the structure housed an old-fashioned coffee shop for travelers, but it is now a favorite of jet-setting fashionistas who want to sip cocktails in style before their fashion-week flights. Walt Disney Imagineering revamped the interior a few years back, converting it into the Jetsonesque restaurant and bar it is today. Even the entrance shoots you through to the middle of the building in a space age elevator playing a sci-fi soundtrack. The interior is groovy and futuristic, complete with psychedelic carpeting, colored lava lights, an opalescent bar, moon-cratered walls, and a wraparound patio where you can watch the planes depart. Dining here will make you feel like a character in *Logan's Run*, and it just so happens that this has been used as flight control in the film *Airplane!* and the James Bond film *Moonraker*. The building itself is more of an attraction than the food, which is pretty overpriced and mediocre.

209 World Way, Los Angeles
(310) 215-5151
encounterlax.com

PANN'S

If you happen to know the secret shortcut to or from LAX Airport, you're sure to pass this classic, family-owned 1950s diner. It was designed in 1958 by Armet & Davis, the most innovative of all the "Googie" coffee shop architects. Elvis struts his stuff through the speakers, and you've entered a total time warp. Pann's was a favorite diner of Marilyn Monroe and can be seen in the film *Bewitched*, starring Michael Caine and Nicole Kidman. As for the grub, they serve perfect blueberry pancakes, great burgers, fried chicken with biscuits, and banana splits.

6710 La Tijera Blvd., Los Angeles
(310) 337-2860
panns.com

LONG BEACH AIRPORT

L.B. Airport is another old-fashioned landing pad. You can picture Lana Turner landing here after a glamorous Palm Springs weekend. It's not only easy as pie to find your way around, but it's adorable, with an Art Deco inspired gift shop and coffee stand. Long Beach also features great vintage shopping. So, if you're a hard-core hunter, go straight from your flight over to 4th St. and go crazy!

4100 E. Donald Douglas Dr., Long Beach
(562) 570-2600
longbeach.gov/airport

MEOW!

Meticulously decorated like an old department store, the shop features California's best selection of dead-stock vintage clothing and funky accessories for guys and dolls—from the 1940s to the New Wave '80s. Try to avert your eyes from the salvaged neon signs that adorn the walls, the fun array of sparkly go-go dresses, platform shoes, and pop-culture pins and collectibles. Give yourself a few good hours for this store alone. You'll wind up buying everyone you know fun presents.

2210 E. 4th St., Long Beach
(562) 438-8990
meowvintage.com

CHAPTER TWO

BEACHES

Santa Monica ✦ Malibu ✦ Topanga Canyon ✦ Venice

YACHT HARBOR, SANTA MONICA

Santa Monica

There are many people who envision Los Angeles as one big beach town populated by Jeff Spicoli-type surfers. If this were true, Santa Monica would be the perfect example of L.A. life. The beaches surrounding Santa Monica are actually what first brought the film community to the West Coast in the early 1900s. The weather was perfect for shooting outdoors. Silent-film director Mack Sennett was one of the first to use Santa Monica's dreamy weather in his early shorts.

They starred "Mack Sennett's Bathing Beauties"—future glamour icons Gloria Swanson and Carole Lombard. When the movie community was off work, Santa Monica was where they lived and played, and by the 1920s, the whole coast was dotted with glamorous cottages occupied by the stars. It was then dubbed "The Gold Coast." Many of these homes still exist, including those once belonging to Cary Grant, Greta Garbo, Mae West, and screenwriter Anita Loos (*Gentlemen Prefer Blondes*).

FATHER'S OFFICE

This is the Santa Monica locals' favorite chilled-out neighborhood pub, and the line that sometimes trails down the block is a testament to it. Originally opened in 1953 by a local volleyball player nicknamed "Dad," they serve over 45 international beers as well as a small selection of wines, tapas, soft-shell crabs (in season), and wicked sweet-potato fries. They are most famous for their notoriously perfect, dry-aged "Office Burger." Top it with melted Gruyère if you prefer.
**1018 Montana Ave., Santa Monica
(310) 393-2337
fathersoffice.com**

AERO THEATRE

Originally built in 1939 as a movie house for the employees of Douglas Aircraft so they could see first-run films during World War II, the theater has been a favorite neighborhood hang out ever since. It's a hidden gem for cinemaphiles with its small neon marquee and old-fashioned ticket booth. Though you may think it's the size of a shoebox, the theater is actually quite large. It has 400 seats, adorned by the original architectural carvings. Recently restored to its original Art Deco charm, there's always something cool happening here. It features art house flicks, including many not available on video—like Joan Didion's *Play It as It Lays* and Robert Altman's *Thieves Like Us*. The theater also hosts independent film festivals as well as screenings of classics, featuring Q&As with cast and crew members, like *California Split* attended by George Segal and Elliott Gould. It is the sister theater of the Cinematheque's Egyptian Theater in Hollywood, so it also shows continuations of their comprehensive festivals.
**1328 Montana Ave., Santa Monica
(310) 260-1528
aerotheatre.com**

ARCANA BOOKS ON THE ARTS

Specializing in rare, out-of-print editions on almost every artsy book under the sun, and a favorite stop for designers and artists in need of visual inspiration (I once spotted Tom Ford), Arcana Books has an inventory of over 100,000 books on modern art, architecture, fashion, photography, and film. It also specializes in tracking down any rare book or art-related information you seek—no matter how obscure your request may be. It's so well organized that I'd even recommend it to an OCD-diagnosed art snob. Arcana also sells limited-edition signed lithographs and art pieces by icons like Claes Oldenburg, Andy Warhol, Edward Ruscha, and Keith Haring. It's the perfect place to buy a gift for the discerning aesthete in your life.

1229 Third Street Promenade
Santa Monica
(310) 458-1499
arcanabooks.com

BERGAMOT STATION

This unique, industrial-looking structure is like a little community or campus with a very artsy vibe. An outdoor arts center that first began life as a trolley station in 1875, it is now an arts complex that houses 30 galleries, 10 shops, the Gallery Cafe (that displays works by upcoming artists), a fine jewelry boutique, a Japanese paper store, and the Colleagues Gallery, which is a designer resale charity boutique. Most of the galleries host their openings on the first Saturday of every month, and it is a fun spot for beautiful-people watching while scoping out fabulous pieces to adorn your walls. With a variety of galleries such as these, you'll find both affordable and astronomical art. Make sure to visit the Santa Monica Museum of Art in building G1, where they always have great exhibits from cool eras. Check out the recent collage works of X singer Exene Cervenkova, as well as pieces from California's groundbreaking Semina art movement of the 1960s.

2525 Michigan Ave., Santa Monica
(310) 829-5854
smmoa.org or bergamotstation.com

CHEZ JAY

This legendary restaurant opened in 1959 and has remained virtually unchanged since. Located only blocks from the beach, it is the perfect restaurant to visit after a day at the beach. With its Christmas lights, checkered tablecloths, and nearly the same original menu, stepping into Chez Jay is a trip back in time. Jay's has a dark, misty marina vibe that attracts a local crowd looking for steak, sand dabs, and steamed clams. It's the kind of joint any modern Gidget and Moondoggie would love. This seaside relic is complete with a ship's wheel, sawdust on the floor, and an authentic stacked jukebox.

It's a place filled to the brim with history. Frank Sinatra, Marlon Brando, Vivien Leigh, and Jayne Mansfield were regulars. There are rumors that John F. Kennedy and Marilyn Monroe would rendezvous here, and it's a known fact that astronaut Alan Shepard took a Chez Jay peanut on his historic trip to the moon. Hollywood's new regime continues to make up the clientele—George Clooney, Drew Barrymore, and Al Pacino have been known to grab a beer at Jay's.

1657 Ocean Ave., Santa Monica
(310) 395-1741
chezjays.com

LEFT
Though the lobby is no longer painted jadeite green, the Georgian Hotel still retains much of its original Art Deco pizzazz.

THE GEORGIAN HOTEL

With its striking seafoam green and butter yellow facade, the Georgian Hotel looks more like it belongs in Miami than L.A. It's quite a dazzling sight from the street and is rich in history. It dates back to 1933, when Hollywood's elite frequently visited to escape the city heat. Even Rose Kennedy lived here for a time. Sitting on the bay-facing veranda, ideal for afternoon cocktails, you can gaze at the panoramic views of rainbow-hued ocean sunsets. The Georgian was also one of the very first "skyscrapers" along a then sparsely populated Ocean Ave. At one time, its basement restaurant, with red leather banquettes and flocked velvet wallpaper, became one of the last vestiges of Prohibition. Known as a popular "speakeasy," it hosted the infamous likes of Charlie Chaplin, Bugsy Siegel, Clark Gable, Fatty Arbuckle, Carole Lombard, and other Hollywood stars.

Sitting on one of the city's most beautiful, palm-lined streets, the Georgian is a short walk from the restaurants and shops of the Third Street Promenade, as well as the historic Santa Monica Pier. It's the perfect location for vacationing beach bunnies and bums (the surfing kind, not the homeless ones—although they're around too) who want to stay someplace where they won't have to do much driving.

1415 Ocean Ave., Santa Monica
(310) 395-9945
georgianhotel.com

HOTEL CASA DEL MAR

Opened in 1926, Casa del Mar was originally called Club Casa del Mar, an exclusive, members-only beach resort catering to the famous and high-falutin'. The brick and sandstone hotel was built in ornate Renaissance revival-style and is nestled smack dab in the sand. Step inside the foyer and notice the intricately tiled floors, exposed stenciled wood beams, and forest-green velvet drapery. The opulence continues in every sherbet-colored guest room and suites with plushy four-poster beds, hand-painted armoires, and marble baths. Sultry silent-film vamp Theda Bara was a frequent guest, and it's no wonder why.

1910 Ocean Way, Santa Monica
(310) 581-5533
hotelcasadelmar.com

PARIS 1900

Proprietress Susan Lieberman has been collecting treasures of romantic finery from sources in the United States and Europe since 1974. She opened Paris 1900 in 1976, and it's a true vintage classic. Upon my last visit, I bought a faded wall map of Paris and lusted over intricately embroidered pillows, miniature handmade seashell ships from the 1920s, and a Victorian Battenburg lace tea jacket. The store houses antique Victorian white dresses that would make any cynic hear wedding bells, dainty jewels, tiaras, and accoutrements that could fit in your purse or sit atop your Art Deco vanity. Every item is feminine, romantic, and in pristine condition. By appointment or chance.

2703 Main St., Santa Monica
(310) 396-0405
paris1900.com

THIS SPREAD
Paris 1900 is filled with items fit for a royal trousseau, from exquisite Gibson Girl-era lingerie to 1920s floral headpieces that are beaded with delicate wax flowers.

SANTA MONICA PIER

Many young people visiting L.A. or living here for the first time seem to pass up visiting the Santa Monica Pier because they fear that it's too "touristy." But I always talk them into it, and they always thank me. After all, how many old-fashioned American amusement boardwalks still exist? The kind with roller coasters, carnival games, vaudeville-style street performers, skee-ball, and cotton candy? The kind that Rodgers and Hammerstein could write a musical about? Not many—which is exactly why it deserves our attention. It's been here since 1909 and has the antique details to show for it. You can picture men with curly, handlebar mustaches courting ladies with parasols and ruffled bloomers. And if it's romance you seek, I can't think of a better L.A. date than a stroll on the pier as the sun sets its orange and pink cast over California.

The amusement part of the pier is dubbed Pacific Park, and it features a 1922 merry-go-round (listed as a National Historic Landmark), and a Ferris wheel (dubbed the The Pacific Wheel) that stands nine stories tall at the edge of the ocean with glittering, colored lights. During the summer months, the pier offers awesome outdoor entertainment, like classic movie screenings under the stars and Amoeba Music's Twilight Dance Series, where eclectic musicians, like surf guitar legend Dick Dale, soul singer Mavis Staples, and punk band Agent Orange, play free shows to raise awareness for the Santa Monica Pier Restoration fund.

200 Santa Monica Pier (at Colorado Ave.), Santa Monica
(310) 458-8900
santamonicapier.org

SANTA MONICA AIRPORT OUTDOOR ANTIQUE & COLLECTIBLE MARKET

Flea market veterans are always dazzled by the huge selection of quality antique furniture and home accessories they can find here. Upscale vendors assemble entire rooms with shopper-friendly displays to help customers visualize items in a living space. Although jewelry and small decorations are available, these vendors rarely clutter their tables with trinkets. Instead they focus on larger, quality antiques with staple pieces like natural wood tables, painted cupboards, and carved bureaus. Though there may be room for negotiation, prices on particularly unique items can be high. A set of 1940s leather armchairs from France can cost anywhere around $4,000. This market also hosts many specialty stands, selling bejeweled sari skirts, Chinese antiques, gold leaf–edged rare books, and colorful African beads. On the first and fourth Sunday of every month.

South side of Santa Monica Airport
Airport Ave. & Bundy Ave.
(323) 933-2511

INSIDE SCOOP

The Santa Monica Pier has been used in many classic films, including *Funny Girl* (where it doubled as Coney Island), *The Sting*, *They Shoot Horses, Don't They?*, and *Inside Daisy Clover*. It also appears in the opening credits of *Three's Company*. If you recognize the pier's bumblebee ride, it may be that you've seen the cover of Elvis Costello's album, *When I Was Cruel*. And the carousel was used in 1963 as a setting for an Andy Warhol wrap party for his film *Tarzan and Jane Regained . . . Sort Of*, where he celebrated his first trip to L.A.

VINTAGE FASHION EXPO

Three times a year, die-hard collectors come to find treasures that range from the turn of the century to the New Wave '80s. More than 100 carefully selected dealers assemble their busy booths, featuring their best vintage couture, clothing, jewelry, textiles, and accessories. You'll find alligator pumps from the '40s, Schiaparelli gowns, Dior turban hats, Art Deco Bakelite buttons, mod go-go boots, Kenneth Jay Lane brooches, Duran Duran badges, and Victorian lace capelets. It's always quite a scene, where attendees range from major costume designers to stylists to actresses and rock stars.

Santa Monica Civic Auditorium
1855 Main St., Santa Monica
(707) 793-0773
vintageexpo.com

WERTZ BROTHERS

Antiques collectors come to Wertz to find quality furniture and larger decorative items. Wertz has two locations—Wertz Brothers Furniture and Wertz Brothers Antique Mart. "Furniture" is located in West L.A. and is 55,000 sq. ft. with 196 dealers. Santa Monica's "Antique Mart" is a 20,000 sq. ft. antiques mall set in an old barnlike structure. It features 106 dealers, showcasing their best Victorian, French Deco, midcentury, and modern furnishings. Find Spanish rugs, paintings, rusty old '30s patio furniture, tiki-style rattan, sterling serving sets, '40s framed floral Turner prints, Bakelite jewelry, ceramic objets d'art, estate jewels—just about every imaginable decorative item for your home. Decorators and collectors frequent both large locations.

Wertz Brothers Furniture
11879 Santa Monica Blvd., Los Angeles
(310) 477-4251

Wertz Brothers Antique Mart
1607 Lincoln Blvd., Santa Monica
(310) 452-1800
wertzbrothers.com

McCABE'S GUITAR SHOP

Since 1958, McCabe's has presented the folk music elite with the largest and most drool-worthy selection of new stringed instruments. It's not only an L.A. institution for the world famous to shop for guitars, banjos, and dulcimers; it's also a cool place to catch acoustic rock shows. Just a few of the hundreds of legends who have graced the tiny stage of McCabe's cozy back room include Les Paul, Emmylou Harris, Etta James, Aimee Mann, Allen Ginsberg, Nico, Jeff Buckley, John Lee Hooker, Beck, The Bangles, Jonathan Richman. P. J. Harvey, X, Cat Power, Robyn Hitchcock, Alex Chilton, John Cale, and Sun Ra. And if you are so inspired by the craftsmanship of some of their merchandise, they also offer private lessons. Think of it as "The School of Folk."

3101 Pico Blvd., Santa Monica
(310) 828-4497
8mccabes.com

FAR LEFT
From Marie Antoinette gowns to Doctor Zhivago-esque fur hats . . . anything goes at the Santa Monica Vintage Clothing Show.

LEFT
Fabulous dead-stock high heels and vintage angora sweaters at the Santa Monica Vintage Show's Meow! boutique.

On the Roosevelt Highway, U. S. 101, near Malibu

Malibu

About 10 miles north of Santa Monica, Malibu (or "The Bu" as locals and wannabe gangstas like to call it) is where much of Hollywood hangs on the weekends to breathe its clean salt air and catch some rays. It has what is said to be the highest concentration of celebrity residents of anywhere in the world, which is why, in its original heyday of the 1930s, it was called "The Movie Colony."

Strolling around the quaint Malibu Country Mart, which features a great health food stand, many designer boutiques, and the überpopular West Coast incarnation of Nobu sushi, you may spot Goldie Hawn, Kate Hudson, John Cusack, Drew Barrymore, Diana Ross, Pamela Anderson, Farrah Fawcett, Shirley MacLaine, the Osbournes, or the Arquettes.

ABOVE
If all this vintage hunting has put your chakras out of whack, Lake Shrine is the perfect place to sit in a lotus pose and say "Namaste."

GETTY VILLA

This historic, Mediterranean-style villa sits on 64 acres of Malibu dreaminess. It holds a stunning art museum and cultural center focused on Greek, Roman, and Etruscan works. Originally purchased by J. Paul Getty in 1945 to house his astonishing art collection, he first opened it to the public in 1954, and after years of seaside wear and tear, it closed in 1997 to undergo a meticulous eight-year renovation, reopening in 2006 to rave reviews. Visiting the Villa is a more romantic and intimate experience than the one you'll have at its much larger, more modern sister site, the Brentwood Getty Center. Even if the ancient arts, suits of armor, or Trojan War mosaics aren't your bag, no other L.A. museum can compete with the surrounding scenery. Feel the ocean breeze as you stroll through Roman-inspired gardens to a courtyard surrounded by priceless marble statuary. The museum also hosts classical music performances, plays, tours, and lectures. Reservations required.

17985 Pacific Coast Hwy., Pacific Palisades
(310) 440-7300
getty.edu

LAKE SHRINE

Gracing the basin of Santa Ynez Canyon lies the truly stunning Lake Santa Ynez, now called Lake Shrine. It's L.A.'s only natural spring-fed body of water. Spanning over 10 acres and covered in tropical trees, ducks, koi, and lotus flowers, the land was used throughout the 1920s as a location for many silent Westerns, and in 1940, an eccentric contractor named Everett McElroy purchased it to live on after he helped build the 20th Century Fox Studios. He even had his giant double-deck Mississippi houseboat called "Adeline" transported onto the lake as a temporary home. He later added a Dutch-style wooden mill house, equipped with a working waterwheel, stained glass windows, and Tyrolean carvings. In 1950, McElroy dedicated the land to world-renowned Swami and yoga pioneer Paramahansa Yogananda, who built a temple and an open-air shrine to honor all religions. Through his Self-Realization Fellowship, he lectured and conducted meditative services for the public and luminaries like George Eastman, Leopold Stokowski, and Mahatma Gandhi (who also has some of his ashes enshrined here). George Harrison contributed funds to build the main chapel, and he frequently went there for meditation. Think of it as L.A.'s enlightenment HQ.

17080 Sunset Blvd., Pacific Palisades
(310) 454-4114
lakeshrine.org or yogananda-srf.org

NEPTUNE'S NET

When it comes to beachy seafood joints, this is the real deal. It attracts stoner Spicoli types, industry shakers, bearded bikers, and the Juicy Couture crowd. Scene aside, the food is pirate worthy. Take a seat on a shabby (but charming) picnic table and pick up your plastic forks. Enjoy clam chowder, lobster, crab, clams, and the freshly grilled catch o' the day. Have a killer view of the Pacific and a cold beer after a long day of hanging ten and baking in the sun. This is hunger heaven, brah!

42505 Pacific Coast Hwy., Malibu
(310) 457-3095
neptunesnet.com

REEL INN

Less of a tough Hell's Angels vibe than Neptune's Net, this is an ideal romantic date spot—if you make sure to go after all the bratty Malibu kids have gotten their dinners. It's a cute Hawaiian shack with a perfect outdoor patio adorned with twinkle lights. You can sip hard-to-find ales and dine on one of the many delicious seafood meals scrawled on the chalkboard menu. They serve the freshest grilled ahi and Cajun-spiced tuna, and the dishes come with a side of mashed potatoes and 'slaw.

18661 Pacific Coast Hwy., Malibu
(310) 456-8221

Topanga Canyon

Topanga Canyon is a gorgeous road that winds all the way from the Pacific Coast Highway through the Santa Monica Mountains, leaving you off in the San Fernando Valley.

It has a legendary rock 'n' roll lineage and evokes visions of surfers driving beaten-up Studebakers with surfboards peeking out the back and long-haired girls wearing prairie dresses. Canyons are hidden away and so full of nature that you forget you're anywhere near a buzzing metropolis. In Topanga Canyon, birds coo, rare flowers bloom, and the Malibu Creek gently rolls along behind the cabin-style homes. This haven for creative inspiration is the second-most famous of the L.A. canyons (Hollywood's Laurel Canyon is the most famous).

Old Topanga began attracting artsy bohemians in the 1940s, and when folk troubadour Woody Guthrie settled here in the '50s, its fate was sealed as the perfect spot for those who wanted to pretend to live in the Wild West. Since then, it's always been inhabited by characters as colorful as its sunsets and has had many musical hits penned within its borders. Tunes by Bob Dylan (who moved here to be like his idol, Woody Guthrie), Mick Fleetwood of Fleetwood Mac, John Densmore of the Doors, Linda Ronstadt, and unfortunately, Charles Manson, have lived in the canyon. It is here that hippie band Spirit wrote "Topanga Windows" and John Phillips (of the Mamas and the Papas) wrote "Topanga Canyon." But the king of the rock 'n' roll canyon was Neil Young. While he was living in a redwood house at 611 Skyline Trail., he wrote the hit tune "Cinnamon Girl," as well as the classic LPs, *After the Gold Rush* (1970), *Harvest*, and *Tonight's the Night* (both in 1972), and *Zuma* (1975).

Topanga even had its own '60s art movement dubbed "Semina" after artist Wallace Berman's handmade magazine of collages and beat poetry. Berman's brilliant circle of friends included Dennis Hopper, Peter Fonda, Jack Nicholson, and Dean Stockwell, who, together in the canyon, wrote the classic '60s antiestablishment film, *Easy Rider*. Breathe deeply enough, and you're sure to leave Topanga Canyon with some divine inspiration of your own.

HIDDEN TREASURES

Among an actual tepee commune, giant wooden hula dancers, and taxidermied animals wearing top hats, you'll find a magical cottage covered in seashells and filled to the rafters with incredible vintage finds (and I'm not making this up). As the name suggests, Hidden Treasures is like a pirate's chest full of charmingly shabby additions to your wardrobe and hippie home—and I've never seen anyone leave empty-handed. Rock 'n' roll-inspired fashion stylists have been raiding this Topanga Canyon hangout since its opening about 15 years ago. Located in what was Topanga's only drugstore in the 1940s, it's set up like a rickety little ol' house where you can wander from room to room, picking up everything from handmade Victorian quilts and silk and velvet 1930s glamour gowns, to tea-stained doilies, animated 1950s waterfall lamps, and beaten-up Keith Richards-worthy leather jackets. Merchandise is displayed with a devil-may-care California attitude, and you can have fun sitting on the patchwork of Indian floor rugs while digging through antique steamer trunks billowing over with silk scarves and slip dresses. Most items run about $10 to $30, so it's well worth the detour through the long and winding canyon.

154 S. Topanga Canyon Blvd., Topanga
(310) 455-2998
hiddentreasuresla.com

LA HORSEBACK RIDING

Embark on either a daytime ride, which provides stunning views of the Valley and Santa Monica Mountains, or a nighttime, full-moon ride, complete with fog rolling over the hills and falling stars. Friendly wranglers will escort you down the trails while riding beautiful Arabian horses. Hi-ho Silver!

2623 Old Topanga Canyon Rd., Topanga
(818) 591-2032
lahorsebackriding.com

SADDLE PEAK LODGE

If you're trying to seduce a carnivore who smokes a pipe, collects taxidermy, and reads '60s issues of *Esquire*, this is the perfect place. But if you're attempting to woo a vegetarian, don't go here. To get here from the beach, you'll drive along twisty canyon roads, passing horse ranches and creeks along the way, which just adds to this restaurant's Robert Mitchum-worthy appeal. Along with the Malibu mountain views, moose heads, and gamy gourmet cuisine, this historic restaurant resides in a landmark, three-story building from 1920, with a woodsy, Catskills clubhouse vibe. It's the type of place where you see someone proposing at the next table. Stars of the golden era, as well as today's front-page headliners, have adored this romantic hideaway. They have cozy seating by stone fireplaces in winter months and a gorgeous, tree-lined upper terrace for dining on warm starry nights.

419 Cold Canyon Rd., Calabasas
(818) 222-3888
saddlepeaklodge.com

Venice

Watching Olivia Newton-John roller-skate in the 1980 cult classic film _Xanadu_ is enough to make anyone want to hang out here. I'm still inspired every time I visit this laid-back beach community. Venice was developed in 1905 by a cigarette manufacturer and real estate baron named Abbot Kinney, who happened to be obsessed with the Italian Renaissance.

He decided to build his own Venetian fantasyland just south of Santa Monica, with neo-Italian structures and colonades arcaded along Windward and Pacific Aves. There are also 16 miles of actual canals that were occupied by gondolas navigated by singing gondoliers in full costume.

Kinney also had a 1,600-foot amusement pier built, as well as an attraction called Ocean Park, which garnered Venice the nickname "Playland of the Pacific." From the '20s through the '30s, this is where Hollywood stars loved to ride roller coasters, eat hot dogs, drive bumper cars (as Charlie Chaplin frequently did), and throw parties. There was a legendary night on the pier in 1935 when actress Carole Lombard and William Randolph Hearst's mistress, Marion Davies, let their hair down and had fun with fellow glamour icons, Marlene Dietrich and Claudette Colbert. Sadly, by the 1950s, Venice was in desperate need of a renovation, as you can see in Orson Welles' 1958 film noir, *Touch of Evil*, which used Venice's decaying buildings as a sleazy Tex-Mex border town. As Venice became more populated over the years, the 16 miles of canals became only four blocks, and Ocean Park, along with the amusement pier, was destroyed by fire and neglect. Venice has had its highs and lows and is now experiencing a renaissance of its own. Old buildings are being restored and chic new vintage boutiques, design studios, art galleries, restaurants, and watering holes are popping up daily.

OPPOSITE
Through Bazar's unique steel gate you enter a chic environment, filled with expertly curated vintage home décor—from tastefully kitschy 1940s figural lamps to an oversized chemist's jar from the late nineteenth century advertising rhubarb.

ANIMAL HOUSE

It's a spacious boutique with vintage and up-and-coming designer duds for guys and dolls, housed in the same historic Venetian-style building that Orson Welles used as a main location in his classic film noir, *Touch of Evil*. For guys there is day attire, like '80s rock tees and Levis that are already perfectly worn. For the babes, there are flirty floral slip dresses, embroidered tops, and a wall covered in collectible Pucci and Peter Max Pop Art print apparel. Be sure to check out their bitchin' section of hard-to-find art books and the tiki-tacky Hawaiian home accessories.

66 Windward Ave., Venice
(310) 392-5411
animalhousevenice.com

BAZAR

This is a vintage home boutique specializing in unique décor from the 1930s through the 1970s, with much of the selection hailing from Europe. Everything here is spectacular and rare—like the antique canoe hanging from the ceiling or the gold-flecked, oxidized glass apothecary jar from the nineteenth century ($2,400). On my last visit, I told the owner I'd been searching high and low for a vintage Lucite vanity chair with a leopard fur cushion, and she not only had one designed by Charles Hollis Jones in the '70s, but it swiveled.

3108C Abbot Kinney Blvd., Venice
(310) 314-2101

INSIDE SCOOP

For film buffs, Rydell High (from the classic 1978 film *Grease*) was actually Venice High. Feel free to sneak onto the bleachers and pretend that you're Sandy and Danny belting out "Summer Nights."

13000 Venice Blvd., Venice
(310) 306-7981
venicehigh.net

BOUNTIFUL

Interior designer Sue Balmforth's shop looks as if Miss Havisham decided to open a home décor store instead of having a wedding. Entirely designed in a palette of original worn chipping whites and adorned overhead with a rainfall of beaded chandeliers, the selection is shabby French country chic. Let this 10,000 sq. ft. boutique be your destination for ornate iron bedframes, mercury glass, Victorian oil paintings, Venetian mirrors with perfect silver patina, birdhouses, old American press-back chairs, British china, and more. With mile-high, mazelike displays of dreamy treasures that nearly topple over, Bountiful's huge space feels like a scene from *Alice in Wonderland*. Hidden in the middle of the maze is a romantic boudoir loft that is actually the proprietress' personal boudoir, where everything is available for purchase. Decorators and serious collectors can't get enough (neither can Pamela Anderson or Shabby Chic's Rachel Ashwell), but despite the extraordinary prices, everybody can walk away with something they love because the store also has a great selection of seashells, soaps, candles, picture frames, and apothecary jars.

1335 Abbot Kinney Blvd., Venice
(310) 450-3620
bountifulhome.com

EQUATOR BOOKS

This is one of my all-time favorite stops for collectible and cool out-of-print titles, focusing on literature, art, photography, design, architecture, and poetry. Much of the merchandise is written by the Beats, which is perfect because Venice has a rich Beat Generation history. They also have sections devoted to books on special subjects, such as amusement parks and prostitutes. Harking back to the creative explosion of the 1980s in Manhattan's SoHo, Equator is not only a bookstore and publishing house, but an art gallery, featuring exhibits by artists such as Ed Ruscha, Edmuch Teske, and Raymond Pettibon. Located in an open, architectural showplace that was originally an auto garage in the 1920s, it is still equipped with its original roll-up door and is as inspiring a space as the contents of its tomes. It's fully constructed of eco-friendly materials, and above its center island there is a dazzling floating birch wall that displays rotating art. For literary nerds like me, this place is pure perfection.

1103 Abbot Kinney Blvd., Venice
(310) 399-5544
equatorbooks.com

FRENCH 50S–60S

Owner Michele Sommerlath has been collecting and dealing French antiques for over 30 years, but at this whimsical and colorful store, midcentury modern furniture rules the roost. She ships every wonderful piece directly back from her native France, and she perfectly curates all the furniture you'd need to decorate a Neutra (or Neutra-esque) house into a minimalist dream—but with a sense of humor sprinkled on top. Furniture, lighting, abstract art, shaggy rugs, and accessories are abundant here, and every piece looks like it could decorate the set of Brigitte Bardot's boudoir in a Godard film. *Vive le Français!*

1427 Abbot Kinney Blvd., Venice
(310) 392-9905
french50s60s.com

MADLEY

Madley is a magical store, decorated with a large carousel horse in the front window and chock-full of 1980s rock 'n' roll-inspired apparel and handmade one-of-a-kind accessories. Much of the merchandise is designed by the boutique's owner, the adorable Coryn Madley. She is influenced by the 1986 fantasy film *Labyrinth*, starring David Bowie, as well as her deep-rooted love of nature. Her clothing is mostly comprised of handknits, some with pouffy princess sleeves, in romantic shades of metallic gold, mauve, midnight black, and shadowy gray. They are like the colors of Venice Beach at sunset, which also happens to be Ms. Madley's hometown. Her jewelry designs are vintage findings strung together—Victorian jet beads, cameos, raw crystal, seahorses, shells, feathers, and broken chains. These findings become stunning necklaces, brooches, and bracelets. She also stocks clothing by young neighborhood designers and displays works by California artists she admires. Items run from $40 for a vintage dress to $700 for a hand-crocheted shawl.

1227 Abbot Kinney Blvd., Venice
(310) 450-6029
madley.com

LEFT
Madley regularly hosts art exhibits for L.A. artists, like Echo Park's Kime Buzzelli, who did this whimsical painting.

ABOVE AND OPPOSITE
Hand-painted windows and handcrafted fashion by local artisans adorn the window display at Madley.

INSET, OPPOSITE
Madley's owner and label designer, Coryn Madley, always stocks her unique Venice boutique with gorgeous knitted sweaters, dresses, and '80s suede boots, fit for any California bohemian beach bunny.

INSIDE SCOOP

Take a fun, beachy drive to Laguna Beach, located on the rocky cliffs south of Newport. It was once known as a bohemian artists' colony, but it's now too chi-chi for starving painters to inhabit (though it still sports a dedicated surfer scene). Its twisty, sandy roads are lined with gorgeous beach cottages, boutiques, art galleries, and waterfront cafes.

It still has a great late '60s vibe, and it's where my groovy parents bought matching wedding rings in the '70s with big, raw, and rare purple stones from a custom jeweler that is still in "biz."

THIS PAGE
Sixties California beach culture is alive and well at Surfing Cowboys in Venice. Their furniture selection is sure to give any midcentury collector good vibrations.

NEPTINA

Neptina features twentieth-century modern design, with an eye toward the whimsical side of the machine age. It's the perfect place to look for Art Deco furniture and streamlined home accessories—if you're going for that Metropolis-meets-Disneyland vibe. Aside from furniture, they've got killer lamps, salvaged architectural details, and a mind-boggling selection of fluted glass decanters. Yet the thing that bowled me over upon my last visit was the featured playground toys that owner Lianne Gold has dubbed her "platinum zoo." They are aluminum rides, found in East Coast schools and playgrounds, that were discarded to be replaced by modern resin rides. They weigh about 50 pounds and come in shapes like seahorses, rocking horses, hound dogs, snails, and bumblebees. Lianne has stripped, polished, and priced them from $850 to $2,200. They work brilliantly as striking conversation pieces or as yard sculptures.

1329 1/2 Abbot Kinney Blvd., Venice
(310) 396-1630
neptina.net

SURFING COWBOYS

Donna and Wayne Gunther are the über-cool married owners of this bitchin' home décor shop. They first met when he was a fashion photographer and she was an art director for Elite models. As they worked and traveled together, they found they shared a common love for "junking" and would sneak off after shoots to look for undiscovered thrift stores. Sick of the drama, they soon dropped out of the fashion world and, thankfully, opened this awesome shop. They are now the greatest purveyors of vintage beach culture memorabilia on this side of sunny California. You can buy enough midcentury furniture and accoutrements to deck out any pad in authentic surf style. Their genius lies in that they not only know how to mix different eras together in a room, but they specialize in mixing West Coast with European style—like placing '60s California pottery atop a Danish coffee table. They have superb eyes for the unusual, including in their mix a 1960 Ducati Brio scooter ($2,500), a Tim Blake paddle board from the 1930s ($25,000), and a giant filter from a '50s Boeing jet that would make smashing wall art ($2,000). They also have atomic-age coffee shop-style swag lights, vintage Hawaiian surf photographs professionally framed and matted, Italian film and advertising posters, mosaic-tiled tables, vintage '60s surfboards, and freestanding, metal, wood-burning fireplaces.

1624 Abbot Kinney Blvd., Venice
(310) 450-4891
surfingcowboys.com

WORLD ON WHEELS

This is the best, old-school, '70s skating rink, and it hosts a rad monthly roller disco-themed party called Space Is the Place. The party is a '70s-inspired "dance and skate," and World on Wheels is rare in that it has a full bar (most roller rinks do not serve any liquor—roller boogying is dangerous enough sober). It also features an upstairs dance floor that plays funk, disco, and rare grooves. There's also a video game arcade to complete the vibe. Note: Thursday and Sunday nights are 21 and over. Space Is the Place is every fourth Saturday of the month.

4645 1/2 Venice Blvd., Venice
(323) 933-5170
wowsk8.com

INSIDE SCOOP

To view World on Wheels and the Venice Beach roller-skating scene during its disco heyday, watch the so-bad-it's-hysterical 1979 film *Roller Boogie*, starring Linda Blair.

CHAPTER THREE

WESTSIDE

Bel Air ✦ *Brentwood* ✦ *Culver City* ✦ *Westwood*

Bel Air

BEL AIR HOTEL

Originally built in 1922 as the planning offices for Bel Air developer Alphonzo Bell's exclusive estates, this 12-acre hotel hideaway is much like the Beverly Hills Hotel. It's a pink, Spanish mission-style mansion, and it mostly caters to guests with the last name Moneybags. Yet this place is more like a private woodsy paradise, with its lavish fairy-tale gardens, towering sycamore trees, secret stone pathways, and an actual "Swan Lake" stocked with friendly feathered friends. Hidden in the residential hills of Bel Air, away from the hustle and bustle of the city, it was once home to Cary Grant, Grace Kelly, and Marilyn Monroe (whose favorite bungalow is now the gym and who adored swimming in its famous oval pool). It was visited by Greta Garbo, Clark Gable, Marlene Dietrich, and Andy Warhol (on his last trip to L.A.). It will forever be a haven for the rich and royal, due to its plush, cushy suites, and regal clubhouse piano bar. If your name happens to be Miss Moneybags, and you'd like a reservation, be sure to request a room with a fireplace and private patio (perfect for the most gorgeous brunch of your life).

701 Stone Canyon Rd., Bel Air
(310) 472-1211
hotelbelair.com

PREVIOUS SPREAD
Oscar-winning actress Claudette Colbert lived in this dreamy Bel Air estate for many years of her glamorous life.

BRENTWOOD COUNTRY MART

Designed in 1948 to look like a big red barn, and recently restored, it's a quaintly adorable outdoor mart with about 20 boutiques and several eateries, which in its early days was frequented by Elizabeth Taylor, Shirley Temple, and Joan Crawford (they all lived nearby). Brentwood Country Mart has a *Beverly Hillbillies* vibe that attracts sophisticated locals, since it's the perfect weekend hang where you can stroll around eclectic boutiques, eat at the classic BBQ chicken joint (Reddi Chick), sip killer hot chocolate at Manhattan's famous City Bakery, or chill at the picnic tables in the quiet courtyard, which surrounds a giant birdcage.

225 26th St., Brentwood
(310) 458-6682
brentwoodcountrymart.com

THE GETTY CENTER

Though it's not housed in a vintage building (unless you consider 1997 vintage), it contains a bunch of pre-twentieth-century art. High above Los Angeles rests the J. Paul Getty Museum at the Getty Center, and on a clear day you can literally see forever—from the snow-capped mountains of Big Bear to the Pacific Ocean. That's not to say the view is the star attraction here, because the art's pretty breathtaking too.

The complex is made up of interconnecting pavilions of Italian travertine that follow the natural ridge of the hills and enclose a large courtyard (Meaning: This is a totally hot place to take an artsy date you're trying to woo). Its construction allows you to wander in a free-form pattern through various exhibits, moving you from outside to inside in a natural and organic way. The collection here is quite diverse, featuring classical statuary, Greek vases (they possess one of the most important collections in the world), and pre-twentieth-century manuscripts, photography, and decorative arts. Be sure to wander the unique gardens designed by Robert Irwin.

1200 Getty Center Dr., Los Angeles
(310) 440-7300
getty.edu

INSIDE SCOOP

The Westside of L.A. is made up of many posh 'hoods between Santa Monica and Beverly Hills. All are ripe with Hollywood folklore, and if you're a fan of ritzy historic architecture, then it's fun enough just to drive around and explore. Westside living is not about the in-your-face rock 'n' roll glam of Hollywood. It's more gilded manor and iron gates and fragrant bougainvillea—that type of glamour.

Through all the lush foliage, you lose the raucousness of L.A.'s busier enclaves—much to the delight of its many famous residents. This side of town has been populated by stars since the 1930s because the movie industry's two most important film studios are located here in Culver City, which has been nicknamed "The Heart of Screenland." They are MGM (now Sony Studios) and 20th Century Fox. What I love most about the Westside is that it will eternally be the most decadently glam part of town.

H. D. BUTTERCUP

This is a unique furniture mart housed in L.A.'s historic 100,000 sq. ft. Helms Bakery building, and it features 50 individual shops, many of which sell antiques. Of the goods here you'll find exquisite Persian and Turkish rugs, Moroccan lanterns, mod textiles, midcentury steel desks, cabinets and chairs, French '60s cafe ashtrays, lustworthy Venetian chandeliers, and ancient Asian accessories. H. D. Buttercup was founded by the former CEO of N.Y.'s fabulous ABC Home & Carpet, so if you've been there, you know this has to rock.

3225 Helms Ave., Los Angeles
(310) 558-8900
hdbuttercup.com

HOLY CROSS CEMETERY

As is typical with most L.A. cemeteries, this one is as star-studded as an Oscar ceremony. While I understand visiting cemeteries may be considered quite morbid by some, for film buffs it's just the closest they're ever gonna get to meeting their silver-screen idols. This is a nice place to take a peaceful stroll around eternity, while spotting the resting places of '40s pinup girl Rita Hayworth, iconic crooner Bing Crosby, film star Rosalind Russell (star of my all-time favorite film, *Auntie Mame*), the great lover of the '30s Charles Boyer, the tragically murdered (and stunning) actress Sharon Tate, glam tap dancer Ann Miller, and the original Dracula, Bela Lugosi (who is buried here in his signature black cape).

5835 W. Slauson Ave., Culver City
(310) 776-1855

THE MUSEUM OF JURASSIC TECHNOLOGY

Okay, there is seriously no possible way to describe what this museum holds until you've experienced it for yourself. Everything contained within its black walls and cabinets of curiosities is juxtaposed—just like the words "Jurassic" and "technology." Upon first glance at many of the displayed artifacts, you would think that you were just looking at someone's collection of old magic tricks, but upon closer inspection (I highly recommend you watch the short introductory film as you enter), you see that the ancient oddities on display are artifacts predating the 1800s. See everything from ridiculous Victorian remedies for ailments (which included whispering specific rhymes into a basket of bees before doing anything of importance), floral radiographs (X-rays of flowers), and micromosaics made of butterfly wings that are so minuscule, you have to look through a magnifying glass to see them.

This museum is an homage to the visionary early scientists, who found truths in quaint, aesthetically driven experimentation. The museum provides us with a specialized repository of relics and artifacts from past eras that delve deep into the mystical meaning behind things that most people would mistakenly dismiss as mundane. After you're done exploring, visit the upstairs Tula Tea Room with its vaulted ceiling, hanging votives, and gurgling baptismal fountain.

9341 Venice Blvd., Culver City
(310) 836-6131
mjt.org

SONY PICTURES STUDIOS

This is where glamour was actually invented! Originally MGM Studios, which boasted that it was home to "more stars than there are in heaven," this is the most historic movie studio lot in the world, which turned out more classics in the 1930s (about one a week in its heyday) than any other studio in history. They offer an informative and fun daily walking tour, which gives you a rare glimpse of Old Hollywood's golden age, as well as an insider's view of how a state-of-the-art motion picture studio is currently run. My favorite stop on the tour is the historic Thalberg Building, where Louis B. Mayer (the second "M" of MGM) and his head of production, Irving Thalberg (dubbed the "boy wonder") green-lit some of the most classic films ever to grace a silver screen. These were films like *Grand Hotel* (starring Greta Garbo), *A Night at the Opera* (starring the Marx Bros.), *Dinner at Eight* (starring Jean Harlow), *The Thin Man* (starring William Powell and Myrna Loy), and *The Wizard of Oz* (starring Judy Garland). Sadly, the physically frail Thalberg died in 1936 at the age of 37, but MGM still flourished in the '40s and '50s with a stream of timeless dramas and lavish musicals. These classics included *Meet Me in St. Louis*, *Singin' in the Rain*, *An American in Paris*, and *Gigi*. Many relics of its gilded, Art Deco past remain, and you can see them adorning the buildings, in the historic commissary, and in the sound stages haunted by ghosts of Hollywood past. The tour is a must-do for film fanatics. Reservations necessary.

10202 W. Washington Blvd., Culver City
(323) 520-TOUR
sonypicturesstudios.com

Westwood

20TH CENTURY FOX STUDIOS

Founded in 1925 by William Fox, this historic studio turned out nearly as many classic films as MGM in the '30s and '40s, making it MGM's longtime rival. Fox may not have possessed the number of superstars that MGM held in its arsenal, but the ones they did have were dazzling—like Shirley Temple (who at five years old was not only an amazing tap dancer but the studio's biggest moneymaker), pinup girl Betty Grable, Technicolor queen Carmen Miranda, handsome Gregory Peck, and smoldering Elizabeth Taylor. But Fox's most famous asset came in the 1950s—in the buxom-blond shape of Marilyn Monroe, who made some of my favorite films here on the lot, including *All About Eve*, *Gentlemen Prefer Blondes*, and *The Seven Year Itch*. Sadly, Fox does not offer guided tours, but even driving by can be exciting if you're a fan of its colorful history. If you do happen to get an invite one day, make sure you dine in their marvelous private commissary—and check out the walls painted with an original 1930s mural depicting all the studio's most glamorous stars.

10201 Pico Blvd., Century City
(310) 369-1000

APPLE PAN

Every time I push through the Apple Pan's shabby old screen door and sit on one of their red vinyl swivel stools at the wraparound Formica counter, I feel like a character out of an Edward Hopper painting or a Preston Sturges film. Apple Pan looks a lot like the diner where Joel McCrea woos Veronica Lake in his 1941 Hollywood farce, *Sullivan's Travels*. This is the quintessential, family-owned L.A. diner, and for a better visual, imagine if Dorothy's white clapboard house from *The Wizard of Oz* was dropped 60 years into the future by a time-traveling tornado—across the street from a Godzilla-sized mall. My favorite thing about "The Pan" is that everything is as it was when they first opened in 1947, including the 90-year-old waiters. So stop in, be prepared to wait a little, and order up some of the best old-fashioned diner food on the Westside—or in L.A. for that matter. Los Angelenos love their hickory burgers, tuna salad sandwiches, legendary banana cream and apple pies, and their farm-fresh ingredients. All the details here are totally World War II-style—they serve your grub on little brown paper plates after they've wrapped your order in wax paper, and even the sodas are served in paper cones. They will be serving "Quality Forever," as their original neon sign states.

10801 W. Pico Blvd., Los Angeles
(310) 475-3585

MATTEO'S

Opened in 1963, this is L.A.'s most *Goodfellas*-style Italian joint. Matteo's ambience is East Coast meets Old Hollywood—where the booths are red leather, there's always a Rat Pack soundtrack playing, and the dimly lit décor includes Christmas lights and wine bottles. They are famous for their old-school, hearty Italian dishes, like mozzarella marinara, chicken parmigiana, linguini with clams (my favorite), and veal Milanese (Sinatra's favorite). It was Frankie's favorite L.A. haunt, and he always sat in the same back-corner booth, which is now marked by one of his own abstract paintings.

2321 Westwood Blvd., Los Angeles
(310) 475-4521

UCLA AND ITS FILM AND TELEVISION ARCHIVE

On the lovely UCLA campus, which was built in 1928, you can either hang out, fondly remembering your college days, or if you're like me and never attended college, you can wear some penny loafers, find a nice bench to read on, and feel truly collegiate. Miraculously, the colors here feel like fall—they are romantic shades of amber, even in the yellow heat of a scorching L.A. summer. But aside from pretending I'm late for class, there's something magical about coming here at night, tea in hand—to find their quaint little theater and see a rare film alongside fellow classic film nerds and inquisitive students. Their calendar is filled with everything from rare '60s French New Wave to German Expressionist horror films of the 1920s. They also have an annual festival of features they themselves have restored in their film preservation facilities.

Did you know that 50 percent of all films produced in the United States pre-1950 have disappeared forever? That number grows daily, with 90 percent of our country's films currently deteriorating from age. Even our earliest television shows are on deteriorating tapes, but lucky for us, the UCLA Film and Television Archive has committed itself to the preservation of these invaluable moving images.

The James Bridges Theater
1409 Melnitz Hall, UCLA Campus, Westwood
(310) 206-8013
cinema.ucla.edu

ABOVE
UCLA's campus is just as idyllic today as when this postcard was printed in the 1930s. It's the perfect place for a lovely afternoon walk.

WESTWOOD MEMORIAL CEMETERY

This is where our country's most beloved legends lie. This is Marilyn Monroe's final resting place, the saddest of all the lonely starlets. When she died in 1962, at the young age of 36, her former husband, baseball legend Joe DiMaggio, chose this as her resting place because it was secluded. He had red roses placed on her crypt three times a week from her death until 1982. Her grave now lies in the shadow of (ironically) a movie theater. If in cemeteries all the spirits would sip champagne on their tombstones after midnight, this place would have the most otherworldly guest list. Those who would surely be on the V.I.P. list would be Natalie Wood, Dean Martin, film director John Cassavetes, Truman Capote, Peggy Lee, Frank Zappa, Carl Wilson of the Beach Boys, Walter Matthau, Jack Lemmon, and director Billy Wilder.

1218 Glendon Ave., Westwood
(310) 474-1579

"Los Angeles is a large city-like area surrounding
the Beverly Hills Hotel."

— *Fran Lebowitz*

CHAPTER FOUR

BEVERLY HILLS

Beverly Hills is a fancy fantasyland where you'd expect the streets to be paved with gold. It's a souvenir postcard of a golden era, a reminder of when Hollywood stars were really stars—not just paparazzi fodder, and they built their own residential sets to prove their power.

These homes rivaled even their most elaborate fictional film abodes. B. H. was developed as a city in 1907, but it was a financial failure until silent-film stars Mary Pickford and Douglas Fairbanks built their dream home named "Pickfair" in 1920, and the rest of Hollywood soon followed. This is where the very first gods and goddesses of the silver screen hung their designer hats. Beverly Hills is wrapped in historic architecture since actors frequently employed the actual studio set designers to build their own custom castles. In effect, Beverly Hills became a palm tree–lined kingdom of gilded gates, blue swimming pools (like the ones immortalized in David Hockney paintings), and platinum Rolls-Royces purring in the driveway. It's the kind of place where glitz sneaks up behind you, pulls you in, and makes you feel glad to be alive.

PREVIOUS SPREAD
Glamour icon Marlene Dietrich lived in this Art Deco mansion throughout the 1930s, followed by pinup goddess Rita Hayworth in the 1940s.

FAR LEFT
The Beverly Hills Hotel was featured on the cover of The Eagles' 1977 hit LP, *Hotel California*, in all its hazy, dreamy, California splendor.

LEFT
The author sips a perfect strawberry milkshake at her favorite legendary lunchtime haunt, The Beverly Hills Hotel's Fountain Coffee Shop.

THE BEVERLY HILLS HOTEL

If you love old-school Hollywood glamour, then the Beverly Hills Hotel is mecca. It's the tip of L.A.'s diamond iceberg, on which all other buildings just float by in a sea green with envy. It was a favorite home-away-from-home for Charlie Chaplin, Greta Garbo, Clark Gable, Carole Lombard, Ava Gardner, Liza Minnelli, John F. Kennedy, and Elizabeth Taylor (who has spent six of her honeymoons at the hotel). Designer Tom Ford has said, "When you pull up under that canopy you can't help but feel like Ricky and Lucy pulling into Hollywood from New York in their Cadillac. It's so glamorous!" This hotel is the perfect place for anyone who craves the sight of green-and-white-striped awnings, red carpets for your arrival, pink Spanish stucco, and custom banana-leaf wallpaper, which itself has become a recognizable icon. It was designed in 1949 by Paul Williams (the esteemed L.A. architect, not the *Muppet Movie* soundtrack composer). It is owned and was gorgeously renovated by the Sultan of Brunei, who bought it in 1987 for $185 million and put over $100 million into bringing it back to its gleaming pink glory. Though the furniture and paint are shiny new, it still retains a total 1950s glammy Hollywood pastiche.

Dubbed "The Pink Palace," this Spanish mission-style landmark was built in 1912 to lure potential residents to a new development called Beverly Hills. The hotel houses lavish rooms and private bungalows, original artwork on the walls, and pink marble powder rooms. It's a full-service resort with a day spa, a tearoom, boutiques, a pool as famous as the guests who swim in it, and the legendary Polo Lounge restaurant, where I've spied Sean Connery, Michael Caine, and Yoko Ono. There's no reason to leave—ever. Just call your friends to come visit you. It's much cheaper, though, to just pretend you live there and hang out every day. But my favorite thing about the Beverly Hills Hotel is the Fountain Coffee Shop, a favorite of Marilyn Monroe. I can just picture her sipping a vanilla milkshake with a cashmere coat wrapped around her shoulders and Ray-Bans to shield her eyes.

The best time to visit the Beverly Hills Hotel if you're a star-struck looky-loo is Oscar week. Just mill about in the lobby in your fanciest finery and kill some time smelling the spectacular floral arrangements until, bingo—the stars come waltzing in. And don't forget to tip the valet guys. They are not only sweet and will greet you with a warm hello even if you arrive in a backfiring jalopy, but they are cute to boot.

9641 Sunset Blvd., Beverly Hills
(310) 276-2251
beverlyhillshotel.com

BEVERLY HILLS RENT~A~CAR

Instead of a piña colada spray-scented Taurus (aka sofa on wheels), when cruising L.A. for vintage you need to ride in something vintage. Check out the Beverly Hills Rent-A-Car's small selection of swanky vintage convertible boats. Cruise in a mint-green 1959 Cadillac, a late '60s Cadillac DeVille, a 1975 Lincoln Continental pimpmobile, or a 1976 Cadillac El Dorado.

9732 S. Santa Monica Blvd., Beverly Hills
(310) 274-6969
bhrentacar.com

INSIDE SCOOP

Howard Hughes had all his Betties shacked up in the bungalows of the Beverly Hills Hotel so he could spy on them more conveniently. In the 1940s, surrealist art king Salvador Dalí and his fabulous muse wife, Gala, stayed in the hotel while Dalí painted portraits of Beverly Hills. During the 1960 filming of *Let's Make Love*, Marilyn Monroe was rumored to have conducted a secret affair with her irresistible costar Yves Montand, while they shared neighboring bungalows. Both stars were married at the time—he to actress Simone Signoret and she to playwright Arthur Miller. We do know that soon after wrapping the film, Marilyn's marriage quickly deteriorated. The Beverly Hills Hotel is always abuzz with scandal and excitement!

Q&A

Vintage

The Observer

DOMINICK DUNNE

Dunne is the author of five bestselling novels, including *The Way We Lived Then: Recollections of a Well-Known Name Dropper*, which is a wonderful scrapbook of his star-studded life in Beverly Hills. He has also produced several great films, including *Play It as It Lays* (1972), starring Tuesday Weld. He writes a long-running and always riveting column for *Vanity Fair*, where he uncovers the darker side of the rich and powerful. After surviving the loss of his daughter, actress Dominique (who was tragically murdered in 1982), he has become an important champion for victims' rights, covering many high-profile trials. Dunne is now working on his latest novel, *A Solo Act*.

JENNIFER BRANDT TAYLOR: What are your favorite L.A. haunts?

DD: The Beverly Hills Hotel. It evokes so many memories. It's where Howard Hughes had a bungalow with a guard outside. It's where a stool at the counter of the coffee shop was, and still is, the best seat in town.

The Church of the Good Shepherd in Beverly Hills. In the old days, mass on Sunday was the one the movie stars attended...Gary Cooper, Rosalind Russell, Loretta Young, Cesar Romero, Jayne Mansfield and her daughter, Mariska Hargitay. It's the church where my daughter was buried after she was murdered in 1982. Whenever I drive by, I bow my head.

Book Soup on Sunset Blvd. My favorite bookshop anywhere.

JBT: Have you ever had a starstruck moment?

DD: I produced *Ash Wednesday* (1973), in which Elizabeth Taylor starred with Henry Fonda. She was at the time married to Richard Burton. The picture was shot in the Italian Dolomites. None of us could speak Italian, so we clung together. The picture was not a hit, but the life experience was one of the most fascinating I've ever lived through. Except for Fonda, we were all drunk and stoned the whole time. Elizabeth was simply magnificent. She and Richard were the most famous couple in the world. Our lives were more interesting than the characters in the movie we were making.

JBT: What is the quintessential L.A. film?

DD: *Chinatown.*

GREYSTONE MANSION

Greystone Mansion is one of L.A.'s best-kept (and prettiest) secrets. In 1928, oil tycoon Edward Doheny built this posh estate as a gift to his son, Ned Jr., at a cost of over $4 million. Many people hail this massive home as one of the grandest mansions on the West Coast (second only to William Randolph Hearst's San Simeon.) Ned and his family moved into the mansion in 1928, and the spread included 55 rooms, tennis courts, a pool, a greenhouse, and its own fire station. Despite their fortune of over $100 million, the Dohenys had their share of tragedy. Edward Doheny was publicly accused of bribery, and his son's life ended in a bizarre murder-suicide at Greystone when Edward Sr.'s personal secretary killed Doheny Jr. and then himself when he was denied a raise. The son's widow lived at Greystone until 1955 (along with a couple of ghosts, no doubt). In 1954, the property was sold to "Trousdale Estates." In 1955, the remaining 18.3 acres of land, including Greystone Mansion, were sold to a businessman who never occupied it. The mansion remained vacant until 1965 when the City of Beverly Hills purchased it, and in 1971, dedicated the site as a public park. In 1976, Greystone Mansion became a historic landmark, since it was the largest home ever built in Beverly Hills, and the first in the fancy tradition of White House-sized, overly extravagant, Aaron Spelling-worthy manors everyone seems to adore.

Many movies have been filmed at Greystone Mansion, including *The Witches of Eastwick*, *The Big Lebowski*, *Death Becomes Her*, and *Ghostbusters II*. It has also been the set for memorable and beautiful music videos. Elton John's great music video where Robert Downey Jr. wanders around lip-synching takes place at Greystone as well as the Guns and Roses' *November Rain* video, where Axl Rose weds Stephanie Seymour in true rock 'n' roll decadence.

The coolest thing about Greystone is that while it's semi-fun to drive past all the grand mansions of Beverly Hills, this one you can actually stroll around without getting arrested. The mansion is guarded with wrought-iron gates, and the 16-acre grounds are a maze of lush landscaping, winding stone walkways, brick stairways, sweeping green lawns, wonderful vistas, sculpted hedges, and hidden courtyards. Peek through the dusty windows of the mansion, and you'll see thick gray limestone walls, heavy wooden doors, glorious old ballrooms, crystal chandeliers, massive marble fireplaces, and sweeping stone archways—like a giant castle abandoned in some tragic fairy tale. There is an undeniably beautiful sadness to this deserted mansion. The grounds are dotted with numerous swimming and reflecting pools, fountains, waterfalls, and ponds, but many of these now stand dry and spooky. The grounds are open daily, and Music in the Mansion performances are held in the unique and intimate setting of the historic Greystone Mansion's living room.

905 Loma Vista Dr., Beverly Hills
(310) 550-4654
greystonemansion.org

THE PAPER BAG PRINCESS

If you've ever dreamed of discovering a time machine that could take you to shop for designer clothes at Saks Fifth Avenue in the 1960s, then this boutique will surely give you heart palpitations. Glamour-puss owner and former model Elizabeth Mason stocks one of L.A.'s most dazzling collections of classic vintage—not to mention that she's a total doll! Her retail philosophy is as follows: "If they come in and behave like a celebrity, I'll treat them like a person. If they behave like a person, I'll treat them like a celebrity." Needless to say, she treated us like Oscar winners. This is where fancy Beverly Hills ladies with overflowing closets come to unload their treasures. You'll be awestruck by minty items from all eras of iconic designers like Chanel, YSL, Givenchy, Chloe, Dior, Ceil Chapman, and Pucci. She also stocks consignment pieces, showstopping baubles, and a shoe department to make any girl's heart melt. The "Princess" is also the only boutique in L.A. that has a bridal trousseau room. Her celebrity-studded client list includes Donatella Versace, Winona Ryder, Courtney Love, Molly Ringwald, and Madonna. Prices range from $195 for a collectible pair of never-worn 1950s glittered Schiaparelli stilettos, in the original box, to $12,000 for an Adrian jacket once belonging to Theadora Getty.

8818 W. Olympic Blvd., Beverly Hills
(310) 358-9036
thepaperbagprincess.com

LEFT
Elizabeth Mason (aka The Paper Bag Princess) glams it up in a 1940s Ceil Chapman dress (Marilyn Monroe's favorite designer), accompanied by the boutique's official mascot, Robbie.

ABOVE
An extraordinary collection of vintage couture chapeaux from the estate of Betsey Bloomingdale.

AVALON HOTEL

If the B.H. pink palace is a little over your budget, try this midcentury gem of a hideaway. Once called the Beverly Carlton, it has since been revamped by über interior designer Kelly Wearstler with her signature inimitable, vintage-inspired flair. Many rooms feature classic furniture by Eames and George Nelson and include groovy touches like bubble lamps, shag carpeting, and Keane-inspired paintings. This hotel was a favorite of Marilyn Monroe in the 1950s, and you can just picture her swimming in their fabulous hourglass-shaped pool, after sipping screwdrivers in a private poolside cabana. Minutes from Rodeo Drive, you can take a beautiful walk to some killer shopping.

9400 W. Olympic Blvd., Beverly Hills
(310) 277-5221
avalonbeverlyhills.com

NATE 'N AL

This is a serious Jewish delicatessen with an old-school clientele that has been serving great pastrami sandwiches, bagels with lox, and matzoh ball soup since 1945 to three generations of power-hungry agents and retired Hollywood geezers. Their tough waitresses remind me of Flo from the '70s show *Alice*. And for you film fanatics, this happens to be Roman Polanski's favorite American breakfast joint.

414 N. Beverly Dr., Beverly Hills
(310) 274-0101
natenal.com

THE PLAYBOY MANSION

Built in 1927 by Bullock's department store scion Arthur Letts Jr., the gorgeous English-style stone manor features 18-inch walls, an Italian marble entryway, a built-in pipe organ, stunning gardens, an infamous pool grotto, a zoo of exotic animals, and quite a few buxom "Bunnies." Good luck getting an invite.

10236 Charing Cross Rd., Beverly Hills

VIRGINIA ROBINSON GARDENS

If you're into strolling along rare and beautiful blooms while in the shadow of a historically beautiful six-acre estate, boy, have I got a sight for you! Virginia Robinson's Estate and Gardens is a well-hidden secret sanctuary of gorgeousness, and it's open to the public! In 1911, when Beverly Hills was still mostly barley fields, Harry Robinson (of Robinson's Department Stores) had this magnificent estate built for him and his wife, Virginia. It was designed in a classic Mediterranean-style by developer Nathaniel Dryden, Virginia's father, who is also responsible for the glorious Brand Castle (p.184) in Glendale. Robinson Gardens is very significant to the growth of this part of the city; its deed actually reads, "The first residence in Beverly Hills." The Robinsons also inspired the development of downtown Beverly Hills by opening their department store, in turn encouraging others to invest, which led to Beverly Hills' current status as one of the most ritzy retail areas on the planet. The fabulous couple shared a passion for gardening and collecting rare plants, fueled by their travels around the globe. You can see these plants gracing the landscaped paradise to this day! They were also known for their glamorous soirees, during which dignitaries and movie stars such as Fred Astaire and Charles Boyer would drop by, which no doubt lured more stars to become neighbors. Virginia, who lived to be 99, graciously donated her estate to the public so that it could remain a reminder of the elegant style in which people once lived. Tours Tuesday through Friday. Call for reservation.

1008 Elden Way, Beverly Hills
(310) 276-5367
www.robinson-gardens.com

802:—Willat Studio, Washington Blvd., near Los Angeles, California.

LEFT
The infamous "Witch's House" was first built as a silent-movie studio in Culver City, and is now a private residence—and popular Halloween trick-or-treating spot.

THE WITCH'S HOUSE

This was originally built in the 1920s by studio art director Harry Oliver, to be used as a silent film set for the Willatt movie studio in Culver City. It hails from an era when architects began letting their imaginations run wild, turning pockets of L.A. into the surreal fantasyland it is today. And in this land of mixed-up, screwed-up home design, there sits a witch's cottage—with towering peaked roofs, crooked shutters, a magical overgrown English garden surrounded by a moat, and a very long candy line on Halloween. It was moved to B.H. in 1934 and converted into a real home, named the Spadena House (after the first family to reside there). It's now owned by a real estate agent who is restoring it to be once again the most magical storybook castle in all of Hollywoodland.

N. Walden Dr., Beverly Hills
(310) 271-8174

FRANCIS KLEIN

Established in 1960, they display (and sell to those with deep pockets) vintage estate jewels covered in glimmering gems. These are the kind of rubylicious pieces you'd see Jean Harlow wearing in *Dinner at Eight*. In their Art Deco display cases, you'll be dazzled by Victorian, Edwardian, Art Deco, Art Nouveau, and modern-era accoutrements—nothing less than extraordinary.

310 N. Rodeo Dr., Beverly Hills
(310) 273-0155

TRADER VIC'S

Looking for the perfect place to get cocktails served in coconuts and adorned with pineapple slices and plastic swords? Aloha! Trader Vic's has been rockin' Polynesian style in the Beverly Hilton since 1955, and it's one of the last great remnants of L.A.'s tiki lounge culture. It's a little paradise of mai tais and mink coats, candlelight and clamshells, Asian fare and flaming drinks to share. It's a fantasy island of taxidermied blowfish, red pleather booths, brass menus, and wooden canoes floating overhead.

Beverly Hilton Hotel
9876 Wilshire Blvd., Beverly Hills
(310) 274-7777
tradervics.com

CHAPTER FIVE

WEST HOLLYWOOD

La Cienega Blvd. ✦ *Robertson Blvd.* ✦ *Santa Monica Blvd.*
Sunset Blvd.

BLACKMAN/CRUZ

To know the true nature of West Hollywood (WeHo to the locals) is to know that it is the only community in L.A. County that voted against being annexed into the City of Los Angeles.

Due to this rebellion, it's more accepting of artistic and alternative lifestyles, not to mention that the sexy Sunset Strip is a part of its turf so it also boasts most of L.A.'s coolest rock 'n' roll history. If you want a real architectural treat, drive down Fountain Ave. between Crescent Heights Blvd., and La Cienega Blvd., which is a historic district, and you will see some gorgeous architecture, in all-mixed-up styles from Moorish palaces to Spanish haciendas to French châteaux and Art Deco towers. Many of these are legendary apartments where countless stars once lived, including Marilyn Monroe, Joan Crawford, Bette Davis, Dorothy Dandridge, and Al Pacino.

This store has an otherworldly, unique selection of modern and antique objets d'art and architectural pediments, which would've looked perfect as set décor for the futuristic silent film *Metropolis* (1927). The store's owners, David Cruz and Adam Blackman, are personally responsible for starting the machine-age silver-steel hospital and industrial furniture craze. They have exquisite taste and an eye for uniqueness, and the store features items you'll never find anywhere on Earth, except maybe the Museum of Jurassic Technology. They delight in taking things that were once thought of as friendly and turning them into something more sinister, like a miniature salesman's sample of a saw from 1910 ($950), a Victorian-era wooden baby rattle ($550), a Buck Rogers Disintegrater gun from 1939 ($650), or a dilapidated Carl Zeiss camera ($550). More obviously wicked in nature are the rusty ol' Colt 45s on display and the real iron and leather shackles similar to the ones Anthony Quinn wore in Fellini's *La Strada*. This is the perfect place to come gift shopping for the eccentric collector who already has everything. They also sell exquisite and historically inspired pieces of their own design, under their label BC Workshop, which includes my most currently desired décor items—black metal bat incense burners that gracefully hang from the ceiling ($4,750), Bauhausesque leather and oak lounge chairs ($5,200), simple lamps with iron skull bases ($2,200), and the giant hand-shaped andirons (*Hand-irons*. Get it? $10,200).

**800 N. La Cienega Blvd., West Hollywood
(310) 657-9228
blackmancruz.com**

OPPOSITE
BC Workshop limited edition hand andirons and large aluminum architectural panels from the 1960s grace Blackman Cruz's spellbinding shop.

CHAPMAN RADCLIFF

Proprietress/interior decorator Ruthie Sommers curates this cottage-like jewel of a shop like a dream. Favored for its well-kept '60s and '70s furniture and lighting fixtures, she tactfully places exquisite pieces alongside more tongue-in-cheek affairs, like original chinoiserie writing desks (price upon request, yikes!) next to a very Liberace-style poodle dog statue ($950). Check out the large 1940s lantern from San Francisco's Chinatown and the pristine Chinese Chippendale dining set for a sophisticatedly groovy home.

517 N. La Cienega Blvd., West Hollywood
(310) 659-8062
chapmanradcliffhome.com

REFORM GALLERY

Picture Joni Mitchell and Graham Nash going furniture shopping for their Laurel Canyon love pad, circa 1968, and you have a pretty good picture of the kind of organic vintage home décor Reform has on hand. Their serious and sometimes whimsical selection of rare furnishings is modernistic with a warmly mellow California vibe. Everything here seems to be inspired by nature and many were passionately handmade by West Coast artisans, like Jerry and Evelyn Ackerman, who together made many colorful Fantasia-esque wall tapestries, tile mosaics, and hooked rugs in the '50s and '60s. Some other pieces I most adored upon last visit were the '60s ceramic vases and necklace beads by California-based artist Doyle Lane (who is also said to be the first African American ceramist), giant sculptural mixed-wood doors from 1965 by Mabel Hutchinson ($32,000), a stereo cabinet from 1958 by Glenn of California ($4,500), and a groovy sofa from 1965 with rich, patterned velvet upholstery by Jack Lenor Larsen.

816 N. La Cienega Blvd., West Hollywood
(310) 854-1033
reform-modern.com

WEIDMAN GALLERY

Established in 1963, this gallery is home to original vintage film and advertising posters and limited-edition contemporary posters and art from all over the world. The works are in pristine condition, and they offer custom framing services.

811 N. La Cienega Blvd., West Hollywood
(310) 657-5286
weidmangallery.com

TOP RIGHT
Whimsical 1960s wall weavings by Evelyn Ackerman.

BOTTOM RIGHT
A 1965 sofa with Jack Lenor Larsen velvet upholstery, and a 1966 painting by Juan M. Sanchez at Reform Gallery.

OPPOSITE
Clean, natural and groovy seventies California living at Reform Gallery.

BARNEY'S BEANERY

Built in 1927, it is one of the last original Route 66 roadhouses, and it's about as close as you're gonna get to a real, old-time billiards joint without it getting too scary. It's like a vintage sports bar with American comfort food, karaoke, a pool table, and pinball machines. Check out the cool '70s decoupaged tables, extremely faux-Tiffany lamps, photos of Mick Jagger, psychedelic Peter Max art, and license plates on the ceiling. Because of its proximity to all the Sunset Blvd. clubs, West Hollywood art galleries, and record labels, Barney's Beanery has attracted the counterculture of every generation—starting with the flappers, through to the Beats, and up to rock stars and actors. It was frequented by Jean Harlow, Clark Gable, Clara Bow, Errol Flynn, and Bette Davis in the '30s. In the mid-'60s it became a Beat and pop artists' hang. Regulars included Ed Ruscha, Dennis Hopper, Mel Ramos, Marlon Brando, and Charles Bukowski. Also a favorite of musicians, Jimi Hendrix, Janis Joplin (favorite booth #34), Jim Morrison, and Led Zeppelin were frequent guests. Now the crowd is more college frat boys and rowdy rock stars, but it's always a great time to go with friends and hang with Hollywood's ghosts.

8447 Santa Monica Blvd., West Hollywood
(323) 654-2287
qsbilliards.com/barneysbeanery

Robertson Blvd.

INDIGO SEAS

Lynn Von Kersting has created a romantic, unique, and identifiable home décor style all her own. Indigo Seas is where she sells exquisite, turn-of-the-century French antiques. You'll find antique Eiffel Tower statues, Venetian glass chandeliers, and gorgeous antique furniture—all in the most romantic colors you've ever seen. Check out the rose-strewn tablecloths and the mishmash of glorious throw cushions. French music wafts through the speakers while you admire the feather-stuffed chairs, rustic dining tables, ashtrays, and cocktail glasses. She also stocks a wonderful selection of rare, first edition books by stylish authors like Cecil Beaton. It's not cheap, but there are little trinkets almost anyone can afford, like soaps, seashells, and paper lanterns. And if shopping has made you work up an appetite, you must try lunch at Lynn's notoriously romantic restaurant next door, The Ivy. It is mostly known for being the eatery of choice for Hollywood's A-list, but the food is the star attraction if you ask me. For a delightful meal, sit on cushy, overstuffed floral pillows on the cute front porch of this rickety old house, and try their honey-fried chicken (a longtime favorite of mine) accompanied by mango chutney, veggies, and perfect mashed potatoes. I also adore ordering their mint juleps on warm summer nights, and every Sunday they serve the most heavenly, freshly baked scones with homemade raspberry spread.

123 N. Robertson Blvd., West Hollywood
(310) 550-8758

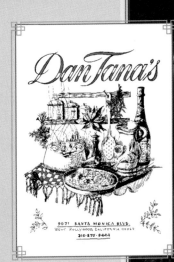

CHERRY WEST

Just like a cherry, the current stock at this vintage paradise is always ripe for the pickin'. This sister store of two well-regarded NYC locations, Cherry West specializes in mod, disco, and '80s glam styles for men and women. It also features more structured American designers like Anne Klein and Bonnie Cashin. Owners Cesar Padilla and Radford Brown also stock '80s Japanese lines like Yamamoto and Kansai. Though a bit too pricey, they have a fun selection of trendy vintage—from Gunne Sax prairie dresses to never-worn Joseph La Rose '50s spike heels, '80s Chanel sunglasses, and many leather cinch belts with patched appliqués. The men's selection has everything from Gucci jackets to rock tees and bell-bottom rocker pants. They claim that they can locate anything—quiz the owners and be surprised.

8250 Santa Monica Blvd., West Hollywood
(323) 650-4698
cherryboutique.com

DAN TANA'S

If you're an old-schoolie, you call it "Tana's." Opened in 1964, Dan Tana's has a dark, warm, old-fashioned vibe—with real waiters (read: not actors). This is an old-school Northern Italian hang and celebrity haunt (Madonna loves the grilled swordfish). Come here for hearty steaks and chops, linguine with clams, and mozzarella marinara. Look for the canary yellow exterior and then languish in the lacquer red room with white iron leaf accents. This is the closest thing to L.A.'s Little Italy—Chianti wine jugs hang from the crimson red ceiling, the tables are covered in checkered tablecloths, and white ironwork of acorns adorn the walls. It's small, crowded, and lively—with lots of middle-aged guys who've watched *Goodfellas* one too many times and are checkin' out all the Beverly Hills blondes at the bar.

Come here for star spotting—it's favored by Johnny Depp, Jennifer Aniston, and Springsteen himself. It is also said that Tana's was where John Belushi had his last meal. Be mindful of the strong cocktails—especially the martinis. Reservations recommended.

9071 Santa Monica Blvd., West Hollywood
(310) 275-9444
dantanasrestaurant.com

FORMOSA CAFÉ

Declared a historic landmark, this cafe looks like a Chandleresque red and ebony, Chinese-themed watering hole with a great neon sign, a black-and-white awning, and great make-out lighting. It's a setting straight out of film noir—with hundreds of autographed photos lining the ruby walls that date back to Hollywood's golden age. It's the perfect place to show off that little black dress and '40s Carmen Miranda platforms, and it's more famous for its drinks than its food (trust me on this one).

Originally built in 1925 as a trolley car, it emerged as a restaurant in 1939. Hollywood myths say that here is where old-time gangsters like Bugsy Siegel and Mickey Cohen kept their gambling wins safe in a hidden box in the floor. "Ol' Blue Eyes" (Sinatra) ate chow mein here after winning his Oscar for *From Here to Eternity*. It's also been immortalized in several films, including *Swingers* and a key scene from *LA Confidential*, where a detective mistakes the "real" Lana Turner for a hooker. Ironically, this was where the *really* real Ms. Turner loved to go for chop suey.

7156 Santa Monica Blvd., West Hollywood
(323) 850-9050
formosacafe.com

THE TROUBADOUR

While Sunset Strip's Roxy and Whiskey-À-Go-Go still showcase up-and-coming bands nightly, they are mostly pretty bad. But Doug Weston's Troubadour still only books the best. This rock club is almost as legendary as the artists who have debuted on its small stage. It's the home of Elton John's first live show in the United States, John Lennon and Harry Nilsson partied here on John's famous lost weekend away from Yoko, and Carly Simon played her very first show in 1971 while opening for Cat Stevens (she met James Taylor on that same fabled night—they later married).

They have a fun, hall-of-fame bar, and it still launches and showcases great new artists today—the Ravonettes, Lavender Diamond, the Like, Rilo Kiley, Quintron and Miss Pussycat, and Phantom Planet. It's a guitar slinger's heaven, and they still sell out the little space with more well-known acts like the Yeah, Yeah, Yeahs, Patti Smith, and Franz Ferdinand.

9081 Santa Monica Blvd., West Hollywood
(310) 276-6168
troubadour.com

BOOT STAR

Boot Star has an amazing selection of cowboy boots, both vintage and new. They also specialize in custom-made boots—with inlaid leather flowers, birds, or moons. There's something romantic about those worn-out stitches, stars, and butterflies. Custom boots start at about $495 and get pricier (depending on how many details you request—like perhaps, your name in gold old-Western-leather Saloon font). Yee haw!

8493 Sunset Blvd., West Hollywood
(323) 650-0475

MYSTERY PIER BOOKS, INC.

I love that amid all the hubbub of the sleazy Sunset Strip, you can find a dark, covered staircase to a hidden cottage in a back alley and unearth sought-after, fine and rare books: coveted and collectible literature—with a focus on American and British classics—signed copies by many reclusive and iconic scribes, Hollywoodiana and antiquarian tomes. The store has a love of mystery, crime, and detective fiction, and this is actually the perfect place to seek out a prized copy of a Nathanael West or Dashiell Hammett novel. Just put on your rain slicker, big black

sunglasses, creep down the hidden alley, and emerge with a suspicious paper bag filled with a first edition classic. It's also a favorite stop for Sir Michael Caine when he's in town and Bono, who they say buys Irish literature to give as gifts. On my last visit with Harvey and Louis, Mystery Pier's brilliant and sweet proprietors, I spied a first edition of *Moby Dick* (for a whopping $110,000), an agency-submission transcript by Raymond Chandler ($55,000), F. Scott Fitzgerald's college yearbook, a signed edition of an Oscar Wilde work, and a book of Warhol Polaroids signed to Ryan and Tatum O'Neal by Andy himself. Oh my word! It's all too much for a book nerd to handle.

8826 Sunset Blvd., West Hollywood
(310) 657-5557
mysterypierbooks.com

RAINBOW BAR & GRILL

This heavy-metal time warp was established in 1972, which may not sound very "vintage," but upon entering, you'll be transported to a land of Aqua Net and Tommy Lee. It's great for heavy-metal–themed birthday dinners. Tease your hair and memorize the lyrics to some Motley Crüe tune (so you can sing along with the rest of the gang). Hair bands still rock here! There's a huge fireplace, framed, signed photos of Led Zeppelin, greasy calamari to soak up the whiskey, cheesy tunes and cheesy pizza, and try the apple burrito for dessert. This is where all the rockers come after all their shows on the Sunset Strip.

9015 Sunset Blvd., West Hollywood
(310) 278-4232
rainbowbarandgrill.com

SUNSET TOWER

> **"I am living in a very posh establishment, the Sunset Tower, which, or so the local gentry tell me, is where every scandal that ever happened happened."**
>
> — *Truman Capote*, letter to Leo Lerman, December 8, 1947

Sunset Tower is an Art Deco landmark with floor-to-ceiling, half-sphere windows that offer sweeping views of Hollywood. This legendary hotel had been known as the Argyle for many years, but it is now back to the first name it was called when it opened as a residential hotel in the 1920s. Even after all these years, the hotel still holds its original flawless elegance. The Sunset Tower graces the commercially tacky Sunset Strip like a pristine diamond on a bed of gold sparkle spandex. On the building's exterior there are Deco scenes of pagan goddesses and centaurs and Adam and Eve. The pure Art Deco lines, muted palette, and use of woods gives the hotel a rich feeling of Old Hollywood. I've been to parties in the glamorous 15th-floor penthouses where I flirted more with the original gold-plated brass fixtures in the stunning black limestone powder rooms than the handsome guests.

Fabulous former residents include Errol Flynn, Claudette Colbert, Ziegfeld Girl Billie Burke, Marilyn Monroe, Elizabeth Taylor, Frank Sinatra, Paulette Goddard, and ZaSu Pitts. Howard Hughes lived in both penthouses as well as the entire 14th floor. John Wayne lived in what is now the Argyle Spa and was rumored to have kept a milk cow out on the spa's back terrace.

Designed in 1929 by prominent Los Angeles architect Leland A. Bryant, the building was a landmark from its opening and a favorite of Hollywood stars for decades. In more recent decades, however, the hotel changed hands several times, and when proprietor Jeff Klein acquired the property in 2004, it was badly in need of a shine. Architecturally, the Sunset Tower represents the moment when Los Angeles, Art Deco, and Hollywood came together. It is considered to be one of the most important Deco structures in Los Angeles and is listed on the National Register of Historic Places. It's now the hotel of choice for artists like glam-rock crooner Bryan Ferry of Roxy Music, and rebel filmmaker Vincent Gallo. Try the utterly chic Tower Bar and restaurant, but be prepared to drop an entire paycheck (it's worth it).

8358 Sunset Blvd., West Hollywood
(323) 654-7100
sunsettowerhotel.com

YE COACH AND HORSES

With its rock-filled jukebox, faux Tudor décor, hunting scene paintings, and friendly folks pounding pints of Guinness, Ye Coach and Horses ensures a night to remember (or forget, if you have one too many). This is the cozy, Disney-version of an old-time British pub. And for all you Smiths fans, Morrissey is said to be a regular.

7617 Sunset Blvd., Hollywood
(323) 876-6900

INSIDE SCOOP

The Sunset Tower has appeared in a number of films, including Robert Altman's *The Player*. Its first literary and screen mentions were in Raymond Chandler's noir novel, *Farewell, My Lovely* and its film adaptation, *Murder, My Sweet* (1944).

CHAPTER SIX

MELROSE AVE.

DECADES

Take the long, leopard-print staircase up to vintage heaven, and you'll find Cameron Silver, Decades' proprietor, playing the world's chicest god. He's truly passionate about his collection and generous with his knowledge. He has the most stylish clientele in all of LaLaLand, and he's responsible for helping starlets find a higher taste level and a sense of fashion history. Check out the Hermès desk accessories, alligator Kelly bags, diaphanous Thea Porter, Dior, and much more. Decades also stocks all my favorite British designers of the '60s and '70s: Ossie Clark, Biba, The Fool, and Jean Muir. The collections come straight from serious movie star estates. This is L.A.'s vintage couture H.Q.!

Cameron is my favorite boutique owner in Los Angeles, but he's more than that—he's a vintage confidant and knows all the best stories, the history of the clothes in his store, and all the socialites who hold their families' collections until they are ready to give them up. They all give their clothes to him because he's not only dashingly handsome, but sweet, genuine, and totally unaffected by his fame in the fashion community (a rarity in this town, where vintage collectors usually have Louis Vuitton-logoed egos).

And for label lovers, on the ground floor you will find Decades Two. It's a designer-resale boutique that offers everything from once-worn Chanel bouclé suits to Versace gowns and last season's leather Balenciaga bags.

**8214 1/2 Melrose Ave., Los Angeles
(323) 655-0223**
decadesinc.com and decadestwo.com

ABOVE AND BELOW
Oscar-worthy vintage couture at Decades.

ABOVE
Decades proprietor Cameron Silver attempts to retrieve the crocodile Hermès Kelly bag the author was dangerously coveting. Aside from that nasty incident, he's a true vintage gentleman, always happy to wax poetic about his remarkable collection. The author is wearing a 1960s Don Loper satin opera coat (a favorite of Lucille Ball), courtesy of Decades.

THIS SPREAD
Decades' dashingly handsome owner and vintage-style connoisseur Cameron Silver (who was once a cabaret singer in Germany) refers to himself as "a storyteller who uses fashion to teach history and to make people feel beautiful." When asked to tell us about his most glam customer, he says "Britt Ekland came in on Valentine's Day in a Burberry trench coat and a big hat. She's such perfect sixties glam!" As for Decades' prices, they range from $95 for a 1970s bangle to $35,000 for a strapless Dior worn to the Oscars by Trudie Styler.

BOO RADLEY'S ANTIQUES

European furniture from the '20s–'40s at amazingly fair prices. Check out the walnut vanities, cool 1930s shortwave radios, and detailed armoires with little plaques on each shelf. Owner Lorca has a true passion for home décor with a history, and many of the pieces come from her own home. I envision furnishing my entire house here—all of the pieces are gorgeous. The store smells like rustic old wood, and there's a rock 'n' roll vibe to the store, despite the selection of streamlined Deco styles.

6825 Melrose Ave., Los Angeles
(323) 939-6909

CHIC-A-BOOM

Pack rats rejoice! Chic-a-Boom sells everything from original Shaun Cassidy lunch boxes to Black Sabbath band pins, and obscure rock magazines to important pieces of signed costume jewels. The shop's glam proprietor, who reminds me of '70s supermodel Dayle Haddon, and her husband, Paul, can find you just about anything your pop culture-loving heart desires. I was searching for an original poster from the obscure '60s film *Wonderwall* starring Jane Birkin, and they found one that was not only a poster, but it unfolded into the booklet that was given out at the original premiere. If you ever need a gift for your memorabilia-collecting boyfriend, who thinks he already has everything, come here.

6817 Melrose Ave., Los Angeles
(323) 931-7441

MAXFIELD

Besides being the first store to bring Yohji Yamamoto and Giorgio Armani to Los Angeles, Maxfield's also boasts that they have the largest selection of vintage Hermès bags and watches anywhere in the world. It remains the city's style pioneer, with a current lineup that includes top-shelf, hard-to-find designers like Rochas, Libertine, Dries Van Noten, and Balenciaga. They also sell my favorite scented candles in the world, by L.A. resident and opera singer/interior designer Rose Tarlow. You'll also discover many out-of-print art, fashion, and photography books, cocktail sets, and an extraordinary selection of oddities, curiosities, and Louis Vuitton trunks. And as a bonus for celebrity watchers, I've spotted more stars here than anywhere in L.A.—from Gwyneth Paltrow to Winona Ryder to Elton John. The store's entrance is hard to miss—just look for the mammoth monkey statues crouched by the parking lot, and you'll know you've arrived.

8825 Melrose Ave., Los Angeles
(310) 274-8800

MELROSE TRADING POST

Head over to the Fairfax High School parking lot, where many designers and savvy celebs pick up fun vintage items at a steal. Melrose Trading Post is an antiques and collectibles market where you can find '50s party dresses, great '70s collectibles, tooled leather purses, shabby chic furniture pieces, chunky costume jewels, hippie oils—the gamut! The market is held every Sunday from 9 a.m. to 5 p.m. and costs only $2.00. The admission price raises funds for Fairfax High School's art and after-school programs.

544 N. Fairfax Ave., Los Angeles
(323) 655-7679
greenwayarts.org/tradingpost.htm

RIGHT
The author and her vintage hunting posse, Moira and Miss Lizzie, have made the Melrose Trading Post their Sunday morning tradition.

MISTER FREEDOM

Just off the cheesy, tourist-infested part of Melrose Ave. lies Christophe Loiron's supercool realm for hard-to-find, new/old stock and casual vintage. Loiron carries clothing, cowboy boots, and accessories from all over the world. The shop is primarily for guys, but there is also a small selection of tomboy-inspired vintage for gals who have a bit of Annie Hall in them—or who are trying to emulate Katharine Hepburn's chutzpah. Check out the workwear, dungarees, original surfwear, and striped Warhol sailor shirts, which sell out immediately. Guys! Look like Marlon Brando in *The Wild One*! Girls! Look like Jean Seberg in *Breathless*!

7161 Beverly Blvd., Los Angeles
(323) 653-2014
misterfreedom.com

NECROMANCE

Attention all goths—or anyone who was obsessed with Siouxsie and the Banshees in high school. With an owner originally hailing from the Bayou, it's no wonder why the store is filled with skulls and bones, mounted bats and butterflies, Victorian mourning jewelry, antique funerary pieces, and medical instruments. I love their selection of gorgeous, turn-of-the century embossed valentines and eerie paper ephemera. This small boutique rivals the Haunted Mansion ride at Disneyland in morbidity, but you'll find no animatronic puppets here. This is all the real deal. Only take those with you who aren't easily spooked. Boo!

7220 Melrose Ave., Los Angeles
(323) 934-8684
necromance.com

OFF THE WALL (ANTIQUES AND WEIRD STUFF)

This is a legendary store that as a kid I actually thought was a museum. During the 1980s Melrose heyday this was the coolest vintage décor store in all of L.A. It's now practically the size of a peanut and almost a landmark. They deal mostly with private clients looking for that one major, showstopping piece—like a 6-foot-high Mutoscope punching bag arcade game from 1910. Many of the pieces they sell are incredible architectural salvages with a sense of either glamorous Art Deco design or intentionally tacky kitsch. Truly "off the wall" items like a 5-foot Virgin Mary church statuette, or a large, bronzed aquarium with sculpted seahorse legs from 1926. The items will cost you an arm and a leg, but it's worth a look.

7325 Melrose Ave., Los Angeles
(323) 930-1185
offthewallantiques.com

THE RECORD COLLECTOR

It's a classic music store—with a sophisticated selection of records—in a quaint space, much less overwhelming than nearby superstore Amoeba Music. Though it may be a bit overpriced (most LPs around $25), and they have only a small selection of pop and rock, they carry amazing classical composers, lounge music, jazz LPs, soundtracks, and rare 78s. I waltzed in thinking I'd stump the owner, Sanders Chase, by asking for an album by a very hard-to-find female vocalist of the 1920s, and surprisingly, he had several for me to choose from—all in minty mint condition. Be sure to check out the gorgeous listening room and the wall of photos documenting all the legends who've stopped by.

7809 Melrose Ave., Los Angeles
(323) 655-6653
therecordcollector.net

RESURRECTION

This is the L.A. headquarters of the infamous NYC-based chain of hot vintage boutiques that specialize in designers. The shops are a little more downtown rock 'n' roll than the rest of the gang. Owners Katy and Marc scour the globe and have vintage-seekers planted globally, like spies. They carry designers like Ossie Clark, Pucci, Courrèges, and Biba—basically, things even clotheshorse Kate Moss would covet. The sweet staff will help you find tons of old-school Gucci logo accessories, Hermès ties and knickknacks, YSL gold chain belts and sunglasses—even 1980s Air Jordans for your Beastie Boys-idolizing boyfriend. Not only designer obsessed, they also stock obscure labels and label-less pieces that are just too fabulous to pass up. They've amassed such a great selection that they sometimes have parties to celebrate the exciting collections they've acquired—like a soiree they recently threw for the unveiling of Vivienne Westwood's groundbreaking '80s pirate collection. Many stylists of modern "it" girls shop here to find those camera-worthy pieces that will surely wind up gracing the tabloids' fashion "do" pages—like Rachel Zoe, who is responsible for the looks of Lindsay Lohan and Nicole Richie.

8006 Melrose Ave., Los Angeles
(323) 651-5516
resurrectionvintage.com

THANKS FOR THE MEMORIES

Maddie and David Sadofski carry great twentieth-century designs—items you think you'd only see in a 1930s *Architectural Digest* or adorning the set of a Cedric Gibbons film. The vibe never ceases to change in here, and the proprietress is always happy to teach you a thing or two about the history of a piece.

This is the cream of the early modernist crop. They sell both femme and masculine furniture and accessories from the Deco period—most of which were inspired by the German Bauhaus movement of the 1920s. Every piece is in the same condition as the day it was originally bought. The mahogany desks, reverse-painted picture frames, and the nude goddess torchères are my favorites. The selection of jewelry is also mind-blowing, tempting you with everything from carved Bakelite brooches to marcasite cocktail rings and ornate Mexican sterling and turquoise cuff bracelets.

8319 Melrose Ave., Los Angeles
(323) 852-9407

WASTELAND

This is a vintage and recent-designer resale outlet (they give the best prices in town for your retro wares and gently worn special pieces). Bring your gold go-go boots, angelic '70s disco Gunne Sax gowns, and '80s Diane von Furstenberg sunglasses, but be warned—the staff is well-educated about fashion and they are quite picky (so leave those old Gap jeans at home, unless they predate 1985). The selection is huge and a bit overwhelming at times, but you can always find something to wear out dancing, and when you get tired of being seen in it, you can sell it back. *Tip: Call first to see what items they are currently buying before you schlep over your entire closet.*

7428 Melrose Ave., Los Angeles
(323) 653-3028

1338 4th St., Santa Monica
(310) 395-2620
thewasteland.com

WANNA BUY A WATCH

This has been a watch collectors' droolfest since 1981. They sell fine vintage and antique watches by Rolex, Cartier, and Hamilton (among others), and they also have a dazzling array of antique diamond engagement rings.

8465 Melrose Ave., Los Angeles
(323) 653-0467
wannabuyawatch.com

CHAPTER SEVEN

BEVERLY BLVD.

ANTIQUARIUS

Located in the heart of West Hollywood's "Avenue of Art and Design" district, Antiquarius is L.A.'s largest collection of antique and estate jewelry stores all under one roof. Find pavé diamonds from the 1800s, sculptural brooches, vintage 1950s Bulgari and Cartier pieces, antique toys, porcelain, and Persian rugs. Neil Lane, every Oscar nominee's favorite jeweler, is at Antiquarius, along with the Estate Collection, which stocks dazzlers from the Belle Epoque to the disco years. When you feel like you deserve a reward or have had a bad day, gift yourself a bauble and feel positively reborn! I plan on doing just that for my next birthday. Screw paying for a party; antique diamonds are forever.

8840 Beverly Blvd., Los Angeles
(310) 274-2363

DOMINICK'S

This joint feels very Old New York—warm brick and white clapboard, unpretentious, and dangerously romantic. This Rat Pack hang originally opened in 1948, and Frankie (Sinatra) and Dean (Martin) were regulars. Frank's bartender opened the restaurant, and at one time you couldn't *get in* to the place unless you were a friend of the Pack. Touch the brass bar rail they'd lean on for good luck, and admire the ebonized wood panels, creamy walls adorned with vintage photographs, and antique glass decanters. Warm, inviting, and wonderful—with old-school fare like spaghetti and meatballs and off-the-charts amazing whitefish piccata. After several incarnations, it has finally been revamped to its original glamour status. There are large, breezy brick patios and an outdoor bar area with olive trees and fireplaces. It's now partially owned by Ben Harper, Laura Dern, Warner Ebbink—all of whom also helped launch the hipster heavenly 101 Coffee Shop—and chef Brandon Boudet (my favorite L.A. chef). Don't miss Sunday Supper at Dominick's (starts as early as 6 p.m.) for an Italian family-style dinner with an extra side of class ($15 for dinner, $10 bottles of wine, and $2 brewskis).

8715 Beverly Blvd., West Hollywood
(310) 652-2335
dominicksrestaurant.com

EL COYOTE (CIRCA 1951)

There's always a long wait at this quirky Mexican restaurant, but it's the perfect place to go for a flirty first date. There's stained glass, waitresses in festive folk dresses, Christmas lights, mood lighting, big, red pleather booths, black velvet paintings, and kitschy art everywhere. The simple, old-school Mexican fare is perfect with their killer margaritas. It is rumored that El Coyote is the site of Sharon Tate's last meal before meeting up with the Manson family that same fateful night. Originally located on 1st and La Brea, the new location is large and can fit a whole slew of Angelenos looking for a festive night and good food.

7312 Beverly Blvd., Los Angeles
(323) 939-2255
elcoyotecafe.com

INTERNATIONAL SILKS & WOOLENS

It's ISW for those in the know. What sets this fabric superstore apart from the others is that the fabric is so out-there not even a psychedelic granny with dementia would approve of it for your prom dress. They have a mind-boggling stock of styles they like to call "theatrical" fabrics. From '60s mod patterns to fine antique lace to awesome 1970s novelty prints. On my last visit I walked away with the very last yards of 1970s movie-star-print fabric with amazingly bad renderings of Groucho Marx, Veronica Lake, and Busby Berkeley dancers. A very famous fashion designer friend of mine (who shall remain nameless) was slack on producing her fashion week show, and the day before the models went out onto the runway, we came here and she picked out several wacky Carmen Miranda fruit prints, sewed the creations on me all night, and voilà!—it was a huge success! If you're a material girl (or guy), meaning that you love to stitch, sew, and dream your way into fantastic creations, this is your fabric fantasyland.

8347 Beverly Blvd., Los Angeles
(323) 653-6453

INSIDE SCOOP

Dominick's is where Billy Wilder first approached Jack Lemmon and asked him to star in *Some Like It Hot*.

KOWBOYZ

This rustic shack of a store carries thousands of vintage cowboy boots from the '40s to the '70s, as well as jeans, leather jackets, snap-button Western shirts, and accessories. There's somethin' about those stitches, stars, and butterflies—even the most worn-out pairs have got a certain romance to 'em. Get a pair all beaten up and slouchy for the cowpunk look or get them pricey in pristine condition.

8050 Beverly Blvd., Los Angeles
(323) 653-6444

NEW BEVERLY CINEMA

They're always saying it's been renovated, and yeah, maybe they got some new speakers and a brighter projector, but it's always been a total dive—and it's glorious! The perfect place to see a Cassavetes film, and it seems like everyone's smoking jazz cigarettes in the theater—just like in '70s art houses—but it's just your imagination. Catch a vintage sci-fi, a film noir, a bad musical, a showing of *Day of the Locust*, or see a rare '70s film that hasn't been released on video or DVD (like *Play It as It Lays* with Tuesday Weld).

7165 Beverly Blvd., Los Angeles
(323) 938-4038
michaelwilliams.com/beverlycinema

RE-MIX SHOES

L.A.'s only dead-stock vintage shoe store that sells never-worn, new/old stock pairs. Come here for amazingly cute vintage heels from the '30s to the '70s. They have a wide selection for guys and dolls. Styles always in demand by the dolls are the pinup girl bow platforms, Marilyn "Baby Doll" pumps, '50s leopard skin Hollywood Stiletto Slides, and Katharine Hepburn-worthy saddle shoes. For the guys, hip wingtip spectators, blue suede shoes, and James Dean-worthy loafers. And they even have sizes to boot! Some vintage styles have proved to be so popular—like their collection of original '40s leather peep-toe wedges with detachable bow clips, as seen on Kate Beckinsale in *Pearl Harbor*—that they had to actually start producing knock offs just to appease the angry mobs of obsessed bombshells. I'm not usually a fan of repros, but with the old-time cobbler quality and perfect-shaped heels, not even a purist would suspect they aren't the real deal.

7605 1/2 Beverly Blvd., Los Angeles
(323) 936-6210
remixvintageshoes.com

SAM KAUFMAN GALLERY

This gallery offers "unusual modern objects of the last century"—an idiosyncratic variety of twentieth-century objects by names both famous and obscure. Every item has been selected for its historical interest, quality, and beauty. Owner Sam Kaufman envisions his enterprise as a salon for design enthusiasts, and he welcomes midcentury lovers to come hang out and chat with him about their collections and obsessions. Many items here are so extraordinarily rare, you'd think they'd be in a museum, but happy for us design nuts, everything here is available for your living room. On display one might find George Nakashima coffee tables supporting Guido Gambone vases, and Stig Lindberg tapestries hanging above Jean Prouvé desks. The inventory will please a wide variety of customers, from a connoisseur searching for an elusive piece to complete a collection, to an interior designer looking for an unusual lounge chair for a client's screening room. When I last told Mr. Kaufman I'd been searching high and low for a rare book of David Bailey's photography, he offered me the copy from his own personal collection, since he saw how passionate I was about finding it.

7965 Beverly Blvd., Los Angeles
(323) 857-1965
samkaufman.com

SHABON

This is where you go if you read *Bazaar* like it's the Bible and want the vintage versions of all the cute current trends. Shop here, and you are still at the height of fashion, but no one will be able to duplicate your look. Shabon offers a playful, happy approach to vintage, with Japanese, rock 'n' roll flavor. They carry cinch belts with seashell buckles, rainbows of leather boots, appliquéd bags, custom-painted leather jackets by South Paradiso, huge sunglasses by Paco Rabanne, '70s wedges, hard-to-find original high-waisted groupie jeans, prairie dresses, and pussy-bow secretary blouses.

7617 1/2 W. Beverly Blvd., Los Angeles
(323) 692-0061

SWINGERS

Located in the lobby of a kitschy '50s motel, this is a fun rock 'n' roll diner with Warhol wallpaper and waitresses in Nirvana cheerleaderesque rah-rah skirts with spike jewelry and morning-after eyeliner. It's perfect for a nice nosh, but the later it gets, the longer the wait. At least they have a great jukebox loaded with everything from Ziggy Stardust to Lee Hazlewood. They have delicious burgers and a variety of options for neurotic vegans and people on master cleanses. It's very New York, but it has a Sunset Strip-ness about it that only L.A. can produce. Don't come here on a first date, unless you're a pro at communicating with your eyes (the later it gets, the louder it gets).

8020 Beverly Blvd., Los Angeles
(323) 653-5858
swingersdiner.com

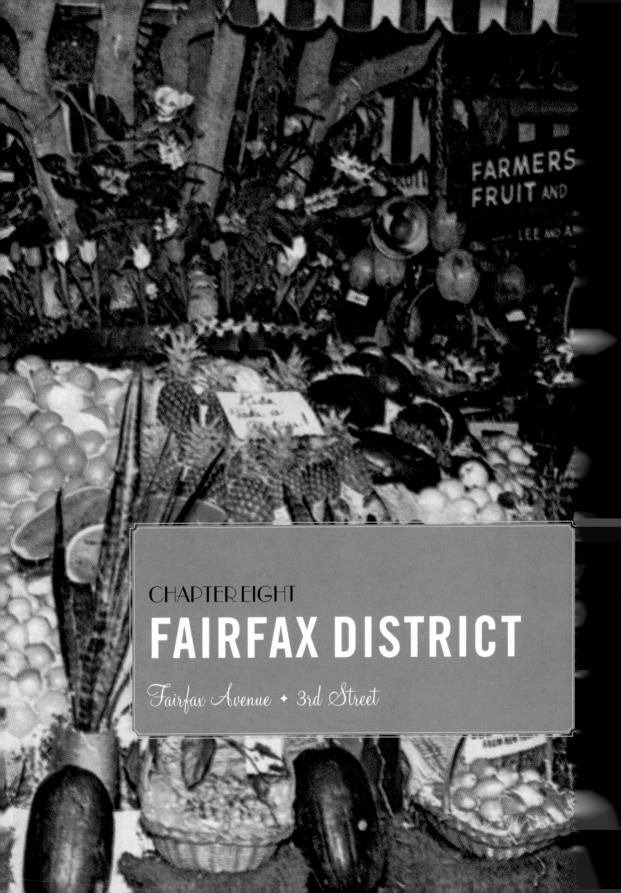

CHAPTER EIGHT

FAIRFAX DISTRICT

Fairfax Avenue ✦ 3rd Street

CANTER'S DELICATESSEN

As far as L.A. delis go, this is an institution. Canter's is a deli, bakery, bar, and one of the most famous restaurants in Los Angeles. Originally the Esquire movie theater, Canter's moved into this location in 1948, and it's hardly changed since. There are grumpy waitresses who are used to serving drunk rock stars and bratty actors; matzoh ball soup; blintzes; waffles; and a psychedelic ceiling of tree branches lit from behind. Show up late for fun, post-club people watching, then pop next door to the Kibitz Room (Canter's bar) where there's always something surreally entertaining going on (or a dance party!). Canter's is open 24 hours, which is one of the reasons it was once a favorite hangout of Frank Zappa and the band Love (as well as a whole slew of 1960s Sunset Strip groupies and rock stars). They even opened a Las Vegas location, but nothing can compare to this one's original kitsch.

419 N. Fairfax Ave., Los Angeles
(323) 651-2030
cantersdeli.com

CATWALK

This is an exquisitely curated collection of fun, designer vintage pieces, and every one is extremely special and unique. Catwalk is overwhelmingly cool, and the owners are a total delight for a chat. Come here for East West leathers, couture Dior, and Gucci galore! They are frequent collaborators with movie costumers, and they sell stunning finds from every decade (designer and non)—all displayed in a collage of looks and eras. Everywhere you look, there are rainbows of heels in perfect condition, boots lined up on the floor, and racks billowing over with mint '60s cocktail dresses and Stevie Nicks-worthy caftans.

459 N. Fairfax Ave., Los Angeles
(323) 951-9255
catwalkdesignervintage.com

Fairfax Avenue

ABOVE
Unlike many other L.A. vintage boutiques, Catwalk stocks items from around the globe, as you can see by this tribal bohemian ensemble.

VINTAGE Q&A

The Mayor of Sunset Strip

RODNEY BINGENHEIMER

VINTAGE L.A. LOCATION
CANTER'S DELI (FAIRFAX AVENUE)

World-famous KROQ disc jockey Rodney Bingenheimer has been dazzling listeners with groundbreaking tunes on his L.A. radio show *Rodney on the ROQ* since 1976. Once dubbed the "Mayor of Sunset Strip" by Sal Mineo, it's the mixture of his soft-spoken Warholesque demeanor and infectious true love of music that attracts celebrities to him like flies to flypaper. The story of Rodney's life is as colorful as a psychedelic album cover.

Upon first moving to Los Angeles as a teen in 1965, he met Sonny and Cher, who gave him a job as their personal publicist, which led to a stint as Davy Jones' stand-in on the hit TV show *The Monkees*. Though he couldn't type, this gained him a regular music column in a magazine—he had Edie Sedgwick take dictation—wherein he coined the catchphrase "It's all happening!" and later exclaimed by Kate Hudson as groupie Penny Lane in the 2000 film *Almost Famous*.

CONTINUED ▶

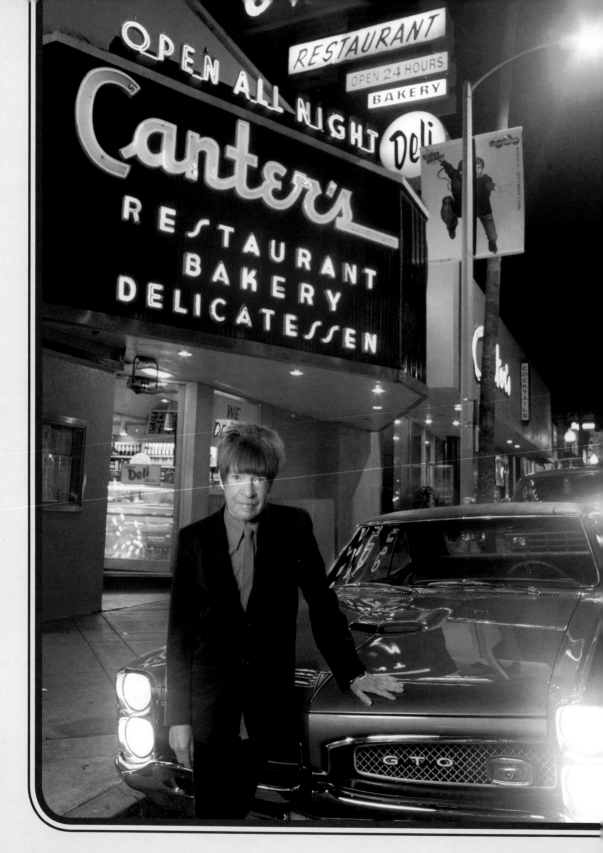

In the 1970s, he opened the legendary Hollywood nightclub Rodney Bingenheimer's English Disco, where Iggy Pop, T. Rex, Led Zeppelin, and Elvis Presley all came to debauch. In 1971 his good friend David Bowie put Rodney in charge of promotion for his LP *Hunky Dory*. Bowie was completely unknown in America at that time, until Rodney helped him work out his Ziggy Stardust persona and brought him into RCA, landing Bowie his first U.S. record deal.

Aside from his glittering past, Rodney is most noted for his uncanny ability to discover the next big thing. On his radio show, he has broken more future-hit singles than any other DJ in history, which is why he's been personally thanked on literally hundreds of LPs. He is a radio revolutionary, being the first ever to play punk rock on commercial radio in the United States. He's the very reason you've ever heard of the Sex Pistols, The Ramones, Blondie, Van Halen, The Clash, The Cure, The Smiths, Siouxie and the Banshees, Duran Duran, No Doubt, Sonic Youth, Nirvana, Oasis, Coldplay, or The Strokes, as he was the very first to play these artists on the radio.

In 2003, Rodney was the subject of the documentary feature film *Mayor of the Sunset Strip*, and in 2006 he was immortalized with a glittering star on Hollywood's Walk of Fame.

Listen to Rodney on the ROQ *Sundays from 12 a.m. to 3 a.m. on www.KROQ.com. myspace.com/rodneyontheroq*

JENNIFER BRANDT TAYLOR: What do you love about this place?

RODNEY BINGENHEIMER: Since I was a kid I'd always go to Canter's. That's where all the hipsters and freaks would hang out: The Byrds and Pamela DeBarres. The Mothers of Invention's album *Freak Out!* had a map inside and they had Canter's on it. It hasn't changed and it's open twenty-four hours. A friend of mine once said, "All roads lead to Canter's."

JBT: What are your favorite L.A. haunts?

RB: Mel's Diner (next to the Hollywood Museum), Denny's (in the Gower Gulch on Sunset Boulevard), The Château Marmont, the Capitol Records Building, the Cinerama Dome.

JBT: What is the quintessential L.A. film?

RB: *I Love You Alice B. Toklas*, *The Player*, *The Graduate*, *Good Times with Sonny and Cher*, *Riot on Sunset Strip*, *True Romance*, *Mondo Hollywood*, and *The Cool One,* where Roddy McDowall plays Phil Spector and runs around Hollywood. It's amazing!

JBT: Essential L.A. soundtracks?

RB: Mamas & Papas' "California Dreamin'," X's "Los Angeles," The Go-Gos' "This Town," Raveonettes' "Old L.A.," Ronnie Spector with the E Street Band's "Say Goodbye to Hollywood," The Kinks' "Celluloid Heroes," and The Beach Boys' "I Get Around," where they sing "tired of driving up and down that same old strip," which I like to think is about Sunset.

LEFT
Rodney and his prized 1967 Pontiac GTO at Canter's Deli, where several nights a week you can find him holding court in his regular booth (marked by a plaque that was dedicated to him by Nancy Sinatra in 1999), along with hopeful unsigned rock bands and legendary friends like Brian Wilson.

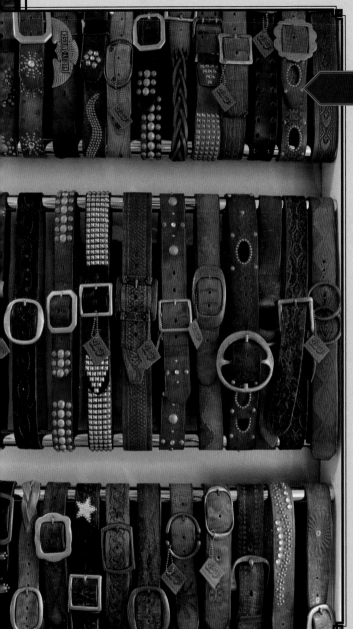

LO-FI

As the store's slogan, "Clothes for Your World Tour" suggests, this is L.A.'s best (albeit priciest) collection of vintage rock tees and unisexy attire. Lo-Fi is like every rocker guy's dream closet, and it's the dream closet of every rock 'n' roll sweetheart who loves to borrow her boyfriend's worn-in tees and jeans. Though there are no bargains here, you don't have to sort through any crap—you head straight for the vintage gold mine (like an original Jimi Hendrix tour tee for $750). The store attracts the who's who of rock 'n' roll with their stellar vintage denim, hard-to-find, original rock-tour tees, hand-tooled leather belts and buckles, and motorcycle leathers worthy of Robert Plant's derrière. They've also started to produce their own cool line of sexy leather biker jackets in a rainbow of colors, their own jeans, and zip-up baseball-style sweatshirts (they fit perfectly, like from back when you were on the softball team). Check out the tight-fitting women's leather jacket, the Iggy ($875), and my favorite men's style, the Starman (about $985).

Owners Kelly Cole and Gary Wagner have created a cool destination for '70s preservationists who are looking to replicate the decadent Zeppelinesque lifestyle. The store is painted Caribbean blue, has an awesome '70s-style fireplace, a silver-tin embossed ceiling, walls covered in rare rock 'n' roll photography by Mick Rock, and Ziggy Stardust blaring on the speakers.

1038 N. Fairfax Ave., Los Angeles
(323) 654-LOFI
lofi.com

THIS PAGE
Along with rare vintage rock T-shirts, and a stellar selection of original tooled leather hippie belts, Lo-Fi sells their own radical line of boot-cut jeans and leather jackets, designed using vintage-inspired patterns.

PETERSEN AUTOMOTIVE MUSEUM

Come here for vintage and new rides, as well as special exhibits to entertain both gearheads and glamour gals. I went to a fab Cars of the Stars exhibit where Greta Garbo's 1925 burgundy Lincoln Brunn limo was on display with Clark Gable's sporty '30s sedan and a 1959 Outlaw hot rod designed by Ed "Big Daddy" Roth.

petersen.org

SILENT MOVIE THEATRE

This is the only cinema in the world strictly devoted to showing films from the silent era. Originally opened by Dorothy and John E. Hampton in 1942, the couple's goal was to have a venue to share their personal collection of silent films, as well as to help those affected by the Great Depression. They dubbed the theater "Shrine of the Old Time Silent Pictures," and in an early manifesto written by the Hamptons, they dedicated the theater to "you who see in the movies the mirror of our life and times—the living history record of our changing styles, manners, and social customs...To you, who find in the movies relief from a war-torn world, and escape into the world of romance through the master storyteller of our times." This is a great place to bring kids, especially for the comedies of Charlie Chaplin, Buster Keaton, and Harold Lloyd. For added authenticity, the films always feature live organ accompaniment. Plus, Johnny Depp is a frequent visitor, which is just another gorgeous reason to love this place.

**611 N. Fairfax Ave., Los Angeles
(323) 655-2520
silentmovietheatre.com**

Farmers Market, Los Angeles, Calif.

INSIDE SCOOP

If you're still not tuckered out after checking out all the glammy goods at Polkadots & Moonbeams, hop across the street to Julian's Vintage Clothing for more secondhand scores.

**Julian's Vintage Clothing
8366 1/2 W. 3rd St., Los Angeles
(323) 655-3011**

ABOVE AND TOP RIGHT
The world-famous Farmers Market still has the same country-inspired white clapboard facade and old-time interior as it did in 1934. It also happens to be where James Dean ate his last breakfast before biting the dust.

FARMERS MARKET

Before its opening in 1934, the legendary Farmers Market was originally a dairy farm where oil was discovered. With its original white wood clock tower, awesomely kitschy signs, and green metal tables from the 1930s, the market is an outdoor maze of cafe counters, serving all different kinds of food—from perfect tacos to chocolate crepes and from sushi rolls to caramels and homemade ice cream. You can walk around and sample tastes from around the world. Witness tourists, rock stars, and locals stocking up their kitchens, Jewish grannies playing canasta, and gramps smoking cigars. Smell the roasting peanuts and baking breads while surveying the best selection of tacky Los Angeles souvenirs.

6333 W. 3rd St., Los Angeles
farmersmarketla.com

DENIM DOCTORS

Want to find the perfect pair of dream vintage denim jeans or cords? Walk into this small, country, rock 'n' roll bumpkin-decorated boutique, and tell any members of the hip and knowledgeable staff the kind of wash, cut, and emotional content of the pair you've been seeking. They'll fit your tush in no time. Pairs usually cost more than $150, but for this dreamy a jeans experience, it's so worth it. Praise this place!!! The staff is always helpful, honest, and friendly—even when checking out your bum. They sell perfectly worn-in pairs, great studded belts, new/old-stock '70s platforms, cowboy boots, and rock tees. There's even an alterations place next door, unrelated to the store, but known for their impeccably undetectable hemming techniques, and a great idea if you want to have your new jeans embroidered or embellished. Kate Hudson and Donovan Leitch are fans.

8044 W. 3rd St., Los Angeles
(323) 852-0171

IMONNI

This Japanese-owned boutique carries very affordable vintage—'60s cardigans, shift dresses in funny novelty prints, big, gaudy-in-a-good-way owl jewelry, Pop plastic rings, huge sunglasses, pointy '50s heels, and plastic animal change purses. They have such a fun selection that it makes you feel like you've wandered into a hip Tokyo closet. They also feature their own line of reworked vintage pieces that retain their original labels, only the shapes are more fitted and modern. It reminds me of how vintage boutiques must've been in N.Y.'s SoHo, circa 1986.

7954 W. 3rd St., Los Angeles
(323) 653-3014

POLKADOTS & MOONBEAMS

Gracing 3rd Street for the past 23 years, you can easily spot it when driving down the street by the rows of pastel petticoats and Technicolor dresses they have hanging outside. This vintage boutique store is violet in hue, powdery pink in vibe, and extremely girly, with great prices for things like flouncy party dresses, rhinestone jewelry, and 1950s crinolines. Also be sure to visit their sister store a few doors down that sells adorable modern wear. After all, there's always room in your wardrobe for some great new basics to pair with your stronger vintage statements.

8367 W. 3rd St., Los Angeles
(323) 651-1746
polkadotsandmoonbeams.com

Q&A

Vintage

FAWN GEHWEILER

VINTAGE L.A. LOCATION

GILL'S OLD FASHIONED ICE CREAM (SINCE 1937) AT THE FARMERS MARKET (FAIRFAX DISTRICT)

Miss Gehweiler is the Alice in Wonderland of the L.A. art scene. She's an artist, fashion designer, and doll maker. Her art is dreamy and nostalgic, influenced by abandoned theme parks, vintage children's books, and alpine kitsch. Her paintings are sought after by a legion of devoted teenage girls, gallerists, and rock stars alike. Her line of collectible dolls, aptly called Sundae Girls, debuted in 2006. Fawn's signature wide-eyed girls and androgynous pixie boys have been exhibited all over the planet—from L.A. to N.Y., Miami to London, Tokyo to Paris, and Berlin to Australia. She has designed and illustrated for high-profile clients such as Nike, Levi's, Screaming Mimi's vintage (NYC) and VH1.

www.fawngehweiler.com

JENNIFER BRANDT TAYLOR: What do you love about this place?

FAWN GEHWEILER: Its adorable pink, stripey ice cream stand with giant light-up cones and fancy hand-lettered signs. One of the very first things we did when we got to L.A. was head straight to the Farmers Market for crepes and pink lemonade. It was like a step back in time—a tiny soda fountain with root beer floats, stalls full of swirly lollipops and old-fashioned candies, glazed donuts, cake stands, picnic umbrellas, and some of the most perfectly imperfect hand-painted signs I've ever seen!

JBT: What do you love about living in L.A.?

FG: That you can see the ocean, the forest, the desert, and the snow all in one day if you wanted. I love random encounters with wild animals in the heart of the city—like a pack of coyotes strolling down Sunset at dusk.

JBT: What about L.A. do you find most inspiring?

FG: The wealth of storybook architecture, and the fact that so many of them were built by Hollywood set designers. I think Los Angeles must have more alpine kitsch than anywhere outside of the actual Alps, which is a major influence on my art.

JBT: What are your favorite L.A. haunts?

FG: The Alpine Villages and gingerbread cottages in Torrance and Rosemead. We go to the one in Torrance to stock up on cuckoo clocks, giant plastic mushrooms for our yard, and Swiss chocolates from the import grocery.

JBT: What is your favorite film genre?

FG: Sixties and '70s cautionary tales about Los Angeles, in the "youthsploitation" vein of *Beyond the Valley of the Dolls*. They always seem to feature either a crazy acid-tinged montage sequence of Sunset Boulevard, an out-of-control psychedelic party scene—or both!

JBT: What is the quintessential L.A. read?

FG: I adore *Hollywood Babylon* and any other book written about Hollywood eccentrics, misspent youths, sixties cults, dead rock stars, or communes in the hills.

JBT: What is the quintessential L.A. soundtrack?

FG: The Beach Boys' "Disney Girls." The lyrics are so great. Also near the top of the definitive summer playlist will always be Love's "Orange Skies." The line "Orange skies, carnivals, cotton candy and you" is totally L.A.!

CHAPTER NINE

LA BREA AVE.

AMERICAN RAG CIE

This is a European emporium of both new designer apparel and selective vintage. They follow current trends and hot items, and they stock racks full of one specific item so you can choose your favorite interpretation. This was everyone's favorite L.A. vintage spot in the '80s. I used to gaze at then teen queen Molly Ringwald trying on '50s tulle prom dresses, and spy John Malkovitch combing the racks for fitted '60s suits. Be sure to stop by their gorgeous home décor store, Maison Midi, next door, and if you have the time, grab a bite at Eduardo's delicious French cafe.

150 S. La Brea Ave., Los Angeles
(323) 935-3154

FAT CHANCE

Vintage purveyors of drool-worthy, midcentury furniture since 1978. Find Jeffrey Schuerholz's '30s machine-age pieces, Herman Miller chairs, George Nelson clocks, walnut, free-form coffee tables, decorative accent pieces, and Murano glass figures—all mixed with a wicked hot collection of modern classics and abstract sculptures.

162 N. La Brea Ave., Los Angeles
(323) 930-1960
fatchancemodern.com

FRANCE TRADITION

This is a small, ivy-covered shop full of antique treasures. You will find no faux French here. All authentic pieces, and upon first glance, pricey, but the items are so exquisite and rare that for those in the know, they are actually priced at a steal. The store is an impeccably curated wealth of beauty. The ceiling is glittered with ornate crystal chandeliers, and you can admire the fine French antiques, all suitable for the fanciest boudoir. They feature a stellar selection of precious etched mirrors, classical paintings, and petite nesting tables. Every piece has a design detail or quirk that makes it quite special.

458 S. La Brea Ave., Los Angeles
(323) 634-0111

THIS PAGE
Golyester stocks everything from glam faux-leopard fur coats, to fancy 1920s flapper dresses, to kitschy John Waters-worthy menswear. They even have a bedding department, swathed in Battenberg lace and Victorian crocheted duvet covers topped with antique boudoir dolls.

GOLYESTER

A large shop of wonderful women's apparel, where you can find fine vintage pieces from every era, including novelty-print dresses, purses, kimonos, '30s bias-cut satin gowns, leopard fur coats, and textiles, as well as funky home accessories and beachwear. This shop is curated by the ever-eccentric Esther, who should technically be a granny, but she is so much cooler and edgier than the young hipsters I know. The last time I saw her she had punk violet, hacked-off, Zandra Rhodes-inspired hair. Some say she's responsible for kicking off the entire vintage L.A. scene. Her private collection, from which she pulls stock for the store, is the stuff of legend. After being in the rag trade for over 30 years, she's still a flea market force to be reckoned with. She can sniff out the good stuff with unparalleled secondhand sleuthing.

She sells tattered ol' gorgeous frocks that need a little TLC as well as museum-quality mint pieces (for a price). She's got everything—'30s silk velvet alongside wacky '60s Pop prints, '40s gabardines, delicate tilt hats, heavily embroidered tops, bohemian-tiered skirts, and rare pieces of Bakelite jewelry, trims, linens, and antique lace. You can also find great lingerie for your inner flapper floozy, and where else can you find an original '60s Pop Art dress that is sold with a matching upholstered chair? They also have a small men's department, which offers up collectible Hawaiian shirts, sharkskin suits, and smoking pipes. Esther's devotees include Mary-Kate and Ashley Olsen, Molly Ringwald, Winona Ryder, Kirsten Dunst, Cameron Diaz, and fashion designer Anna Sui.

136 S. La Brea Ave., Los Angeles
(323) 931-1339

JET RAG

A vintage clothing superstore, with such cheap prices that in high school, I could shop here three times a week with just my lunch money. I'd buy tons of velvet '60s neo-Victorian dresses for about $15 apiece, and though vintage velvet dresses are getting harder to find, they still stock their warehouse-sized shop full of men's and women's apparel. They have a selection of clothes that are either in shabby shape or stellar condition, but either way, everything's easy on your wallet. Whenever I've dated somebody with less than sexy style, I would take them here with $50, and voilà!—stud in a mod skinny tie, '50s Towncraft button-down shirt, and Chet Baker-style skinny pants and a British driving cap (they also sell band pins for a nice finishing touch). They have $1 sales on Sundays where, if you risk getting creepy crawlies on your hands, you can find Holly Hobbyesque Gunne Sax dresses and fun '70s disco gear. Most girls I know buy the cheapie stuff and then tear it apart for the cool graphic fabrics to make something new.

825 N. La Brea Ave., Los Angeles
(323) 939-0528

LITTLE PARIS ANTIQUES

This large shop sells fine antiques and offers lavish custom upholstery. It's filled with ornate pieces from the 1800s to the 1950s, including an authentic horse-drawn Rothschild carriage from 1860 for $15,000. They receive new shipments every two months from an associate in northern France who supplies the store with stunning new finds. There is a gorgeous selection (not cheap), and items that are well worth the dough if you're looking for a bit of rich libertine romance in your home décor. If you'd like questions answered in a seductive Parisian accent, ask for Baptiste, who will also sweetly e-mail photos to you of incoming shipments, for those seeking a specific item.

612 S. La Brea Ave., Los Angeles
(323) 857-1080
littleparisantiques.com

INSIDE SCOOP

Next door to Rock and Rodeo is Liz's Antique Hardware, L.A.'s coolest stop for antique and reproduction architectural fixtures. They will outfit your vintage home down to every minute detail. Many of the items have been salvaged from historic buildings like the Chicago Stock Exchange. Items range here from the Art Nouveau period to the Atomic Age, and beyond!

453 S. La Brea Ave., Los Angeles
(323) 939-4403
lahardware.com

PINK'S

Pink's has been a Hollywood legend since 1939! It's the most infamous hot dog stand in the land! It was founded by Paul Pink and has remained in the same little location for over 65 years. It's a real stand, and there's always a line. It's apparently so good that the whole city could be on fire and there would still be at least a half-hour wait. They offer over 21 varieties of foot-long hot dogs, served steamy hot, and old-fashioned sodas to wash them down. They specialize in made-to-order dogs, and it's unanimously dubbed the best hot dog in L.A.—or perhaps the world. In addition to serving the best dogs, Pink's is also a late-night hang and has been immortalized in many films and even *Vogue* fashion shoots. Expect to wait at least half an hour—even at 3 a.m.

709 N. La Brea Ave., Hollywood
(323) 931-4223
pinkshollywood.com

RAY FERRA'S IRON 'N ANTIQUE ACCENTS

Ray has been L.A.'s vintage lamp king for over 35 years, and he has the lime green shag carpeting to prove it. There's something for every home here, and it's very affordable. Ray specializes in buying and selling a wonderland selection of old lamps, from Art Deco sconces to '70s swags and from $50 '70s plastic table monstrosities to $10,000 6-foot-tall Italian blackamoor torchère floor lamps. He can rewire your vintage lamps, replicate your vintage fixtures, and can even help you with hard-to-find bulbs—from huge, disco gold balls to silk-wrapped flicker flames.

342 N. La Brea Ave., Los Angeles
(323) 934-3953

ROCK AND RODEO

THIS PAGE
From American Indian ponchos, to 1940s hand-tooled cowboy boots, and seventies Bowie-era glam-rock platforms, Rock and Rodeo is like a mind-bendingly beautiful museum of American vintage design.

So, there's good news and there's bad news.

Bad: Rock and Rodeo is a vintage archive and resource library, not a boutique. This means that unless you're a professional stylist or fashion designer, you can't shop here, let alone get an appointment. Rock and Rodeo's client list is a veritable who's who of the fashion world (a list they keep very private). For these regular clients, and newcomers with the right credentials, they present visual vintage inspiration for future collections, usually working two seasons in advance of the upcoming trends. Since 2001, owners Robin Fauser, Mary Ossanna, and Aldo Palmieri have extensively combed the United States on long road trips for rare vintage denim, beaten-up cowboy boots, Victorian lace dresses, and East West leather jackets—all perfectly worn-in and one-of-a-kind. They have amassed an awe-inspiring array of antique and vintage wares, specializing in Americana, Western, Victorian, Ethnic, and Native American styles. Also, the actual design of the space is a rustic dreamworld of old Art Deco display cabinets salvaged from mom-and-pop stores around the country, tapestries strewn about, religious artifacts, taxidermied buffalo, Nina Simone blasting through the speakers, and an entire wall of glorioius opalescent seashells. Basically, if Keith Richards were a store, he would be Rock and Rodeo.

And for the good news: The Rock and Rodeo team does indeed have an open-to-the-public vintage boutique, directly

next door, called 86 Vintage, where you *can* buy a piece of the action. It features high-quality romantic, hippie-style women's vintage and reconstructed pieces. They have a fun selection of beaten-up jeans, cowboy boots, Gunne Sax printed prairie dresses, '30s velvets, and lots of '70s tees. 86 Vintage also offers tailoring and customization.

Rock and Rodeo
459 1/2 S. La Brea Ave., Los Angeles
(323) 937-8450 (by appt. only)

86 Vintage
463 S. La Brea Ave., Los Angeles
(323) 954-8686
rockinrodeovintage.com

SVENSKA MOBLER

Svenska Mobler (Swedish Furniture) sells Art Deco, Art Nouveau, Functionalist, and midcentury home décor from 1840 to 1940, mostly in rich Swedish woods like golden flame birch, elm root, and alder. The selection here is so beautiful, you get the same feeling as when you enter an art gallery. Everything was hand picked in Sweden and shipped over. Sink into deep blue Art Deco velvet club chairs ($6,900), or a Swedish cubist sofa from 1930 ($4,900). Check out the original framed prints of Mark Shaw's fashion editorial photos from the '50s and early '60s ($800), including an amazing color photo of Nico as a young model (before becoming the Velvet Underground's famous chanteuse). I would sleep, eat, and write on the birch Functionalist-era desk I spied for $7,500 (someday!).

154 N. La Brea Ave., Los Angeles
(323) 934-4452
svenskamobler.com

THIS PAGE
From Native American ponchos, to 1940s hand-tooled cowboy boots, and seventies Bowie-era glam-rock platforms, Rock and Rodeo is like a mind-bendingly beautiful museum of American vintage design.

THE WAY WE WORE

This shop is chock-full of vintage gorgeousness—all housed under a spectacular gold lamé ceiling. Proprietress Doris Raymond has been collecting for over 30 years, and she stocks over 20,000 pieces of pristine-condition clothes and jewels. This is where Hollywood's costume designers come to dress iconic characters, such as Kate Hudson in *Almost Famous*, and Hollywood stars like Courtney Love and Winona Ryder love to scour. The shop carries casual to high-end couture, ethnic clothing, and textiles from the eighteenth century to the early '80s. Find white lace Victorian blouses, glittering signed costume jewelry, '50s cocktail dresses and spiked heels, wood box purses from the '70s, scrunchy leather boots, pencil skirts perfect for work, and peasant shirts. There is also an appointment-only second floor that carries mint vintage couture. If in need of musing for a creative project, be sure to inquire about Doris's Inspiration Space next door at 336 La Brea Ave. This is her private research library of historic garments, textiles, trims, and paper ephemera from the 1800s to the 1980s. She estimates that she has over 500,000 pieces in her archive, which is why many designers, like Marc Jacobs, drool to sneak a peek. But be warned—you must pay for that peek. It's a minimum of $500 a session where Doris acts as your fashion fairy godmother, pulling items at your request. That doesn't include the cost of actually buying pieces of the fabrics or swatches, which start at about $75 and go up to the thousands.

334 S. La Brea Ave., Los Angeles
(323) 937-0878
thewaywewore.com

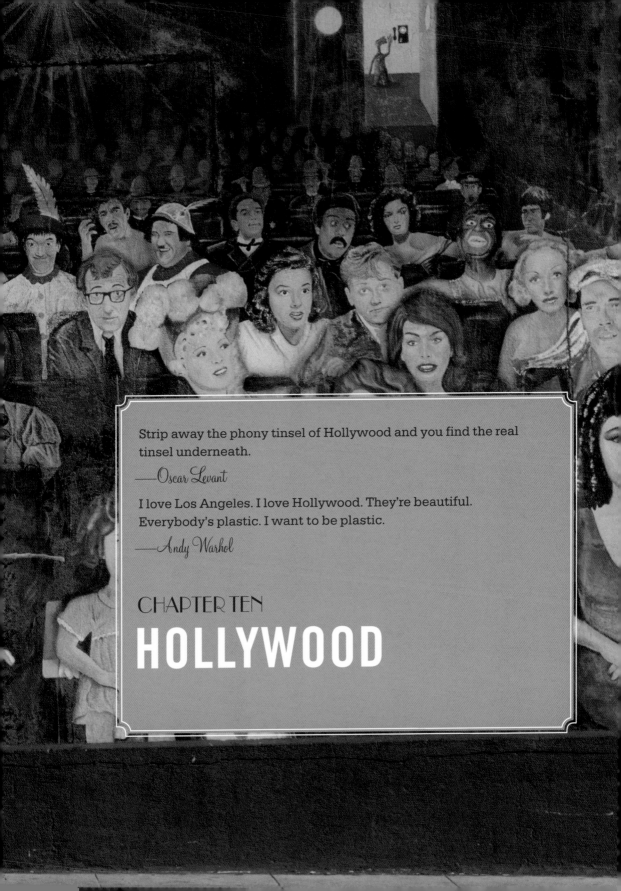

Strip away the phony tinsel of Hollywood and you find the real tinsel underneath.

—Oscar Levant

I love Los Angeles. I love Hollywood. They're beautiful. Everybody's plastic. I want to be plastic.

—Andy Warhol

CHAPTER TEN

HOLLYWOOD

Hollywood has always been the birthplace of fantasy. It's home to the world's most glamorous ghosts, and their spirits dust the city's brick and mortar like otherworldly glitter.

The "boulevard of broken dreams," which acts as its zenith, has recently undergone a complete revamp. On a single city block, you can see a film at the legendary Chinese Theatre; shop at a mall, which features giant Babylonian elephants in homage to D. W. Griffith's 1916 film *Intolerance*; and walk down the gray and salmon-pink glitter walk of fame (the very same one the stars glide down to their Oscar ceremony at the Kodak Theater). For me, Hollywood is the axis on which this whole surreal city spins. It's also where the action is. End scene.

THE 101 COFFEE SHOP

Named after the 101 Hollywood freeway, this old-school, Howard Johnson-style coffee shop has been remodeled in recent years, but is in such perfect keeping with its original, tricked-out early 60s décor that you'll swear it was the real deal. I love the huge brown vinyl wraparound booths, the New Wave and classic rock-stocked jukebox, and soda fountain-style counter. Owner Warner Ebbink, also of the fabulous Dominick's restaurant, grew up loving the classic Los Angeles coffee shop architecture of designers Armet & Davis, and has perfectly emulated their Googie style with The 101. They serve classic diner food, but with a health-conscious twist (this is in Hollywood, after all). Menu favorites are the mac and cheese, blackened-chicken sandwich, fried chicken, and burgers accompanied by crispy sweet potato fries. And for dessert, I insist you experience the truly decadent waffle brownie sundae at least once in your life. It's located on the ground floor of a 1960s Best Western, which has been the room and board for many musical and creative minds, including Ryan Adams, composer/producer Jon Brion, and Vincent Gallo.

6145 Franklin Ave., Hollywood
(323) 467-1175

PREVIOUS SPREAD
L.A.–based fashion designer, and rock 'n' roll muse, Miss Kimme says, "I love Hollywood because it is home to the ghosts of tragic, pin-curled ingenues, pining away in the boudoirs of Art Deco towers." Here she reads a 1970s issue of *Star*, in front of Thomas S. Furiya's 1983 *Hollywood Legends* mural on Wilcox Avenue.

AMOEBA MUSIC

This is the world's largest (and greatest) record store, and I challenge you to prove me wrong. With an unparalleled selection like this, it's no wonder that, when you look next to you, you can spot Jimmy Page, Winona Ryder, Joni Mitchell, or Meg White of The White Stripes combing the bins. They have a vinyl selection that will make even the staunchest record nerd shed a tear. They have great deals on LPs, and they also sell new and used CDs, DVDs, vintage rock posters, and memorabilia. Go to the trade-in desk if your apartment is toppling over with CDs you never listen to, and they'll give you a fair deal, for cash or trade, even on the most embarrassing of albums. Be sure to tell them I sent you, though it won't get you any more dough, but it may get you some true record nerd points (I'm an old-school customer). Amoeba even has live DJs spinning while you browse, and in-store performances by amazing acts like Flaming Lips, Jon Brion, and PJ Harvey. It will blow your musical mind!

64 Sunset Blvd., Hollywood
(323) 245-6400
amoebamusic.com

TOP CENTER AND ABOVE
Amoeba Music, a music lovers' heaven on this rock 'n' roll earth, with enough rare records to make a grown DJ cry.

TOP RIGHT
The author, who also moonlights as a DJ, never leaves Amoeba empty-handed. You can frequently find her, along with her record-collecting sister, Miss Lizzie, in the "Pop Vocalists" section.

BOARDNER'S OF HOLLYWOOD

Serving both the seedy and the stars since 1942, Boardner's is right off the boulevard, and the perfect place to sink into shabby red leather booths and play songs at the classic rock jukebox. Once a favorite hangout of W. C. Fields, Errol Flynn, and Robert Mitchum, it's moody and dark with an outdoor fountain patio. Next door is Boardner's B52 Club, which once was a cabaret in the early '30s known as My Blue Heaven. It's now a nightclub that hosts the city's most popular mod and goth clubs.

1652 N. Cherokee Ave., Hollywood
(323) 462-9621
boardners.com

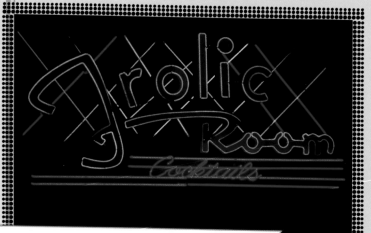

BOB'S FROLIC ROOM

Enter under the fabulous neon sign, and go straight into a surreal smorgasbord of intoxicated Hollywood noir. You'll be shocked by the melting pot of characters. During one recent visit, I was surrounded by actual Hell's Angels and their leather-clad old ladies, a bus driver in uniform, hookers, a guy in a turban, tourists lost from their Hollywood Blvd. adventure, an after-theater crowd in fancy attire (the Pantages next door shows touring Broadway musicals), and a couple of senior swingers all swaying to the same Stones tune on the jukebox. Basically, the joint is always hopping at Bob's Frolic Room, and you'll never leave without some kind of story to tell your friends back home. Check out the gloriously gaudy cigarette smoke-faded celebrity wall mural by Al Hirschfeld, which depicts Joan Crawford, Albert Einstein, Charlie Chaplin, and Marilyn Monroe whooping it up!

6245 Hollywood Blvd., Hollywood
(323) 462-5890
bobsfrolicroom.com

BRONSON CANYON AND CAVES

This canyon is the most perfect nature walk in all of L.A. You can take your pup or practice your yoga breathing techniques, and though it can sometimes be a total fashion scene (the last thing you want when you're all sweaty), you can look over the entire city and zen-out—it's always a rare retreat from the lightning-fast life below. Located deep in the canyon are the famous Bronson Caves, which are man-made and were probably created around 1900 when the area was a rock quarry. They are the perfect spot for a sci-fi make-out session with a fellow film nerd. They have been used in countless movies and TV shows, like *Bonanza, Fantasy Island, Little House on the Prairie, The Lone Ranger*, the original *Invasion of the Body Snatchers*, and as the Bat Cave in the classic *Batman* TV series. Jim Morrison also hung out in them with his wife Pamela in the '60s. They were probably tripping out, but it's a magical spot even without the magic "shrooms."

From Hollywood Blvd., turn north up either Canyon Drive or Bronson Canyon (which merges later with Canyon Drive). Take Canyon Drive through the gates into Griffith Park to where the road seems to end. Park at the end of Bronson Road and prepare for a short hike.

INSIDE SCOOP

Some say the caves were created especially for the 1922 version of *Robin Hood* with Douglas Fairbanks.

CAT & FIDDLE RESTAURANT & ENGLISH PUB

This magical location is full of history. It was originally a movie studio commissary and wardrobe house in 1929, then it was Edgar Bergen's (father of Candace Bergen) studio in the '30s, and then it was a restaurant called Le Gourmet through the '40s and '50s (frequented by legendary stars like Humphrey Bogart, Katharine Hepburn, and Ava Gardner). Finally in 1982, British rocker Kim Gardner (who played with The Creation, The Birds, and Mitch Mitchell) opened it as an authentic pub. The Cat became infamous in the '80s when the entire L.A. glam metal scene like Guns 'N' Roses and Motley Crüe adopted it as their late-night HQ. It's now a less-hairsprayed pub with a pretty, circular outdoor courtyard, indoor fireplace, faux Victoriana, and a Casablanca-themed room (parts of the film were shot at this historical location). Along with the wacky mix of regulars, Drew Barrymore, Charlize Theron, Rod Stewart, members of The Who, and countless others have drifted in for wicked fish 'n' chips and British ale.

6530 Sunset Blvd., Los Angeles
(323) 468-3800
thecatandfiddle.com

INSIDE SCOOP

A very cool, classic Hollywood thing to do is to drive north on Gower from Melrose Ave. You will pass the corner of Paramount Studios (once RKO Studios and where you can still see the old RKO signature globe on the edge of the roof—it's now painted to blend into the building, acting as an aide memoire that Fred Astaire and Ginger Rogers used to dance there). After passing the studio, drive toward the hills and look straight up and ahead— you are in perfect alignment with the Hollywood sign. This is the very same view that all the stars would see when driving to or from the studio. Hooray for Hollywood!

ABOVE

The Château Marmont is a great example of L.A. "storybook style," which was a very popular form of architecture here in the 1920s and 1930s. The hotel is reminiscent of a fairy-tale castle, with gorgeous hand-painted coved ceilings, cobblestone courtyards, overgrown ivy, magical fountains, and a rose garden.

THE CINERAMA DOME

This landmark movie theater is where you can see first-run films in a radical geodesic shell, on an ultrawide Cinerama screen, equipped with the most jaw-dropping sound ever. The Cinerama was recently restored and incorporated into a theater complex called the ArcLight. This is one of L.A.'s most famous vintage theaters, and they show great classic movies, as well as new blockbusters. They even have special screenings introduced by the stars and filmmakers themselves. I once saw *Coal Miner's Daughter* followed by a Q&A session with the Oscar-winning director and writer Michael Apted and screenwriter Tom Rickman. They even have a gift shop with non-cheesy Hollywood souvenirs and a cafe. It's a special place for film nerds and a welcome respite from all the modern, boxlike movie megaplexes.

6360 W. Sunset Blvd., Hollywood
(323) 464-4226
arclightcinemas.com

TOP
The Cinerama Dome is like a giant golf ball that landed on Sunset Boulevard straight from Mars.

CHÂTEAU MARMONT

Look for the fabulous vintage neon sign with an arrow pointing to the hotel's driveway, and you'll find this historical Hollywood landmark. The Château is a faux-French hideaway—a decadent Art Deco dream with antique and midcentury furniture in each room. If you're a hotel guest, it's easy to crash magical parties, drink champagne, dance, and romance here till dawn.

Since 1929, the Château has been home to many stars, like Greta Garbo, Jean Harlow, Andy Warhol, Marlon Brando, Marilyn Monroe, James Dean, Robert De Niro, Drew Barrymore, and Lindsay Lohan. The hotel even refers to Lohan as their own Eloise. Led Zep partied here, John Lennon composed here, and Jim Morrison dangled off the balconies.

Sadly, the Château has also had its share of celebrity deaths, like John Belushi's sad overdose in bungalow number two, and legendary fashion photographer Helmut Newton's car crash while leaving the hotel. They've placed a plaque at the site to memorialize him forever at his all-time favorite home away from home.

The eats are wonderful here too. Either grab a bite in their elegant dining room or at the outdoor French bistro that overlooks the city. It's the perfect place to wear your best vintage Balenciaga cocktail dress. They also serve food until the wee hours.

8221 Sunset Blvd., Hollywood
(323) 656-1010
Châteaumarmont.com

COUNTERPOINT RECORDS & BOOKS AND HARMONY GALLERY

Counterpoint has been around since long before the amazing, super, über-record store Amoeba existed. Sometimes when the enormity, long lines, and fluorescent lights of Amoeba just turn me off, or when I'm feeling more old-fashioned, I go to the place where I hung out in my teens. I go to Counterpoint. It smells like a public school classroom (i.e., dusty), and it looks like a highly cultured grandpa's dream. Counterpoint is a great neighborhood record shop that also buys and trades. It specializes in used books, mostly on the arts, and I always end up buying an out-of-print biography on a jazz musician, like Chet Baker, or biographies of forgotten Hollywood stars like Louise Brooks. Come here for hard-to-find vinyl LPs (including rare 78s), great jazz, classical, opera, and rock records (you can find a pristine two-LP set of Maria Callas singing *Tosca* for about $4!), and miscellaneous memorabilia. It's also a great place to find beaten-up, original copies of Jacqueline Susann novels and other fiction at a fraction of the price. They have a small space next door called Harmony Gallery: Fine Books and Art, that sells pricier and more collectible first editions. The Harmony Gallery also hosts art openings. They recently had a show of paintings by Warhol superstar Mary Woronov, and a photography exhibit by Vintage L.A.'s very own Jeaneen Lund.

5911 & 5911 1/2 Franklin Ave., Hollywood
(323) 957-7965
counterpointrecordsandbooks.com

THE DRESDEN ROOM

The Dresden is a hip bar that reminds me of the nightclub that Walter Matthau and Goldie Hawn go to go-go dance in the 1969 film *Cactus Flower*. It became the Dresden Room in the '50s, and to this day the interior is perfectly preserved. This vintage spot has coral walls, faux Nouveau glass panels, and white wraparound booths with high backs. They also have the best Cobb salad I've ever had and a signature drink called The Blood and Sand, named after the 1941 Tyrone Power movie. The Dresden Room was immortalized in the '90s when it was featured in the hit film *Swingers*. In effect, it was ruined for all of us when it was discovered, but enough time has passed that it is no longer overrun by tourists. Now it's back to its low-key, yet totally psychedelic, Rat Pack roots.

1760 N. Vermont Ave., Hollywood
(323) 665-4294
thedresden.com

TOP LEFT
The author, in her element, surrounded by dusty old books, at Counterpoint.

CENTER
The swanky dining room at the Dresden was designed in 1964 by Guy Moore and Sara Ferraro, with mother-of-pearl accents, cocoonlike white leather booths, and a groovy cork-walled bar.

THE EGYPTIAN THEATRE

Los Angeles is an industry town, and the product we produce is film. Not going to see one of this city's first movie palaces would be like going to Philly and not trying a cheesesteak or driving by the Grand Canyon without a peek. Built in 1922 by Sid Grauman (the same year King Tut's tomb was discovered), this is where Hollywood's very first star-studded premiere took place, which was *Robin Hood*, starring Douglas Fairbanks. At Hollywood's Egyptian, you can step onto the same floor that Ava Gardner glided across, her arm linked with Sinatra's, and gaze up at the giant pharaoh's scarab adorning the theater's spectacular ceiling.

Today, the theater is run by the American Cinematheque, and hosts a variety of screenings, tours, and events for those who live for cinema. The Egyptian's calendar is always filled with awesome film festivals, like a recent Marx Brothers retrospective, the annual Mods and Rockers festival of '60s rock 'n' roll flicks, or the Can't Stop the Musicals fest, where they show so-bad-they're-good cult classics, like 1980s *Xanadu*. You can also attend great film tributes with legendary stars and special Q&A sessions following the films. Jane Russell has dished on *Gentlemen Prefer Blondes*, Terence Stamp charmed the audience about making *The Collector*, Carroll Baker chatted about *Baby Doll*, and Leigh Taylor-Young gossiped about Peter Sellers' superstitions. And if hungry after the flick, the Egyptian courtyard hosts two places to chow. You can grab a pint and a nosh next door at the renovated landmark Pig 'n' Whistle Grill (great crab cakes), or if you are craving something sweet, try the delicious old-fashioned frozen custard at Lickety Split.

6712 Hollywood Blvd., Hollywood
(323) 466-3456
egyptiantheatre.com

EL CAPITAN

Originally opened in 1926 as a vaudeville house, this stunning East Indian–themed theater is now owned by Disney, who has painstakingly restored it to its original movie palace glory—the kind of theater where even the opening of the sparkly curtains before the film is part of the show. Also, before the film, a gorgeous, gilded Mighty Wurlitzer rises out of the floor, with an organist playing the film's soundtrack. Now that's worth the admission alone! My favorite time to visit the El Capitan is around Halloween when they show Tim Burton's *Nightmare Before Christmas* to an audience of enthusiastic goths. Though they mainly show Disney flicks, they sometimes host classic film festivals. The first time I saw Orson Welles' classic *Citizen Kane*, which first premiered here in 1941, it was at this theater. It was the perfect setting for such a mind-blowing film.

6838 Hollywood Blvd., Los Angeles
(323) 467-7674
www.disney.go.com/disneypictures/
el_capitan

EL CHOLO

This is the original location of L.A.'s favorite, and oldest, Mexican restaurant chain. Opened in 1927, it's still a popular choice for perfect margaritas, green corn tamales, and nachos (which are believed to have been invented here), with its stellar, old-fashioned Spanish cooking in a kitschy, old-world, fiesta-inspired setting. Bing Crosby, Harold Lloyd, Elizabeth Taylor, Marlon Brando, Warren Beatty, and Madonna have all dined here.

1121 S. Western Ave., Los Angeles
(323) 734-2773
elcholo.com

TOP RIGHT
In recent years, The Egyptian Theatre has been lovingly restored to its original design by the American Cinematheque.

GRAUMAN'S CHINESE THEATRE

This is one of Hollywood's most famous landmarks, built in 1927 by the movie palace developer Sid Grauman. As a child of vaudeville performers, Grauman watched the birth of cinema occur, and become obsessed with movie magic. As a child he dreamed of building a golden palace to showcase the pictures that he so dearly loved. As an adult he was the first to use floodlights, and thus he invented the Hollywood premiere as we know it. The design of Grauman's Chinese Theatre was inspired by Sid Grauman's travels through China, and it is one of the most important architectural structures in movie history—there's even a replica of it at Disney World. Regardless of the casually attired tourists that crowd the courtyard (along with bad Elvis and Batman impersonators), I always doll myself up for a date with the Chinese in homage to its dazzling past. It's actually Mann's Chinese now, but I prefer to call it by its original name, in respect for the visionary man who conceptualized and invented the movie palace as we know it. In an age when movie theaters are about as glamorous as jail cells, it is nice to go someplace special like Grauman's. It's a theater where you can still dream in the dark, and where you can dress up and make moviegoing a special occasion.

The theater's slogan in the '40s was, appropriately, a shrine to art. Charlie Chaplin broke the first ground at the Chinese in 1927, and it is home to so many historical film experiences. The first film to premiere here was Cecil B.

DeMille's *King of Kings*, as well as the premieres of Howard Hughes' *Hell's Angels* (which also marked the debut of Jean Harlow), *Singin' in the Rain*, *Ninotchka*, and hundreds more. It even hosted the Academy Awards in the 1940s.

Honorary mayor of Hollywood Johnny Grant told me how his good friend Sid Grauman began the longtime tradition of the cement footprints. It started when silent-film star Mary Pickford's dog, Zorro, ran across the wet cement of her new driveway, and when she told Grauman about it, laughing, "now we'll have Zorro forever," a lightbulb went off in Grauman's head. Naturally, Mary and her husband, Douglas Fairbanks, were the first to leave their prints, followed by Hollywood legends like Betty Grable, the Marx Brothers, Sophia Loren, Ava Gardner, Sean Connery, Bette Davis, Shirley MacLaine, Rita Hayworth, Elizabeth Taylor, Jean Harlow, Frank Sinatra, Bogie (who wore his lucky shoes from *Casablanca*), Judy Garland, Clark Gable, Natalie Wood, Steve McQueen (who, always the rebel, left his prints upside down), and even Shirley Temple and her tiny feet. Don't think just because the courtyard is full of tourists in bad shorts with cameras around their necks that this isn't worth stopping by to pay homage to film history and to be dazzled by the structure's chinoiserie beauty. After all, where else on Earth can you literally walk in Marilyn Monroe's footsteps?

**6925 Hollywood Blvd., Hollywood
(323) 464-8111**

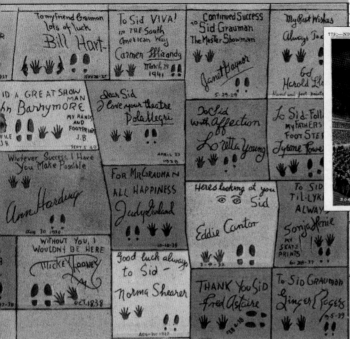

779:—NIGHT SCENE HOLLYWOOD BOWL, HOLLYWOOD, CALIF. "SYMPHONY UNDER THE STARS"

160   GRAUMAN'S CHINESE THEATRE, HOLLYWOOD, CALIFORNIA

HOLLYWOOD BOWL

One of L.A.'s most recognizable symbols, this world-famous, concentric shell-shaped stage is a symphony under the stars, as it reads in a 1940s Hollywood tourism pamphlet. Built in 1922, this outdoor amphitheater has held thousands of musical acts of every possible genre, from classical concerts conducted by Stravinsky, to reggae festivals, to rock shows for bands like Radiohead and Belle and Sebastian. Nearly every legendary American performer has graced the Art Deco stage, including Judy Garland, Sinatra, Streisand, Billie Holiday, and The Beatles. Their calendar is always wonderfully eclectic, listing not only the Playboy Jazz Festival, but performances by The Strokes, Willie Nelson, and sing-alongs to classic musicals like *The Sound of Music*. Many shows are even followed by spectacular fireworks. It's truly one of the most magical live venues in the world, and even the nosebleed seats are good, not to mention dirt cheap if you're on a budget.

2301 N. Highland Ave., Hollywood

(323) 850-2000

hollywoodbowl.com

THE HOLLYWOOD MUSEUM

Finally, Hollywood has a shrine to connect fans with its magical past. With more than 500 displays, this fabulously glitzy museum with a showstopping pink marble entry hall brings Hollywood history to life. Real estate developer, memorabilia collector, and native Los Angeleno Donelle Dadigan spent eight years creating and curating the Hollywood Museum. Located inside the historic Art Deco-style Max Factor building, it's a museum based in the capital of filmmaking that has been perfectly restored to its original Art Deco splendor. Creating the museum was truly a labor of love.

Dadigan has a deep-rooted passion for the motion picture and television industry that stems from her youth. Dadigan grew up as the goddaughter of the renowned concert pianist José Iturbi, who performed in glossy MGM musicals like 1941's *Anchors Aweigh*, starring alongside Frank Sinatra and Gene Kelly. So as a little girl, Donelle watched Hollywood stars parade through her living room. When Dadigan set out to find a space for the Hollywood Museum, she convinced the most recent executor, Procter & Gamble, to sell her the legendary Max Factor building. In 1996, Dadigan became the first individual owner since Max Factor himself.

In 1934, Max Factor turned this former car garage/speakeasy into HQ for his cosmetics empire. Factor's life story is cinematic in itself: he began as the hairdresser to Czar Nicholas II of Russia, and when warned of an impending revolution, he fled to America to begin a new life. At the Chicago World's Fair in 1905, he showcased a line of his greasepaint makeup to be used on the stage, and in 1913 he provided hair and makeup for Cecil B. DeMille's *The Squaw Man*, the first feature-length Hollywood movie. Within these walls, he literally transformed unknown starlets into Hollywood icons. Factor dyed the hair of promising young actresses in individually designed color-specific rooms marked Blondes Only (Lana Turner and Marilyn were first dyed platinum here), Redheads Only (where Lucille Ball and Rita Hayworth became legends), Brunettes Only (Elizabeth Taylor and Dorothy Lamour), and Brownettes Only (Bette Davis and Judy Garland).

Dadigan's Hollywood Museum features Factor's actual makeup case, not to mention over 5,000 pieces of rare Hollywoodiana, original costumes, and movie props. Some of my favorite displays at the museum are Greta Garbo's gowns, Sonny and Cher's stained-glass skylight, Hannibal Lecter's reconstructed jail cell, the iron gates to Jayne Mansfield's sadly demolished Pink Palace, Elvis' bathrobe, Cary Grant's Rolls-Royce, the original three-strip Technicolor camera used to film *Gone with the Wind*, and costumes and miniature models from *Moulin Rouge*. The museum also has rotating exhibits that focus on legends like Marilyn Monroe, Bob Hope, Barbra Streisand, Mae West, and costumer Edith Head. Warning! If you're a film buff, set aside an entire day for this.

1660 N. Highland Ave., Hollywood
(323) 464-7776
thehollywoodmuseum.com

HOLLYWOOD HERITAGE MUSEUM

This museum was built in 1895 and was declared a historic landmark in 1956. If you're interested in the birth of motion pictures and are really a film-lovin' nerd, visiting this museum is a must. The museum's building was once director Cecil B. DeMille and Jesse B. Lasky's movie studio where Hollywood's first full-length feature, *The Squaw Man*, was filmed. The building looks like a little barn in the parking lot of the Hollywood Bowl and is now home to this silent-picture museum. Come look at archived photos from the history of film, including props from silent films, camera equipment, historic documents, and great bits of ephemera from Hollywoodland's early years.

2100 N. Highland Ave., Hollywood
(323) 874-2276
hollywoodheritage.com

TOP
Max Factor's original "color harmony" room at the Hollywood Museum, where he beautified famous brunettes, like Elizabeth Taylor and Hedy Lamarr.

HOLLYWOOD FOREVER CEMETERY & CINESPIA FILM SOCIETY

HOLLYWOODLAND ANTIQUES

Look closely. This antiques shop is hidden away in a small, dark cottage next to the old Beachwood Coffee Shoppe, at the original entrance to the Hollywoodland real estate development of the early 1920s. Owner Jeffrey Meyer is passionate about Old Hollywood, and he sells vintage Tinseltown souvenirs and antiques, along with wonderful items taken directly from the estates of legendary stars, like silent-film comedian Harold Lloyd (my biggest movie star crush). The stock includes several pairs of Lloyd's iconic eyeglasses and photographs from his personal albums (I took home a gorgeous black-and-white head shot in a great vintage black '40s frame). Sort through the silent-film posters, fine timepieces, pottery, oil paintings, lamps, and rugs.

**2699 1/2 N. Beachwood Dr., Hollywood
(323) 962-2438**

ABOVE
Marilyn Monroe frequently took afternoon walks at Hollywood Forever, always stopping to visit Rudolph Valentino's crypt (as seen here), and the cemetery's beautiful replica of Canova's

With a view of the Hollywood sign, Hollywood Forever rests on a plam tree–lined street and is probably the best place to see stars in all of Hollywood—the only thing is, they're stuck in Hollywood forever. Yes, folks this cemetery's jumpin'! I'm always surprised that there's no V.I.P. list to get in. It's located directly next door to Paramount Studios' back lot (how perfect is that?). Latin lover Rudolph Valentino, '20s jazz baby Norma Talmadge, *Wizard of Oz* director Victor Fleming, Johnny and Dee Dee Ramone of the seminal punk band The Ramones, swashbuckler Douglas Fairbanks, silent vamp Barbara LaMarr, MGM's tap dancing queen Eleanor Powell, William Randolph Hearst mistress Marion Davies, spooky film star Peter Lorre, and famous director Cecil B. DeMille, are only a few of the glamorous residents of Hollywood Forever.

The cemetery is also home to the most innovative technology in the history of funerals. The cemetery's Forever Life Stories is a digital database that features what creators call the Library of Lives. This database provides visitors with access to biographical documentaries of those who are buried on the grounds. They are filled with photos, video clips, documents (like letters from loved ones), and sound clips (which are a bit too creepy for me to handle). You can find the life stories of over 1,100 individuals buried at Hollywood Forever.

Aside from its famous ghosts, one of the coolest things about Hollywood Forever is that from April to October, the Cinespia film society hosts popular Saturday night screenings of classic movies, from *Lolita* to *Dressed to Kill*. Set up a picnic on the spacious lawn with your film nerd friends, listen to DJs spin rare soundtracks before sundown, and enjoy the film as you try to dodge the hands popping out of the soil. All kidding aside, if you're easily spooked, don't fret—the actual gravesites are on another lawn. Then again, if you're easily spooked, don't go—the film is projected on the side of the cemetery's main mausoleum.

**6000 Santa Monica Blvd., Hollywood
(888) FOR-EVER
hollywoodforever.com or cinespia.com**

HOLLYWOOD WAX MUSEUM

This is totally cheesy, but it's been a great date place since 1966, especially if you pretend you're scared of the ghouls that pop out in the Chamber of Horrors, or if you smooch on the bench in front of the spooky Jesus in the *Last Supper* scene. As a little girl, I once ran out of here screaming upon turning a corner and being faced with giant wax figures of the band KISS. The wax representation of Jean Harlow is looking shabbier all the time—so visit her soon to make sure she's not forgotten.

6767 Hollywood Blvd., Hollywood
(323) 462-8860
hollywoodwax.com

THE JUNK MARKET

Their motto is "you'll always find something," and upon first visit, I did (and I'm one picky dame). Find extremely romantic vintage home décor if you love the look of worn-down, seafoam green paint on antique wooden chairs that look like they once lived in the kitchen of a Victorian-era California farmhouse. Uncluttered and affordable, this charming shop carries an exquisite collection of vintage pieces—picnic-style dining room tables, Art Deco fixtures, distressed white bookshelves, 1920s wooden tennis rackets, and piles of French linens. The Junk Market offers another great perk: You don't have to think about getting up early on a Sunday to attend the swap meet—they do it for you. And you won't have to take out a second mortgage just to afford a little interior decorating expertise. Owners Nick and Carri Dillon love to help shoppers mix things up, whether your budget is large or small.

6408 Selma Ave., Hollywood
(323) 461-6747
thejunkmarket.com

Q&

Vintage A

The Day-Glo Doll
GO GO GIDDLE PARTRIDGE

VINTAGE L.A. LOCATION
CAPTIOL RECORDS BUILDING, 1750 N. VINE ST.

Go Go Giddle is a Renaissance doll who not only designs and creates Victorian Libertine lampshades that look like Technicolor feathered corsets, but she is also a journalist, psychedelic makeup artist, and even has her own cult public access TV show. She is also the High Priestess of the infamous Partridge Family Temple, a religion that worships pop culture and TV. She is currently recording an LP of duets with artist Boyd Rice, inspired by pop '60s girl groups. She wants everyone to know that "legendary nutcase record producer" Kim Fowley [of The Runaways] dubbed her the "Queen of Hollywood."

JENNIFER BRANDT TAYLOR: Where do you now live in L.A.?

GO GO GIDDLE PARTRIDGE: In West Hollywood on the same block as Lucille Ball's first home. I live with my boyfriend Dan and our kitties.

JBT: What do you love about this place?

GP: Ever since I can remember, the Capitol Records building has intrigued me. I get chills driving past it just thinking of all the incredible music that has been recorded in that architectural modern masterpiece, in the shape of a giant stack of records. So many artists, including Frank Sinatra, Martin Denny, The Beach Boys, Judy Garland, and Peggy Lee.

JBT: What about L.A. do you find most inspiring?

GP: Being able to walk the streets that so many infamous and influential personalities have. Being an artist here, there are so many opportunities and glamorous parties, you can never get bored.

JBT: Where are your favorite L.A. haunts?

GP: For a nightcap, The Formosa or Trader Vic's—which I sadly hear is going to be torn down. I love dining at

Hollywood's oldest restaurant, Musso and Frank's. So many memorable people have dined in those booths while sipping a martini. And El Coyote where Sharon Tate ate her last meal. I like visiting famous death scenes and graves.

JBT: What is the quintessential L.A. film?

GP: *Beyond the Valley of the Dolls.* It totally sums up the psychedelic and twisted aspect of Los Angeles.

JBT: What is the quintessential L.A. read?

GP: *Hollywood Babylon* by Kenneth Anger.

JBT: What is your favorite song about L.A.?

GP: I really dig "California Dreamin'" by The Mamas and the Papas.

JBT: Who are your vintage muses?

GP: Jayne Mansfield was Hollywood glamour personified. She drove down Sunset Boulevard in a pink car while wearing skin-tight pink satin dresses that were so low-cut, her breasts would tumble out just in time for the paparazzi to get some shots.

LEFT
Go Go Giddle casts a
magic spell on the Capitol
Records Building.

LAKE HOLLYWOOD

Lake Hollywood is the Hollywood Reservoir formed by the Mulholland Dam, which was built in 1925, and the history of its creation was fictionalized in the Oscar-winning 1974 film, *Chinatown*. Lake Hollywood is tucked away behind the Spanish and faux Moorish abodes located at the top of the Hollywood Hills. It's gorgeous, with palm trees everywhere and a direct view of the Hollywood sign, and it's quite a popular hot spot for its 3.2-mile jogging path, which was once a favorite morning ritual of Madonna, who lived in the nearby Casita Del Lago estate. The lake is now a regular hangout for couples on dates, neurotic actresses sweating to their iPods, nannies walking little dogs or little kids, and rock stars sprinting by you much too early in the morning.

Located at the intersection of Lake Hollywood Dr. and Barham Blvd. Consult your Thomas Guide or Mapquest for driving directions.

LARRY EDMUNDS BOOKSHOP

For over 60 years this shop has been shelling out the "world's largest collection of books and memorabilia on cinema and theater." As a teen, I first wandered into Larry's with my weekly allowance of $20 and a peaked interest in Hollywood history. My dough was quickly spent on an armful of 1940s *Photoplay* magazines, and a first edition 1950s biography on the scandalous, smoky-throated star of stage and screen, Tallulah Bankhead. Flash forward to present times, when a friend and I were strolling Hollywood Blvd., and she said she needed to find an inspirational photo for the perfect shag haircut. So, I led her into Larry's and had them pull a file of hundreds of glossies of Jane Fonda in the fashionable '70s film *Klute*. Voilà! They have something here on virtually every star under the sun. You can count on this store to find all books and rare periodicals having to do with any aspect of film history, including thousands of original posters, lobby cards, and more than half a million film stills to decorate your walls. Ask any of the obsessive film nerds your most-obscure query—they won't disappoint.

6644 Hollywood Blvd., Hollywood
(323) 463-3273
larryedmunds.com

859—Lake Hollywood, Mulholland Drive, Hollywood, California

LEFT
Lake Hollywood Reservoir's dreamy landscape.

INSET
No longer accessible by car, this bridge is now used mostly as a jogging path across Lake Hollywood Reservoir.

MAGIC CASTLE

THE MAGIC CASTLE

There comes a moment in every Vintage L.A. adventure when you have to utter "open sesame!" to a bronzed owl with flashing red eyes atop an old bookshelf. This is really how you enter the Magic Castle—which is a hoot and a half, and one of the most bizarre and entertaining nights you'll have in all of L.A. It's a private clubhouse for the Academy of Magical Arts (Est. 1963) and magicians from all over the globe, and you can only gain entry by either a member's invitation or by staying at the neighboring Magic Castle hotel. Get dressed up and smashingly bent in true opulent Old Hollywood fashion, where everything is but an illusion!

This Gothic-style, Victorian mansion is nearly 100 years old and is as close to a haunted house as you can get in L.A. Everything is ornate with red velvet curtains and vintage magic posters. There are stained-glass windows, hidden passageways and staircases, and vintage magician memorabilia covering the walls. The Magic Castle is a melting pot of the magician subculture, like Shriners or goths. Their secret motto is, "the more you drink, the better the magic." But no matter how many drinks you toss back, some shows are better than others—like the guy with sprayed silver hair who juggled CDs and explained that the "props" were called "laser discs." Whether the shows are delightfully cheeseball or mystifyingly good, every minute detail here has been tricked out ALAKAZAM style.

The castle also houses a library of magic books as well as a school and a museum. David Copperfield and Doug Henning got their starts here, not to mention the hundreds of legendary stars who have come to be dazzled, like frequent guests Orson Welles and James Cagney. Cary Grant loved to greet guests at the door as his alter-ego, Carini. Frank Sinatra sang at the piano, and Fred Astaire has tap-danced on a tabletop here. The association of devoted magicians here claim that they have direct contact with Harry Houdini (who died in 1926), at least several times a week, in the round private séance room (where they also hold birthday parties).

If you have the pleasure of visiting the Magic Castle, remember that "elegant attire" is required.

7001 Franklin Ave., Hollywood
(323) 851-3313
magiccastle.com

JANE'S HOUSE AND MEMPHIS RESTAURANT

Jane's House is a Victorian cottage that was built in 1903 when similar Victorian homes lined the boulevard (which was then called Prospect Avenue). It is the last remaining residential house along busy Hollywood Blvd. It's a beautiful little two-story Queen Anne/Dutch Colonial Revival home with shingled gables and fancy turrets. Beginning in 1911, Jane's House was the Misses Jane's School of Hollywood, and its classrooms were filled with the children of the movie industry's royalty, like Charlie Chaplin and Douglas Fairbanks. In 2006, Jane's House reopened as a Southern-themed restaurant called Memphis. This ritzy restaurant and bar serves hush puppies, crab cakes, spicy gumbo, and mint juleps. They even project old movies on the walls, like *Casablanca*, outside the restaurant's windows for a true vintage L.A. experience.

6541 Hollywood Blvd., Hollywood
(323) 465-8600
memphishollywood.com

MICELI'S HOLLYWOOD

Right off the heart of Hollywood Blvd., and steps from the Walk of Fame, is the oldest Italian eatery in L.A. Nowhere else in L.A. will you encounter waiters and waitresses who belt out Italian arias and show tunes as they slice your pizza. Opened in 1949, the restaurant is still owned and operated by the Miceli family. A very traditional Italian spot with spaghetti and meatballs, deep-dish cheesy pizza, stained glass, painted murals, a boozy piano bar, and red checked tablecloths, Miceli's is like the Regal Beagle of *Three's Company*. It's the perfect place to eat after seeing a Claudia Cardinale flick at the Egyptian Theatre around the corner. Even The Beatles indulged in some pizza here on their first trip to L.A.

1646 N. Las Palmas, Hollywood
(323) 466-3438
micelisrestaurant.com

MUSSO & FRANK'S GRILL

Down the glittering walk of fame to the historic heart of Hollywood Blvd. lies not only the oldest restaurant in L.A., but the absolute coolest. Opened in 1919, this was, is, and always will be Hollywood's timelessly glam dining experience. It's like stepping into a film noir classic. And as Musso's (for those in the know) legendary luck would have it, the entire neighborhood is currently going through a major renaissance. Many nightclubs, gimmicky bars, and bistros are popping up all over. While the new joints sport celebrity owners, artsy chefs, and V.I.P. rooms, what they lack, which can't be bought, is a mythology.

To understand its history, you must first know that Musso's is divided into two large dining rooms, East and West. In its heyday (from the '20s to the '60s), the East Room was the more formal. It was adorned with faded, golden toile murals, Art Deco wall sconces, and a massively ornate oak bar. The East Room was the preferred spot for studio heads, producers, and money men. The West Room, with its seductively dim lighting, dark mahogany booths, and carved wood hat racks,

ABOVE
Musso & Frank's is the oldest restaurant in Los Angeles, and the author's favorite dining room in all of historic L.A.

has more of a saloon vibe. Naturally, it attracted the creative types—the actors, artists, and writers. I urge you to stay true to your side because it's tradition, and those are getting harder to find. Essentially, there were cliques. In the East, you'd probably find Louis B. Mayer of MGM bitching about why he had to pay so much for a certain star, and in the West you'd see Orson Welles, furiously writing his *Citizen Kane* screenplay over a gin and tonic with his glamorous wife Rita Hayworth (they both frequented Musso's). Legend has it that this segregation led to some pretty nasty bon mots that were shot back and forth through the rooms, like literary gunfire. Musso's is very close to the Writers Guild, so regulars have included some of the great wits of all time, like Fitzgerald, Faulkner, Hemingway, Dashiell Hammett, John Fante, Dorothy Parker, Charlie Chaplin, and more recently, Steve McQueen and Charles Bukowski, to name just a few genius drunks. Due to all these writers eating at Musso's it became the place where their characters ate as well, and the most written-about restaurant in California literature. It was mentioned in Nathanael West's *Day of the Locust*, and since detective novelist Raymond Chandler drank vodka gimlets at the bar daily, he had his iconic character, Philip Marlowe, do the same in his classic pulp novels *The Long Goodbye* and *The Big Sleep*. The latter was written in one of the restaurant's red leather booths, and was later turned into a film starring Humphrey Bogart and Lauren Bacall, who also happened to be (you guessed it) Musso devotees. Cecil Beaton was seen dining here with Andy Warhol and his "Superstars" in 1963, and Buck Henry, screenwriter of *The Graduate*, has even stated that his last meal would he here, if forced to choose. It's the one restaurant Woody Allen favors on his rare visits to L.A., and it's the place where I spotted Johnny Depp dining with Keith Richards (West Room, of course).

Another thing that sets this institution apart from the pack is the service. Most of the red-coated waiters have been serving here for over 20 years (and they move like it too—be patient and inhale the rich atmosphere). And unlike every other restaurant in L.A., none of them dream of being discovered. They are the real deal.

As for the bartenders at Musso's, their cocktail pouring has been perfected over its 80-plus years—it is now a near holy ritual. Martinis and Kir Royales are served either tableside or at the legendary bar, where it's fun to wonder whether F. Scott Fitzgerald may have sipped away his writer's block at the very spot where you're seated. If you stay long enough to really get lost in the old ambience, every architectural detail starts to set up a cinema-worthy scene in which you are the star.

Finally, eating the food at Musso & Frank's is like getting into a culinary time machine. Straight out of a 1950s *Better Homes & Gardens* cookbook, the menu features lamb with mint jelly, creamed spinach, Crab Louie, avocados blanketed in sweet pink dressing, chicken potpie on Wednesdays, shrimp cocktail, enormous steaks, and delicious sand dabs with the tartar sauce in tiny paper cups. They also have about a hundred different variations of potatoes. For dessert make sure you try the Diplomat's Pudding—I once ate it and still can't explain—it's just delicious! And there's no better way to start a lazy Saturday than sitting at the West Room's counter and watching the chef pour light batter on the original griddle. That first bite—perfectly warm with boysenberry syrup and a touch of butter is heaven!

Don't forget that a dress code is also enforced. On a blind date with a certain rock star, who arrived in a tank top and tattooed sleeves, we were promptly asked to return in a jacket, which he refused to do. So needless to say, given my total devotion to this joint, the date was given the boot, and I rendezvoused with Musso's instead. *C'est la vie.* (Closed Sunday and Monday.)

6667 Hollywood Blvd., Hollywood
(323) 467-7788

ALL OUTSIDE ROOMS WITH PRIVATE BATH—REASONABLE RATES

THE ROOSEVELT HOTEL, HOLLYWOOD, CALIFORNIA   JOSEPH M. SCHENCK, PRESIDENT

PARAMOUNT STUDIOS TOUR

The Paramount Studio is L.A.'s only major movie studio that is still located in Hollywood. Surrounded by palm trees and Spanish Baroque architecture, the studio is full of rich Hollywood history, obviously. The two-hour walking tour focuses on the studio's glamorous past, while showing each visitor a behind-the-scenes look at the movie factory's daily operations. Paramount has had several heydays, starting in the 1920s when it boasted having Clara Bow and Rudolph Valentino on it roster, then again in the 1930s when it was home to Mae West, Marlene Dietrich, Bing Crosby, and Bob Hope, and again in the 1970s, when Robert Evans produced *The Godfather*, *Rosemary's Baby*, *Chinatown*, and *Love Story* for the studio. This is also where Gloria Swanson, star of Paramount's quintessential 1950 film noir, *Sunset Boulevard*, said the immortal line: "I'm ready for my close-up, Mr. DeMille."

5555 Melrose Ave., Hollywood
(323) 956-1777
paramount.com

TOP
The ghosts of Hollywood's dazzling past surely sip champagne at the Roosevelt Hotel.

OPPOSITE, TOP
A groovy 1960s scene at the Roosevelt pool, before it was painted by portraitist David Hockney.

OPPOSITE
The author vamping it up at the Roosevelt's Tropicana bar, steps away from where Marilyn Monroe did one of her very first photo shoots for suntan lotion.

ROOSEVELT HOTEL

Built in 1927, the Roosevelt Hotel boasts a history as dazzling and deep as its David Hockney–painted pool. It has recently undergone a hipsterfied revamp, and while I miss its shabby charm, the magnificent bones of this legendary hotel shall always remain. The original investors of the Roosevelt included Douglas Fairbanks Sr., America's sweetheart Mary Pickford, and studio chief Louis B. Mayer. It hosted the very first Academy Awards in 1929, and has entertained guests and luminaries like Salvador Dalí, Ernest Hemingway, Clark Gable, Carole Lombard, and Marilyn Monroe. Everyone has visited here—Monroe was known to swim in the hotel's pool and did numerous poolside photo shoots, and Andy Warhol and Candy Darling partied here after their premiere of *Women in Revolt*. Guests even claim that Monroe's ghost haunts a hallway mirror. The hotel also claims that Montgomery Clift, who lived here during the filming of *From Here to Eternity*, also haunts the hotel. While filming the movie, Clift had to learn to play the trumpet, and guests have said that they sometimes hear a trumpet in the distance. Yikes!

The Roosevelt Hotel is truly a magnificent structure, with a glittering history. It's a fun hangout with classic Spanish-and-Moroccan-meets-Colonial architecture, and its close proximity to the Oscar ceremony (the Kodak Theater is across the street) makes it the perfect place for the stars to glam up before the extravaganza. Be sure to sip a nightcap under the night sky at the poolside Tropicana bar, and grab a cheeseburger at 25 Degrees, the hotel's diner.

7000 Hollywood Blvd., Hollywood
(323) 769-8881
hollywoodroosevelt.com

ABOVE

If you happen to see this man while visiting the Roosevelt Hotel, be sure to say hi. He is the hotel's most famous resident.... Mr. Johnny Grant, the honorary mayor of Hollywood! He has fabulous stories about Tinseltown's golden age, and he can also give you a star on the Walk of Fame!

JOHNNY GRANT

VINTAGE L.A. LOCATION
THE ROOSEVELT HOTEL

Johnny Grant is the honorary mayor of Hollywood and chairman of the Walk of Fame Selection Committee—so the poor thing is always being stalked by gorgeous actresses who dream of being immortalized by a sparkly pink star. Talk about a cinematic life!

This is a man whose best friend was Bob Hope, who dated all the prettiest blond bombshells in Hollywood, who tap-danced alongside Fred Astaire, and who was always on the VIP list at Frank Sinatra's private recording sessions in the Capitol Records Tower.

In the 1940s Grant became an early television pioneer by hosting the game show *Stop the Clock*. In the 1950s, he hosted a popular L.A. radio show called *The Freeway Club*, where he became the first DJ in the United States to report traffic between the songs. He is also a respected actor, with roles in the film classics *White Christmas*, starring Bing Crosby, and *The Girl Can't Help It!*, starring Jayne Mansfield; in the 1960s he produced *The Lucy Show*, starring Lucille Ball. And if all that weren't cool enough, he's a major supporter of preserving Cinema City's past. In 1997, Johnny was honored with one of Hollywood's most famous traditions—a hand-and-footprint ceremony in the forecourt of the Chinese Theatre, and in 2002, he was honored again with a special one-of-a-kind Walk of Fame star bearing the Hollywood seal. At the same ceremony, a street off Highland Boulevard that leads into the Kodak Theater (where the Academy Awards ceremony is held) was named "Johnny Grant Way."

JENNIFER BRANDT TAYLOR: What do you love about this place?

JG: I've lived in the Roosevelt Hotel for over fifteen years! This hotel has all the history, starting with the first Academy Awards. It was a consortium of movie people that built this hotel—Mary Pickford, Doug Fairbanks, Sid Grauman, Louis B. Mayer—and they would roll out the red carpet onto a dirt street, back when Hollywood Boulevard was called Prospect Avenue. This is where they had the after-party for the TV show *This Is Your Life*. So when they did mine in 1960, they got Jayne Mansfield, and we had our parties together in the ballroom! Errol Flynn used to come here every morning to the barbershop to get a shave. He liked gin. As a matter of fact, they say that the Sloe Gin Fizz originated in that barbershop. I would barbecue on the hotels terrace with Ava Gardner. Marilyn Monroe did her first commercial photo shoot at the pool for suntan lotion.

We used to walk across the street and she would stand in Clark Gable's footprints.

JBT: What is your favorite L.A. haunt?

JG: Grauman's Chinese. Everybody loved Sid Grauman. He was like a wild scientist. He had a sparkle in his eye. He also did the Egyptian Theatre!

JBT: What is your hope for the future of Hollywood?

JG: I hope Hollywood will become the most popular tourist destination in the world! We get about twenty million here a year, but I haven't finished promoting Hollywood yet. I'd like to see more signage telling little anecdotes about all the things that took place here.

JBT: What is the essential L.A. film?

JG: *Sunset Boulevard*.

SQUARESVILLE

You can find kooky, affordable vintage here from every era, but this shop specializes in great '60s to '80s pieces like psychedelic print minidresses, ruffled secretary blouses, funny tees, skinny pants, and leather belts for girls and guys. The top floor is a mess of heels and boots, and they buy and trade.

1800 N. Vermont Ave., Hollywood
(323) 669-8464

SUNSET RANCH

Come here for horseback riding in the shadows of the hills and under the Hollywood sign (which is actually the only giveaway that you're not actually in the Old West). It's "Home of the Famous Dinner Ride," where you ride over the hills, down into the Valley (Burbank specifically), and eat at a historic Mexican restaurant.

3400 N. Beachwood Dr., Hollywood
(323) 469-5450
sunsetranchhollywood.com

VINTAGE GEAR HOLLYWOOD

L.A.'s most inventive song slingers claim that this is the first choice for buying, selling, and trading rare guitars, pedals, and amps. Film composer and producer Jon Brion finds equipment here on which to make heavenly music. Actor and drummer Jason Schwartzman is also a fan of the reasonably priced selection, as is popular L.A. musician Jason Falkner.

7501 Sunset Blvd., Hollywood
(323) 876-9862

WHITLEY HEIGHTS

Before there was Beverly Hills, there was Whitley Heights. Established in 1918, this hidden residential area surrounds the Hollywood Bowl, which was Hollywood's first National Historic District. This posh hood stands virtually unchanged since the early 1900s. When you drive up the windy Tuscanesque roads, you'll find a small Mediterranean-inspired hilltop community. The neighborhood was built by Hobart J. Whitley and other architects—some of whom included set designers and craftsmen from MGM—who intended to have the area resemble an Italian village. No two homes are alike; there are homes with creamy stucco, ornate wrought iron gates, Spanish tile fountains, and balconies straight out of *Romeo and Juliet*. From the '20s to the '40s Whitley Heights was the residential neighborhood of Hollywood's artistic royalty because of its convenient location to all the film studios. Imagine all the following people as neighbors: Greta Garbo, Cecil B. DeMille, Rudolph Valentino, and Bette Davis. Jean Harlow once lived at 2015 Whitley Ave., Rosalind Russell at 6660 Whitley Terrace. W. C. Fields and Judy Garland lived at the legendary Villa Vallombrosa at 2074 Watsonia Terrace and Gloria Swanson leased a mini mansion during the filming of *Sunset Boulevard* at 2058 Watsonia Terrace. William Faulkner later lived in that same house. I can't even begin to imagine the parties that occurred atop those hills! In recent years, it has retained its legacy as home to artists, designers, and preservationists.

Whitley Ave., N. of Hollywood Blvd.
(please do not disturb occupants)
whitleyheights.org

YAMASHIRO

This is a delicious restaurant located in a Japanese-themed mansion that rests high on the hills overlooking Hollywood. Swoon over the stunning views while indulging in Cal-Asian cuisine and sushi, but don't skip out on their mean mai tais. It's quite a dreamy joint, so don't bring an ex that you just want to be friends with—you'll get back together, guaranteed. In fact, don't bring anyone you won't want to kiss at the end of the evening. It's *that* romantic, and most patrons follow dinner with a stroll through the private garden path that leads to a pagoda with the glittering view of Los Angeles below. Sit in the Bonsai garden surrounding the koi pond, and you'll feel like Miyoshi Umeki being wooed by Marlon Brando in 1957's *Sayonara* (which was actually filmed here).

1999 N. Sycamore Ave., Hollywood
(323) 466-5125
yamashirorestaurant.com

If we have to tell Hollywood good-by, it may be with one of those tender, old-fashioned, seven-second kisses exchanged between two people of the opposite sex, with all their clothes on.

—*Anita Loos*
Hollywood screenwriter and author of *Gentlemen Prefer Blondes*

CHAPTER ELEVEN

WILSHIRE DISTRICT

Q&A

Vintage

ABOVE

Liz Goldwyn vamps it up in the historic Los Altos apartment William Randolph Hearst built for his longtime love, the actress Marion Davies. Liz is a major vintage collector, and is seen here wearing an Oleg Cassini dress once belonging to Jayne Mansfield, along with 1970s Charles Jourdan heels and dangle earrings from the 1920s.

LIZ GOLDWYN

VINTAGE L.A. LOCATION

THE APARTMENT WILLIAM RANDOLPH HEARST BUILT FOR MARION DAVIES IN THE
LOS ALTOS APARTMENT BUILDING (HISTORIC WILSHIRE DISTRICT)

Liz Goldwyn is a Renaissance woman in the truest sense. She's a filmmaker, author, jewelry designer, and major vintage collector (she owns gowns once belonging to Jayne Mansfield and Ava Gardner). She also happens to be the granddaughter of Samuel Goldwyn (who puts the "G" in MGM), so naturally Liz Goldwyn romanticizes Hollywood's golden age, and acts as a keeper of the family flame.

Liz Goldwyn has held lucrative professional positions since she was 16, and in 1997 she was hired by Sotheby's fashion department. During her time there, she produced the photography for the Marlene Dietrich Estate auction catalog and mounted the costume exhibition for the Duke and Duchess of Windsor.

Liz's major project of the last eight years has been a documentary film on the topic of burlesque queens. As a teenager, she started collecting glamorous and feathery vintage costumes of burlesque. This collection led to an acclaimed HBO documentary that she directed called *Pretty Things*—where she interviews the buxom grannies of bump and grind and revealed the lives and legends of the last generation of old-fashioned strippers. Liz has recently released a beautiful book on burlesque, also titled *Pretty Things*, which further explores the sultry subject.

JENNIFER BRANDT TAYLOR: What do you love about this place?

LIZ GOLDWYN: I was born in Los Angeles and live in the historic Wilshire District, which is slowly being torn down—landmarks like Perino's and the Ambassador Hotel, sadly. At one point this part of Los Angeles, along Wilshire Boulevard, was where Hollywood lived. The chicest restaurants, nightclubs, and shopping (at the old Bullocks Wilshire down the street) all existed in the neighborhood.

JBT: What about L.A. do you find most inspiring?

LG: Driving at sunset, passing the palm trees and 1920s buildings—some painted with graffiti. It makes me feel as if I'm in a film landscape, both surreal and postmodern.

JBT: What are your favorite L.A. haunts?

LG: The Beverly Hills Hotel coffee shop for grilled cheese, the downtown Los Angeles Public Library, Culver City Ice Rink, taco trucks.

JBT: What began your adoration of the past?

LG: I seem to have always lived in the past. In the house I grew up in, which was my grandfather's, I was surrounded by objects and photographs from an era I always wished to have known, people I would have liked to have met.

JBT: What is one of your most memorable starstruck moments?

LG: Watching Bette Davis apply her own pancake makeup before a dressing room mirror. Old-style film star technique: Do it yourself!

JBT: What are some quintessential L.A. films?

LG: *Los Angeles Plays Itself* (a great documentary about the way Los Angeles has been portrayed in the movies). Film Noir: *The Bad and the Beautiful*, *Sunset Boulevard*, *The Big Knife*, *The Long Goodbye*, *Hustle*. Teen Flicks: *Lost Angels*, *Clueless*, *Foxes*.

JBT: What is an essential L.A. read?

LG: *Ask The Dust* by John Fante and any Bukowski.

JBT: What is your soundtrack to vintage L.A.?

LG: "Los Angeles" by X.

Wilshire Blvd. is one of the most important and historic streets in Los Angeles, and it happens to run through nearly every neighborhood mentioned in this book.

It runs 16 miles, starting at the ocean, ending in Downtown, the architectural climate changing many times along the road from chic marble 1960s Beverly Hills department stores to tough Korea Town karaoke bars. From the gorgeous movie star estates of Hancock Park to the ghostly vacant lots where legendary hotels once stood, Wilshire will always exude a classically film noir vibe that perfectly epitomizes L.A.'s design diversity.

THE EL REY THEATRE

Built in 1936, the El Rey Theatre is located in Miracle Mile, one of L.A.'s best-preserved Art Deco districts. The theater is a registered historical landmark—just look at the to-die-for neon marquee, and you'll know why. The building still holds an amazing vintage aura. The Deco lobby has dramatic staircases, and the ballroom dance floor is lined with huge bronze palm trees. It was a movie theater for over 50 years until it was turned into a live music venue in the '90s. It's now a very popular standing-room-only club, hosting something different and interesting every night of the week.

5515 Wilshire Blvd., Los Angeles
(323) 936-6400
theelrey.com

"The Family"
THE DENMANS
ANGEL-ROSE, JOE DEXTER, KIM, AND PAUL
(In order of seating in portrait)

VINTAGE L.A. LOCATION
HOUSE OF DENMAN, HANCOCK PARK

Much like the Osbournes, the Denmans are a family of British rock 'n' rollers, living within the craziness of Hollywood, while remaining a tight-knit and loving gang of marvelously creative misfits. Kim paints portraits of L.A. glamour girls and designs custom gowns for her line, Goddess. Angel-Rose is also a gifted artist, and Joe Dexter is the singer of L.A. punk band Orange, who released their debut CD, *Welcome to the World of ... ORANGE* in 2006. Paul, along with managing Orange and being a true-blue, old-school punk, plays bass for Sade. The Denmans live with their two dogs, Ziggy and Hollywood, on historic Fremont Place, and cruise Hollywood Blvd. in a fabulous pink 1959 Cadillac. They are L.A.'s own Addams Family.

CONTINUED

LEFT
The El Rey's dazzling historic Art Deco neon marquee.

ABOVE
Creepy and kooky, mysterious, and spooky ... Rose, Joe, Kim, and Paul Denman, at home in their historic Hancock Park manor.

JENNIFER BRANDT TALYOR: What do you love about your home?

KIM DENMAN: Every time I drive through the gates of historic Fremont Place, I think of Edie Sedgwick (Warhol's muse) being driven through the very same gates in *Ciao! Manhattan*. Our house was built in the '20s and I love the fact that Errol Flynn once lived here.

JBT: What do you love most about living in L.A.?

KD: I think of L.A. as a planet revolving on its own axis of glamour and poverty. A place where myth and reality collide. Nostalgia juxtaposed against a futuristic *Blade Runner*-esque landscape, haunted by the golden age of Hollywood. The City of Angels, strippers, and porn stars.

JBT: What are your favorite L.A. haunts?

KD: The Hollywood Forever Cemetery, where Rudolph Valentino and Johnny Ramone lie in peace under the Hollywood sign. When the kids were little we used to go on picnics there. I'd like to be buried there, but until then, my other haunts are Musso and Frank's, evenings spent sipping champagne in the lobby of the Château Marmont, the übermodern Arclight to see a movie, or Encounter at LAX for dinner, with its *Mars Attacks* styling.

RD: Disneyland and Necromance on Melrose Ave.

JBT: What are the quintessential L.A. films?

PD: *The Sweet Smell of Success*, for what L.A. can make you do; *Sunset Boulevard*, for how things used to be; *Crash* for how it is.

THIS PAGE
Their house is a museum, where people come to see 'em. They really are a scream…The Denman family!

TOP LEFT
The Denmans' gothic staircase, watched over by a portrait of Lady Kim and Sir Paul.

Hancock Park

If you're into pretending you can buy several gorgeous, historic houses from the early 1900s–1950s, drive around Hollywood's perfectly preserved Hancock Park area and choose your favorites! Here you can see so much of the city's architectural hsitory. The homes are built in all different magnificently classic styles, from Mediterranean to Tudor and from Colonial to Modernist. Many homes were designed by studio art directors and commissioned by the stars themselves. Architects like Wallace Neff and Paul Williams are featured here. It's a neighborhood where the homes have oak-paneled libraries and bedroom are bedchambers, and backyards have tennis courts and pools with cabanas. You can just picture Claudette Colbert in white linens playing croquet on her lawn. In *Pretty in Pink*, when Molly Ringwald is looking at a gorgeous old colonial home, she says, "I bet the people who live there don't think it's half as pretty as I do." Well, in Hancock Park, they do. The city has strict preservational rules, and unlike Beverly Hills, they will not allow you to tear down old homes to build nouveau riche monstrosities. This is the real Old Hollywood deal.

Hancock Park is bounded by Rossmore Ave. on the east, Melrose Ave. on the north, and Wilshire Blvd. on the south.

H.M.S. BOUNTY

Located in the lobby of the historic Gaylord Apartment building, and across the street from the vacant lot where the legendary Ambassador Hotel once stood, H.M.S Bounty is an eternally classic pub. There is always a great mix of people hanging out—hipsters, sloshy seniors, rock stars, queens, and gangsters. Outside this hoppin' bar hangs a kitschy sign that says it's the place for "food & grog." The Bounty was first called, don't laugh, "The Gay Room," which was in reference to Henry Gaylord Wilshire, who owned the street where the building stands. In the 1950s, the bar's name was changed to Secret Harbour, after Henry tried to sue the building to change its name (can you blame him?). It was then changed to the Golden Anchor, and in 1962 it finally became the Bounty that we love today.

Each of the Bounty's round red pleather booths sports a plaque above it, stating which famous personality liked to sit there. You'll see names like Sir Winston Churchill, William Randolph Hearst, and my favorite booth, dedicated to columnist Walter Winchell. The Bounty is the perfect place to meet a gaggle of your wackiest friends. Order fish 'n' chips, sand dabs, burgers, and Caesar salads. You can also rent out the fun back room for private parties.

3357 Wilshire Blvd., Los Angeles
(213) 385-7275
hmsbounty.com

LOS ALTOS APARTMENTS

Los Altos Apartments were designed by Julia Morgan in 1925, and they lie under the golden eye of Old Hollywood in the Mid-Wilshire section of Los Angeles. They were constructed during the first apartment boom in 1920s, in the Spanish Colonial Revival style with Italian ornamentation. The building was once a luxury "co-op," owned by newspaper magnate William Randolph Hearst. The Los Altos is stunning—there is a fountain in the courtyard, an expansive and cinematic lobby, and hand-stenciled beamed ceilings in many of the apartments. Each unit was individually designed for the tenants, which adds to its mystery. The building is lovingly restored, and even the hallway carpets were custom woven in Ireland to match the original designs. Past residents of Los Altos include Bette Davis, Douglas Fairbanks, Mary Pickford, Mae West, and Judy Garland. But the most infamous resident was silent-film actress Marion Davies, who was publishing tycoon William Randolph Hearst's longtime mistress and lifetime love. He customized a five-bedroom suite for her, which was not her real residence but a secret hideaway for the famous couple and a frequent party pad (evidenced by the hidden liquor cabinets in the living room). The suite has carved mahogany doors, vaulted ceilings with intricate gold leaf scrollwork, two-inch-thick Italian green marble, red oak floors, and a movie room that still features the hidden cabinet that once held Marion's movie projector.

The Los Altos has been through a lot of drama—just as its famous residents have. It went bankrupt during the Great Depression but had a resurgence in the 1950s when Wilshire Blvd. boomed with modern high rises and department stores. From the 1980s to 1993, many of these old Wilshire apartments tragically fell into disrepair and were eventually demolished, and the Los Altos was also in danger of becoming only a memory. Thankfully, it was saved by neighborhood protests, and has since gone through a meticulous restoration process in order to return it to its original grandeur. The only sad news now is that if you want to live here, the waiting list is quite a few years long.

4121 Wilshire Blvd., Los Angeles

THE LOS ANGELES COUNTY MUSEUM OF ART (LACMA)

The LACMA has a permanent collection of over 150,000 works, including an exceptional inventory of American art, 18,000 sq. ft. of European paintings and sculptures, contemporary pieces from Matisse to Ruscha, five centuries of drawings, an inspiring span of Asian art, a decorative assemblage of Venetian glass, 7,000 photographs, and a costumes and textiles department. They have also hosted gorgeously curated special exhibits of rare works by Gustav Klimt, Amedeo Modigliani, and David Hockney's portraits. For cinema lovers, their large Bing Theater hosts great classic, independent, and foreign film festivals. Make sure you go to the free Friday evening jazz performances as well as the fabulous events year-round, including the museum's highly anticipated 24-hour party. You can go to the museum, hear great DJs, and socialize with other artsy locals loving the fact that you're partying for free with the John Singer Sargents at 4 a.m.

5905 Wilshire Blvd., Los Angeles
(323) 857-6000
lacma.org

OPPOSITE
The ornate doorway to Marion Davies' apartment in the Los Altos.

ABOVE LEFT
The hidden cabinet that held Marion's movie projector.

BOTTOM LEFT
The preserved apartment features an original poster from one of Marion's films for MGM (of which the "G" happens to be Liz Goldwyn's grandfather).

CHAPTER TWELVE
EAST SIDE

Angeleno Heights ✦ Atwater Village ✦ Echo Park
Los Feliz ✦ Silver Lake

Before any of the big Hollywood movie studios had been built, this is where the film industry's pioneers first set up shop (including Walt Disney's first studio). So, at the heart of the East Side, you will find an inventive and artistic core. The East Side is comprised of several culturally diverse and artstic neighborhoods between Hollywood and Downtown.

These neighborhoods are actually L.A.'s oldest, and have become popular places for young bohos on budgets to reside, being that you can still find semi-affordable digs in cute clapboard cottages and film noir bungalows (compared to Beverly Hills, anyway). It also boasts crazy historic homes, many of which have been perfectly restored by their passionate, and sometimes famous, owners. Esteemed architects have built groundbreaking Spanish, Moorish, Streamlined Deco, and postwar modern-style structures in these neighborhoods. Some of my favorites were designed by Neutra, Schindler, Lautner, and Wright—to name only a few.

Be sure to schedule an entire day to explore the East Side's many pockets. They are dotted with small boutiques, bookshops, bars, beatniky coffee shops, and art galleries. In these festive areas inhabited mostly by artists and musicians, you'll find colorful surprises around every corner, from L.A.'s best homemade Mexican fare at Silver Lake's Alegria, to fabulous art-to-wear at the Show Pony boutique in Echo Park. Now go get lost!

Angeleno Heights

CAROLL AVE.

On top of a hill overlooking Downtown, you can see a slice of the L.A. that existed in the 1800s, virtually unchanged and worthy of a *Twilight Zone* episode. Caroll Ave. is said to be the largest grouping of original Victorian homes anywhere in Southern California, and it's listed on the National Register of Historic Places. This area of town is truly extraordinary to see. Most of the homes have been perfectly restored, and a few of the shabbier ones are up for sale.

1300 Caroll Ave., Los Angeles

PREVIOUS SPREAD
Echo Park Lake, where rare lotus flowers bloom every summer.

THE BIGFOOT LODGE

L.A.'s only log cabin-themed lounge, you can take off your snow boots and stop by for Happy Hour to enjoy the neighborhoody atmosphere, and the life-size Smokey the Bear. Along with killer faux-pine trees and taxidermy, they have great guest DJs, weekly dance clubs, and rock 'n' roll karaoke nights. It's a kitschy Nouveau-vintage spot, but it has been designed with great flair in homage to the real wildlife extravaganza going on nearby in Downtown's concrete jungle.

3172 Los Feliz Blvd., Los Angeles
(323) 662-9227
bigfootlodge.com

INSIDE SCOOP

Michael Jackson's famous 1983 video for *Thriller* was filmed on historic Caroll Ave. It was down these very streets that the King of Pop and his zombies performed their funky ghoul dance, and scared the bejeezus out of poor Ola Ray.

CARROLL AVE.
Highest Concentration
of Victorian Era
Residences

CULTURAL HERITAGE BOARD
MONUMENTS 51 52 71 74 75 76 77 78 79

TAM O'SHANTER INN

The Scottish-themed Tam O'Shanter Inn is the oldest restaurant in Los Angeles to be owned and operated by the same family in the same location. The food at this old-fashioned eatery is from another decade and the décor is from, well, another century. There's an authentic, retro ambience here, and it's the kind of place where you're not afraid to order a scotch and soda with your meat-and-potatoes. The Tudor-style eatery opened in 1922, but it adopted its signature Scottish theme in 1925. The restaurant went on to become an L.A. culinary landmark, famous for its authentic pub character—try the filet mignon and vegetables baked in Yorkshire pudding, if you dig heart-attack-inducing eats (here, they're worth the risk). Back in the day, L.A. was not the buzzing metropolis it is today, and the Tam O'Shanter was situated on the only road linking Glendale to Hollywood. It was also one of the few restaurants near Griffith Park, which at the time was regularly used by the movie industry for outdoor location shoots. "The Tam" quickly became popular with the likes of actors Rudolph Valentino, Mary Pickford, Fatty Arbuckle, and Douglas Fairbanks. Perhaps its most famous patron was Walt Disney, who regularly ate lunch here in the 1930s.

Currently, the bulk of its business comes from the suit-and-tie crowd, but young Eastsiders love frequenting the restaurant's sandwich bar during lunchtime. They also have a live Irish band perform, to keep the spirits a wee bit rowdy.

2980 Los Feliz Blvd., Los Angeles
(323) 664-0228
lawrysonline.com

Echo Park

BRITE SPOT

Hipsters took over a grubby ol' diner and made it into a ham-and-eggs haven for feeding hungry scenesters. It's a true punk-rock diner where many of the waiters are future rock stars, and they offer up classic diner food alongside yummy vegetarian options, and a mouthwatering array of homemade desserts. It's open 'till 4 a.m., and the later it gets, the more crowded it becomes, mostly due to its being located next door to The Echo, the East Side's most popular nightclub. Apparently their grub is the best cure for a Sunday morning hangover, because the line is frequently out the door on weekends.

1918 W. Sunset Blvd., Los Angeles
(213) 484-9800

ECHO PARK AND ECHO PARK LAKE

Founded in 1891, this is one of L.A.'s oldest public parks, and contains a pretty man-made reservoir, created in 1895. Take a ride in a paddle boat, just as Jack Nicholson did in the classic 1974 film *Chinatown* (though his was more of a rowboat). Don't miss seeing the lake's unique lotus flowers, from June to September. They even throw a huge Lotus Festival in July with food, music, and art that celebrates the lake's mysterious lotus flowers. They only bloom in the summer, and Echo Park Lake has the largest display in the West. Lotus flowers are South Asian, and the Hindus believe they are the most spiritual of all flowers. There is something magical about looking at them, and there is also a mystery surrounding how they even got to Echo Park in the first place—since it is a man-made lake. Go to the Historic Echo Park Web site for details on monthly walking tours and for more of the park's colorful history.

751 Echo Park Ave., Los Angeles
(213) 847-3281
historicechopark.org

GOLDMINE GARAGE

This home décor boutique is full of groovy psychedelic '70s home furnishings and hippie crafts like owl tapestries, macramé potted plant holders, wood butterflies, clown dolls, crocheted crazy quilts, vintage cookbooks, art glass, and kitschy kitchen stuff, like Playboy Bunny swizzle sticks. Owner Cynthia Merino combs the California flea markets so you don't have to. She caters to "anyone looking to put a little groove in their cube, flower power in their dinnerware, mood in their lighting, or pop in their art."

1545 Echo Park Ave., Los Angeles
(213) 250-3954
www.myspace.com/goldminegarage

KOHLMAN QUINN

This shop sells fabulous vintage home décor and offers interior design services, like custom drapery and primo upholstery using high-quality retro fabrics. Kohlman Quinn's spirited owner and curator, Chris Quinn, is only interested in pieces she feels are "fearless" in terms of decorating. They are bold and colorful pieces from the 1930s to the late '60s, and according to Quinn, they are "priced from thrifty to spendy." Furniture and conversation pieces include ornate '50s cabinetry, '40s landscape paintings of woodsy nature scenes, shadow boxes filled with taxidermied insects, swag lamps, art glass, and whimsical barware.

2203 Sunset Blvd., Los Angeles
(213) 413-9900
www.kohlmanquinn.com

LUXE DE VILLE

Luxe de Ville sells used vintage and dead stock items, specializing in New Wave '80s styles for guys and dolls. They have a great selection of vintage rock tees, and I spied a great red velvet Balenciaga tilt hat from the '60s, priced at a steal for less than $100. You can also find revamps of vintage clothes by local up-and-coming designers—like Day-Glo splatter-painted white '80s stilettos and hand-rhinestoned groupie platforms.

2157 Sunset Blvd., Los Angeles
(213) 353-0135
luxedeville.com

THE SHORT STOP

Just like that old joke in the film *Swingers*, this is one of those hidden L.A. bars with no sign indicating the name (it vaguely says "cocktails"). It's called the Short Stop because of its proximity to Dodger Stadium, and it's also near the police academy, so this used to be their playground; but the hipsters have taken over. It is co-owned by singer Greg Dulli of The Twilight Singers, and has recently been swankified with a game room, fully equipped with an Elvis pinball machine, Ms. Pac-Man, a pool table, and a black-and-white photo booth. On weeknights, the Short Stop is a fairly quiet neighborhood spot where work-worn Eastsiders relax at candlelit tables, while Lou Reed seeps out of the jukebox. On Friday and Saturday nights, the place is packed with both locals and bored Westsiders looking for a change of scenery.

1455 Sunset Blvd., Los Angeles
(213) 482-4942

SHOW PONY

Kime Buzzelli owns Show Pony, Echo Park's most magical and influential boutique of reworked vintage apparel by up-and-coming local designers. Buzzelli is also the East Side's very own Andy Warholette. She is an accomplished painter, who also surrounds herself with L.A.'s most creative dollybirds, musicians, directors, and personalities. She is like an anchor for all the sweet, young Eastside artists who are looking for a real craft community—not the hard-edged competition you find in the rest of the L.A. fashion scene.

Her own designs are whimsical, with hints of fantasy, California psychedelia, twisted fairy princess, and gothy Stevie Nicks-inspired glamour. She sells chenille yarn puffball boas, hand-painted '70s artisan-style necklace medallions adorned with her original art, and '80s Pierrot face pins trimmed with decaying gold vintage lace. Waifs with pixie cuts buy her flapper headbands covered in hand-sewn vintage findings and sequins, and other rock 'n' roll girls covet her prom dresses covered with sparkly beads and sculptured felt Danish milkmaid cloches.

1543 Echo Park Ave., Los Angeles
(213) 482-7676

THE DERBY

This is one of the original star-studded Brown Derby restaurants, and it's the only one still standing and functioning as a super club. Its original 1941 wooden Derby dome gives the building a unique, open shape. It has recently been named a historic cultural monument by the L.A. city council. The large circular bar can be spotted in Joan Crawford's Oscar-winning film *Mildred Pierce*, as well as the '90s comedy classic *Swingers*.

4500 Los Feliz Blvd., Los Angeles
(323) 663-8979
derby.com

GRIFFITH PARK

In 1896, the well-to-do Colonel Griffith J. Griffith gifted Los Feliz with this prized piece of woodsy land "to be used as a public park for purposes of recreation, health, and pleasure for the use and benefit of the inhabitants of the city of Los Angeles, forever." Turns out the colonel liked to drink a bit too much hooch, and in fact, he shot his socialite wife one night in a drunken rage because he believed that she was trying to poison him. So appropriately enough, our most beautiful park is named after an insane man whose life was wrapped in scandal. Welcome to Hollywood!

Be sure to visit the park's original 1926 merry-go-round, with its ornate, hand-carved, jumping horses adorned with jewel-encrusted bridles and tails of real horsehair flowing behind them. Ride the miniature-scale locomotive at the park's Travel Town Museum, which was featured in a hysterical scene in Steve Martin's 1979 comedy *The Jerk*. Since 1952 it has displayed antique locomotive cars where you can descend off the steps pretending you're Greta Garbo arriving at Union Station. Another Griffith Park must-see is the L.A. Zoo! And if all these sights have made you hungry, stop by The Trails snack stand for organic eats. Located in the park's Fern Dell, the stand serves homemade vegan chili, fruit pies, sandwiches, and gingerbread bear cookies. The faux-rustic log-cabiney look was inspired by Disneyland's Thunder Mountain Railroad ride.

4730 Crystal Springs Dr., Los Angeles
(323) 913-4688
Travel Town: 5200 Zoo Dr.; cityofla.org/rap/grifmet/tt/
Los Angeles Zoo: 5333 Zoo Dr.; www.lazoo.org

GRIFFITH OBSERVATORY

Built in 1935, this famous planetarium is not only an architectural landmark, but a Hollywood history icon. It was used throughout the classic 1954 teen drama, *Rebel Without a Cause*, starring James Dean, Natalie Wood, and Sal Mineo. Since the '80s, they've hosted popular summertime "Lazerium" shows, to a *Dark Side of the Moon* soundtrack. Note: It's been undergoing extensive renovations over the past five years, so check before you visit to ensure it is now open.

2800 E. Observatory Rd., Los Angeles
(323) 664-1181
griffithobs.org

ABOVE
The Griffith Observatory, overlooking all of Los Angeles and up to the stars.

INSET
The magical, whimsical, and psychedelic Show Pony boutique in Echo Park.

OPPOSITE
Painter and proprietress of Show Pony Kime Buzzelli feels that her boutique is "a nest for designers who incorporate vintage into their work. There is a range of influences—flappers, Cockettes, American Indian, appliqué craftwork, Victorian, gypsy, 1960s babydoll, etc.... I love wearable art!" About Echo Park she says, "I love that I can afford a 1930s apartment and live as a painter and make fancy pillows and not have a real job. You can have the creative time to read books and make things here, and I love roller-skating next to the ocean for miles."

MUSEUM OF THE AMERICAN WEST

I'd never been into playing cowboys and Indians until I came here. This is the only place on Earth where you can view California's entire heritage in a single day. It's now one of my all-time favorite L.A. museums. You'll see antique sharpshooting memorabilia, badass Winchester rifles, ornate Colt revolvers, cowboy movie costumes worn by Steve McQueen, an early California stagecoach, gorgeous hand-tooled leather saddles, a Victorian doctor's medical kit filled with its original apothecary vials, and Annie Oakley's gun and embroidered shooting gloves. They also have special exhibits on decorative arts, like "Totems to Turquoise: Native North American Jewelry Arts of the Southwest" and "California Pottery: From Mission to Modernism." Sometimes the museum even shows films on the expansive front lawn, like Sergio Leone's 1968 spaghetti Western, *Once Upon a Time in the West*. Rawhide!

4700 Western Heritage Way, Los Angeles
(323) 667-2000
autrynationalcenter.org

VISTA THEATER

When architect L.A. Smith began building this Spanish-style theater in 1923, there was the astonishing discovery of King Tut's tomb, which sent the world into an Egyptian design frenzy. So, he switched themes halfway through, and that's how this theater got it's wonderfully odd visual vibe, equipped with giant carved serpents and Cleopatra-esque vamps overhead. It started as a vaudeville house and officially became a movie theater in 1926. From 1916 to the theater's opening in 1923, this land was used as storage for the giant Babylon elephant set pieces from D. W. Griffith's silent film *Intolerance*, and the upstairs offices were once HQ for Ed Wood Productions. In recent years, the Vista has started their own collection of footprints in cement, just like the Chinese, but for indie filmmakers like Ray Harryhausen, Kenneth Anger, and Peter Bogdanovich.

4473 Sunset Dr., Los Angeles
(323) 660-6639

SUNSET JUNCTION

In the sweltering August heat, this stretch of Sunset hosts the annual Sunset Junction—L.A.'s largest street fair and festival. The fair has the best food, handmade goods by local artisans, and amazing live rock 'n' roll shows with delightful, mixed-up lineups. As an example, 2006 headliners included The Cramps, Black Rebel Motorcycle Club, and Ashford & Simpson (what?). It's like a giant fiesta—with too much booze, too many tacquitos, and too many people you know. It's always every vintage-loving hipster's swan song of the summer.

sunsetjunction.org

CASA VICTORIA

Affordable antiques to furnish your abode. You can either be an Eastsider—or just live like one. They've got all the accoutrements you'll need for a rock 'n' roll pad, including a great selection of '60s swag lamps and awesomely shaped modern couches just begging to be reupholstered in Eames fabric. They also have a West Side location on Fairfax.

3212 Sunset Blvd., Los Angeles
(323) 644-5590

1051 S. Fairfax Ave., Los Angeles
(323) 934-3591

COME TO MAMA AND HUNG ON YOU

These two vintage clothing boutiques may share the same Nouveau-psychedelic sign, but they each have their own unique, good vibes at affordable prices. Come to Mama is the girlier of the two stores, with racks of tie-dye slip dresses, I'm-with-the-band-style brocade coats ($75), pastel crinolines, '80s blouses, and trunks of silk scarves. Hung on You has a large selection of menswear, like Nehru collar shirts, perfectly beaten-up cowboy boots, hip-slung pants, and other accoutrements to make you look like Z-Man from *Beyond the Valley of the Dolls*. For girls, they have designery garb, like Gunne Sax dresses, embroidered '70s sweaters, and '70s suede scrunchy boots. Hung on You also sells quirky home accessories, like 8-track players, mod lamps, and plaid luggage sets. At both locations, you'd swear you've taken a time machine back to 1969 San Francisco. Peace!

4009 & 4011 W. Sunset Blvd., Los Angeles
www.myspace.com/hungonyou
www.myspace.com/cometomamavintage

THE DEN OF ANTIQUITY

"Quality people, quality furniture." This is one of my favorite antique furniture shops in L.A., and the prices are so reasonable that you'll want to redecorate right now! Their merchandise is more on the romantic, tufted velvet side of design than modernist, with which L.A. is saturated, so this store is always of breath of fresh (albeit dusty) air. I just spotted a showstopping, ornate Victorian china cabinet with Nouveau touches in mixed woods for $675, extraordinary Art Deco end tables for $85 apiece, and a gorgeous mahogany writing desk from the '30s at a steal for $350. If you're looking to furnish a very bohemian Casanova-vibed space, don't visit here without a truck to haul away your finds. This store is a dream that allows bohos like us, who can hardly pay the rent, to live in glamorous decadence. We can easily acquire pieces that our children will actually *want* to inherit. That is, after we stop being kids ourselves and get down to actually wanting children. And while you're pondering *that*, pop next door to the Moroccan-themed Casbah Café for a mint iced tea and perfectly flaky babaghanoush.

3902 W. Sunset Blvd., Los Angeles
(323) 665-1616

THE EDENDALE GRILL AND MIXVILLE BAR

This beautiful firehouse-turned-restaurant serves up fabulous food, with a side of unique Hollywood history. In the early 1900s, the section of Silver Lake where this structure stands was known as Edendale. This part of L.A. was where the film's earliest pioneers built the first movie studios dedicated to making silent pictures. On these and nearby acres, revolutionary films were made, like D. W. Griffith's *Birth of a Nation*, Mack Sennett's Keystone Kops, and *Cleopatra*, starring Theda Bara (the silver screen's first vamp). Also filmed on these acres were the early comedies of Charlie Chaplin, Roscoe "Fatty" Arbuckle, Laurel and Hardy, and Harold Lloyd. Edendale was also home to the original Walt Disney studios, where Mickey Mouse was born.

In 1924, when the film industry had started to set up shop in Hollywood, this was built as L.A. Fire Station Number 56. After being shuttered for years, in 2002 it was bought by cool Silver Lake restaurateurs, and made into the deliciously romantic Edendale Grill, which takes its name from the city's first incarnation. It's been lovingly restored, and still features the original pressed-tin ceiling, wood floors, truck bay doors. Order old-school American eats, like meat loaf, burgers with applewood smoked bacon, macaroni and brie, flatiron steak, and black-eyed pea succotash.

Connected to the grill is the Mixville Bar, named after the first movie cowboy, Tom Mix (who was actually a bartender before finding fame). During the 1920s he built a faux-Western town and Indian village he dubbed "Mixville," a few blocks south of where the Edendale now stands.

This nearby land was where he filmed his action-filled features, in which Clara Bow and John Wayne were first discovered. This gorgeous, dark-wood-paneled pub features the longest and oldest bar in Los Angeles, and the décor is so velvety and rich, it makes seduction a piece of cake.

Mixville has a great outdoor patio for a late-night rendezvous, and where you can order wickedly good potato skins, crab cakes, or tarragon-blue-cheese fries from a special bar menu. Displays and photos are found throughout the restaurant, citing the location's colorful history. And don't forget to take advantage of the vintage black-and-white photo booth on the back patio!

2838 Rowena Ave., Los Angeles
(323) 666-2000
edendalegrill.com

VINTAGE L.A. LOCATION
MISS LIZZIE AND JUSTIN'S 1960S BUNGALOW (SILVER LAKE)

Aside from being my little sister, and taking photographs for this book, Lizzie Brandt is busy designing clothing for L.A. boutiques like Show Pony, and accessories for designers like Anna Sui. She lives with her DJ boyfriend, Justin, with whom she is also collaborating on a line of psychedelic men's and women's apparel, called "Mr. Hodgepodge." They are serious collectors of 1960s vintage clothing and home décor. They live in a mod apartment in the hills where they watch the Technicolor sunset over the Silver Lake reservoir from their patio.

JENNIFER BRANDT TAYLOR: What are your favorite L.A. haunts?

JUSTIN CHAMPION: The forgotten cages of the old L.A. Zoo, the Petersen Automotive Museum, the Museum of Jurassic Technology, and the Museum of Neon Art, Downtown.

JBT: What are the quintessential L.A. films?

LIZZIE BRANDT: *Thank God It's Friday*, *Valley Girl*, *Xanadu*.

JC: *Beyond the Valley of the Dolls* and *Day of the Locust*.

JBT: What are the essential L.A. reads?

LB: *I'm with the Band* by Pamela Des Barres, *Angels Dance, Angels Die: The Tragic Romance of Pamela and Jim Morrison*, *The Pink Palace: Behind Closed Doors at the Beverly Hills Hotel*, *Hollywood Lolitas: The Nymphet Syndrome in the Movies*.

JC: *Hollywood Babylon* by Kenneth Anger.

JBT: What are your L.A. soundtracks?

LB: "I love L.A." by Randy Newman, "Celluloid Heroes" by The Kinks, "Song Cycle" by Van Dyke Parks, "Surf's Up" by The Beach Boys, "Never Before and Never Again" by Marilyn Monroe, and soundtracks to Busby Berkeley musicals.

JC: "L.A. Blues" by The Stooges.

The Psychedelics
MISS LIZZIE AND JUSTIN CHAMPION

EL CID

If Disneyland had a "Spanishland," this would be the tavern. It was a Hollywood landmark first built in 1900 by D. W. Griffith to film scenes from his controversial film *Birth of a Nation*, and it was one of Hollywood's first sound stages. It was later converted into a swanky supper club in 1950, and in 1961, it morphed into this sexy Spanish hacienda. It has ornately carved wood furniture, a multilevel patio and bar with fountains and flowers, hand-painted murals, iron chandeliers, and a red velvet-framed stage. For years it has entertained patrons with a flamenco dinner theater, featuring guitarists so romantic and good they'll break your heart. On most nights it plays host to fun L.A. dance clubs, opera clubs, and L.A.'s best unknown bands who rock for crowds swaying from too many strawberry margaritas.

4212 Sunset Blvd., Los Angeles
(323) 668-0318
elcidla.com

LOVECRAFT BIOFUELS

They are a cool cooperative of young people getting all L.A. hipsters to be aware of alternative automobile fuels, in order to save our air and planet. They purchase and sell stinky ol' diesel-mobiles, but specialize in converting vintage Mercedeses to run on 100 percent vegetable oil. Their services are becoming so popular that they've started to sell several Benzes a day to happy new owners stoked about saving the planet while still rolling like gangstas. They're currently working on setting up a veggie-oil gas pump, so all the eco-conscious Eastsiders can fuel up more conveniently. I'm excited that the LoveCraft guys are not only saving the planet, but restoring these gorgeous vintage rides so that we can eat their (French fry-scented) dust forever.

(213) 291-8587
lovecraftbiofuels.com

MICHAEL BELANGER ANTIQUES

Come here for eighteenth- to twentieth-century home furnishing pieces. The items are not tongue-in-cheek—no faux-Keane clown paintings here. They sell seriously gorgeous stuff—it's like a museum of modern design. You will leave the store in awe, and will want to leave your shabby chic in the street. They sell jazzy Beatnik-worthy pottery from Danish designers, '60s stone coffee tables, lamps, awesome midcentury chairs by important designers, wood-shelving systems to die for, and stunning marble-inlaid end tables (for a comparatively reasonable $750). Every item is gorgeously curated with an earthy minimalism.

1618 Silver Lake Blvd., Los Angeles
(323) 913-7097

MILLIE'S

Established in 1926, this has been a real artsy neighborhood breakfast joint for generations. It's a greasy spoon hangover cure where they serve comfort food like chicken-fried steak and a devil's mess omelet. It's the kind of place to order old-fashioned brunch and coffee strong enough to power a jet engine. The décor is straight out of a '40s roadside dive, with a rickety ol' screen door, shabby wooden patio tables, and sticky syrup decanters. Catering to the morning-after rock 'n' roll crowd, it's fitting that Keith Morris, singer of seminal L.A. punk band the Circle Jerks, is the chef.

3524 W. Sunset Blvd., Los Angeles
(323) 664-0404

Q&A

Vintage

The Soundtrack

IRVING

STEVEN SCOTT, BRIAN CANNING, ALEX CHURCH, AARON BURROWS, BRENT TURNER

VINTAGE L.A. LOCATION
THE RED LION TAVERN (SILVER LAKE DISTRICT)

Psych-pop-inspired, L.A.-based rock band Irving have toured with Franz Ferdinand and The Polyphonic Spree. Much like The Beatles, they function as a musical collective, each of the five members acting alternately as songwriters, instrumentalists, and vocalists. They sound like the tangerine sunset over Hollywood on a summer afternoon. Be sure to get their melodious third LP, *Death in the Garden, Blood on the Flowers* (Eenie Meenie Records, 2006) for the perfect L.A. exploring soundtrack.

thebandirving.com

CONTINUED

JENNIFER BRANDT TAYLOR: What do you love about this place?

AARON: The ambience—where it's great for a summer beer.

STEVEN: On Sunday afternoons, it's great. They have an outside garden, with all sorts of German beers.

JBT: What about L.A. do you find most inspiring?

AARON: There's a convergence of cultural and artistic influences. We also get to meet and work alongside talented and inspiring people.

BRENT: L.A. is the ultimate collage. Pieces of everything from everywhere. The smallest things end up anchoring your secret love affair with the city.

JBT: What are your favorite L.A. haunts?

AARON: The Château Marmont courtyard and the Huntington Library in Pasadena.

STEVEN: Spaceland, Silver Lake Lounge, Hank's Bar.

BRIAN: Sunday Mornings at Ye Rustic Inn.

JBT: What is the quintessential L.A. film?

AARON: *Blade Runner.*

ALEX: *Chinatown.*

JBT: What is the quintessential L.A. read?

BRIAN: *Ask the Dust.*

STEVEN: *Post Office* by Charles Bukowski.

JBT: What is the quintessential L.A. soundtrack?

AARON: "Valley Girl" by Frank Zappa and "Walking in L.A." by Missing Persons.

BRIAN: "California" by Joni Mitchell.

THE RED LION TAVERN

This has been Silver Lake's favorite authentic German pub since 1962. It houses an outdoor beer garden, a German hall of fame, brews served in beer steins, a menu of schnitzel, sauerbraten, and other items ending in "wurst," and waitresses in adorable Heidi-style dirndl dresses. It's a favorite hangout for rowdy hipsters, college kids, seniors, and baseball fans needing to high-five after games at the nearby Dodger Stadium. And if you have to work in the morning, and need to absorb some of the ale, try one of their doughy hot pretzels with mustard.

2366 Glendale Blvd., Los Angeles
(323) 662-5337
redliontavern.net

RAGG MOPP

This shop is dusty, and the racks of clothes are packed like mad—but true vintage lovers dig that. I recently walked into one of L.A.'s posher vintage boutiques, where every piece is over $200, and the adorable salesgirl was wearing the cutest 1940s mint green Girl Scout jumper. So I asked her where she found it, and she replied "Ragg Mopp. It's amazing!" Whether you're looking for a '50s floral hausfrau muumuu, a delicate '30s veil hat, a '40s swing dress, a '60s polyester men's suit, or a Kurt Cobain-inspired fuzzy cardigan, you need to come here. They carry the truest vintage in all of Silver Lake, nothing here postdating the 1970s. Everything is priced reasonably, and if you're holding on to some oldies but goodies, Ragg Mopp wants 'em. They buy as well as sell.

3816 W. Sunset Blvd., Los Angeles
(323) 666-0550

RUBBISH

In two locations across the street from one another, you can find whimsical furnishings, objets d'art, and fabulous lamps. Rubbish sells classy vintage furniture with a modern, midcentury sensibility. East Side interior decorators swear by these stores for finding one perfect piece to complete a room. All the items found here are timeless—perfect to pass on to future generations (they are definitely not rubbish).

1628 Silver Lake Blvd., Los Angeles
(323) 661-5575

TIKI-TI

This is an eternally happening little tiki bar, smack-dab on Sunset. Open since 1961, every inch of this place has been decked out in fabulous vintage Hawaiian. If you are having trouble ordering from their variety of 85 fruity drinks, you can ask for the famous "Wheel of Tiki-Ti Drinks," which you spin, leaving your cocktail fate in the hands of the alcoholic tiki gods! Originally opened by master mixologist Ray Buhen, who is responsible for starting L.A.'s tropical drink craze after years of pouring at popular L.A. lounges, the Dresden and Don the Beachcomber (which was sadly demolished) in the 1940s and '50s. At the Dresden, he created the "Blood and Sand" cocktail for customer Tyrone Power, named after his 1941 dramatic film of the same name. It's now served here at the Tiki-Ti in homage to Ray's pouring talents (he passed on to Tiki heaven in 1999).

Drinks here have delightfully kitschy names, like "The Ugo Booga," "Skull & Bones," or "Chi Chi," and are either adorned with pineapple slices or set ablaze. It's the size of a small hut, so be prepared to wait a little while outside for entry on busy weekends. Drew Barrymore digs it, and if *Fast Times at Ridgemont High*'s Jeff Spicoli had a favorite bar, this would totally be it.

4427 Sunset Blvd., Los Angeles
(323) 669-9381
tiki-ti.com

INSIDE SCOOP

After browsing the fab home décor at Plethoric and Casa Victoria, stroll down the block for a satisfying brunch, lunch, or dinner at Dusty's Bistro. It's beyond gorgeous, filled with French antiques and serves unbelievable couscous, crepes, crab cakes, and croques.

3200 W. Sunset Blvd., Los Angeles
(323) 906-1018
dustysbistro.com

ZANZABELLE

Proprietress Tracy James has turned a lil' old clapboard house into a whimsical candy shop filled with toys, gifts, and curios. It's a general store for those with a serious sweet tooth, serving hard-to-find old-fashioned candies, Ne-Hi soda pop, homemade cookies, and Fossalman's Ice Cream Co.'s delicious ice cream. Visitors are welcomed to the shop by giant giraffe and octopus statues that look like they were happily rescued from some forgotten theme park. There is a grassy front yard scattered with mismatched tin tables, and a polka dot patio. James also stocks nifty gift items like tees with vintage graphics, new/old stock '70s coin machine toys, never-worn 1940s celluloid hair barrettes, antique windup cars, and pillows silk-screened with owls.

Tip: Don't come here if you're currently on a master cleanse.

2912 Rowena Ave., Los Angeles
(323) 663-9900
zanzabelle.net

PLETHORIC

The word "Plethoric" means superabundant and excessively stylish, which are the perfect ways to describe the aesthetically pleasing and affordable vintage home furnishings you'll find here. In a variety of suave and groovy '60s styles, you'll see original abstract artworks, Danish chairs, sexy leather couches, Swedish teak entertainment cabinets, and dining sets. Most pieces are highly collectible—not to mention cool as Belmondo. They sell at an average of about $1,000.

3208 1/2 Sunset Blvd., Los Angeles
(323) 660-1056
plethoric.com

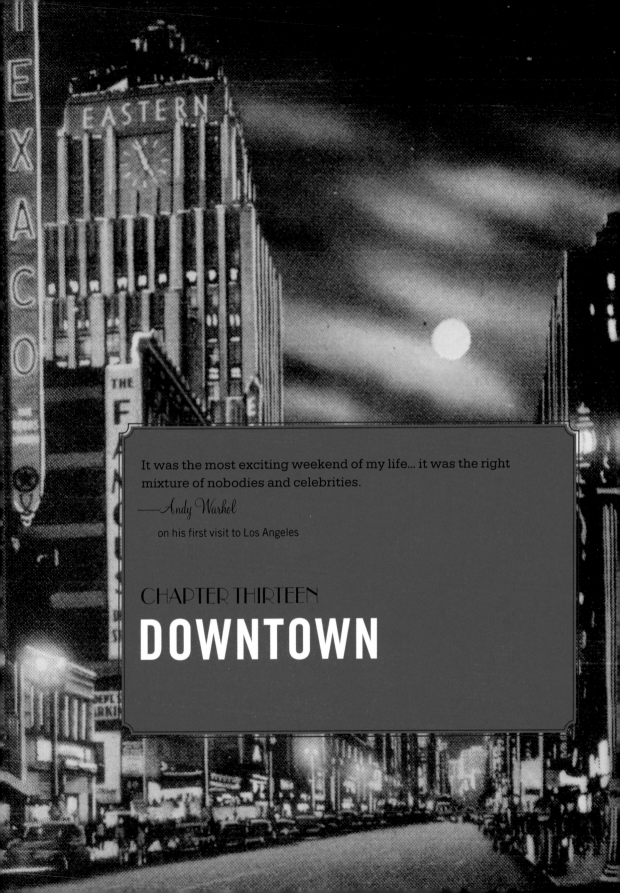

It was the most exciting weekend of my life... it was the right mixture of nobodies and celebrities.

—*Andy Warhol*

on his first visit to Los Angeles

CHAPTER THIRTEEN

DOWNTOWN

This is where Los Angeles truly began. When the first settlers came here from Mexico in 1781, they sought to create political power for themselves in America by building homes and businesses in California, staking claim on a town they named El Pueblo de Nuestra Señora la Reina de los Angeles, which translates to Village of Our Lady Queen of the Angels. Because of this, Downtown is blessed with a deep-rooted Latino heritage, colorful architecture, and cultural diversity.

In the early twentieth century, the first pioneers of the film industry built movie studios all over the East Side of Los Angeles—from Silver Lake to Downtown. For these studios, as well as the ones in Hollywood and Culver City, architects were hired to build lavish movie palaces all over Los Angeles, so the moguls would have showplaces to hold glamorous premieres. In the 1930s, during Hollywood's golden age, Los Angeles boasted to having more movie theaters than anywhere else in the world. Quite a few of the most ornately beautiful ones were built on Downtown's Broadway thoroughfare, which is now known as its Historic Theater District. Spanning six city blocks, it contains the highest concentration of pre-WWII movie palaces in the world! Sadly, most of the theaters no longer show movies. Many are currently being used as churches, swap meets, and filming locations, but even looking at the glorious neon marquees is enough to delight any film fanatic.

If you'd love to actually step inside one of these cinematic stunners, you should attend the annual "Last Remaining Seats" film festival. It's organized by the Los Angeles Conservancy, which is a cool nonprofit group dedicated to preserving L.A.'s architectural history. At these festivals, they screen classic films like *The Seven Year Itch*, and *The Son of the Sheik*. Every year they show one film in my favorite of all the ornate Broadway theaters, The Los Angeles. It was the last one to be built in the district, and it's still referred to by film historians as the most beautiful movie palace in the world.

Built in 1931 by S. Charles Lee, The Los Angeles' opening night party was a premiere of Charlie Chaplin's classic silent film, *City Lights*, and the guest of honor was Albert Einstein! It is a shrine to golden age opulence, and is decorated in a dazzling, Louis XIV-inspired, French Baroque style. Entering the lobby is a gasp-producing experience, from the giant angel sculptures in honor of our city of angels, to the 14-foot-tall crystal chandeliers that hang above the central staircase divided by a grand white marble fountain. Every inch of the theater, down to the gilded powder rooms and the walls, are hand painted with *trompe l'oeil* Heinsbergen murals. It was also technologically advanced for the era, providing an additional periscope-inspired downstairs theater, so patrons on their way to the loo, and mommies with crying babies didn't miss any part of the film.

Another way you can uncover the magical secrets of the Theater District is to take one of the L.A. Conservancy's fun walking tours given every Saturday of the month.

Broadway's Historic Theater District: S. Broadway, between 3rd and 9th Sts.

Los Angeles Conservancy (213) 430-4219 laconservancy.org

BILTMORE HOTEL

"The Host of the Coast" The Biltmore Hotel was known as the finest hotel in the country when it opened in 1923. Many Academy Awards ceremonies were held here from 1931 to 1942, so just about every matinee idol has walked through the Spanish-style lobby. It's a historic landmark, and hundreds of classic films have used it as a location. Films like Alfred Hitchcock's *Vertigo* in 1958 (where it doubled for a San Francisco hotel), *Chinatown* (1974), *The Last Tycoon* (1976), *A Star Is Born* (1976), *Foul Play* (1980), and *Splash* (1983). Get dolled up and visit the Biltmore's gorgeous Gallery Bar and Cognac Room, where ornately carved angels hover above your every sinister sip. It's the kind of place where you'd expect Humphrey Bogart's ghost to pull up a stool and offer to buy you a nightcap. Speaking of ghosts, this is believed to be the last stop of the infamous, unsolved murder victim of the 1940s, the Black Dahlia. They've even named a cocktail after her.

506 S. Grand Ave., Los Angeles
(213) 624-1011
millenniumhotels.com

THE BOB BAKER MARIONETTE THEATER

Bob Baker has been a puppeteer and marionette maker to the stars since the early 1940s. He has created puppets for many movies, including George Cukor's *A Star Is Born*, *G.I. Blues* starring Elvis, Disney's *Bedknobs and Broomsticks*, Saul Bass' Oscar-winning 1968 short, *Why Man Creates*, and countless 1950s sci-fi and monster flicks. Since 1961, Baker's theater and marionette archives have been located in a magical warehouse, hidden away under a freeway overpass. He refers to the building as a "hysterical monument." Upon first entry, you feel like Dorothy discovering Oz—it's so unexpectedly surreal.

The one-of-a-kind marionettes at the theater have all been designed by Bob and his puppet costume seamstress, Ursula, who previously worked for couture fashion designer Galanos. During the performances, the marionettes are brought to life as they are expertly danced and twirled across the stage by trained puppeteers dressed in black, to a wacky soundtrack of old children's records. The shows are performed in a theater-in-the-round-style, where kids sit on the floor, and the parents sit on chairs in the back rows (I prefer to sit on the floor, where the "action" is and where you can have your hand kissed by a fluffy white cat wearing a monocle and waistcoat). Bob's shows change every season, but his most popular show, which also happened to be the first one he debuted in 1963, is *Something to Crow About*. It features tap-dancing bullfrogs warbling "Shine on Harvest Moon," glittery fireflies who sing "Lonely Little Petunia in Her Onion Patch," and

an absolutely brilliant, glow-in-the-dark Dia De Los Muertos skeleton ballet.

The annual *Holiday Spectacular* is a must see! It's a completely tripped-out version of the *Nutcracker Suite*, which takes you on a magic-carpet ride to Christmas in India, where you get to meet dancing candy canes and mop-topped go-go dancers in Day-Glo Pucci dresses. Every show is followed by a puppeteer meet-and-greet, where they serve everyone old-fashioned ice cream on pastel-colored parlor chairs in Bob's actual workshop.

Along with generations of wide-eyed kids and freaky artists, Bob has gained legions of devoted fans over the years, including celebrities like Walt Disney, Gracie Allen, Debbie Reynolds (would throw daughter Carrie Fisher's childhood birthday parties here), and Judy Garland. When Judy was away filming, she would drop her daughter, Liza Minnelli, here to watch Bob's shows all day. Bob even escorted a very nervous Judy to the first L.A. screening of *A Star Is Born*, since he also created puppets for a scene in that film, which sadly wound up on the cutting room floor. Bob told me that one of his all-time favorite moments at the theater was when little Liza Minnelli came up after a show, hugged him, and said, "Puppet man, I just love you!"

1345 W. 1st St., Los Angeles
(213) 250-9995
bobbakermarionettes.com

LEFT
Vintage marionettes wait patiently to work their magic backstage at Bob Baker's Marionette Theater.

ABOVE
The author doing the Charleston with one of Bob Baker's creations, along with the legendary man himself.

BRADBURY BUILDING

If you were to ask me what the most spectacular example of corporate architecture in the entire city of L.A. was, I would say the Bradbury Building. Just entering the central court of this 1893 landmark is breathtaking. It is blessed with Oz-worthy yellow brick walls, highly detailed foliate wrought-iron railings, Belgian marble stairwells, and two Victorian bird cage-style elevators—topped off with a heavenly skylight overhead.

In 1887, after reading Edward Bellamy's *Looking Backward*, a popular book about a utopian civilization circa the year 2000, real estate magnate Louis Bradbury was inspired to build a manifestation of this futuristic vision. He wanted to experience this world firsthand before passing away—sadly, Bradbury died before the building was completed. He hired draftsman George H. Wyman to make his dream a reality, and Wyman only took the job after consulting a Ouija board. He claimed that his deceased brother communicated with him from beyond, spelling out "Take the Bradbury, it will make you famous." This only adds to the mystifying feeling you get as you wander the storied halls.

304 S. Broadway, Los Angeles

BROADWAY BAR

Though it screams "Vegas!" much more than it does "Hollywood," it's still very vintagey. There are patterned carpets in the Baroque-meets-LSD-style, mismatched, upholstered brocade chairs, '70s swaggy chandeliers, flocked velvet wallpaper, an outdoor smoking balcony, and a jukebox stocked with Bowie and Johnny Cash tunes. The circular bar acts as a giant roulette table, and they have ladies pick numbers randomly throughout the evening to offer the winners free drinks. There are also great DJ nights where they play strictly vintage tunes. Check out the tattooed burlesque queens who dance on Broadway Bar's dramatic staircases, and the performer who does a great Josephine Baker routine, complete with a banana tutu. There's also a cool female magician who studied at the Magic Castle and dresses like a bunny.

830 S. Broadway, Los Angeles
(213) 614-9909
thebroadwaybar.net

INSIDE SCOOP

Sci-fi film buffs will surely recognize the Bradbury from Ridley Scott's 1982 cult classic *Blade Runner*, starring Harrison Ford and Daryl Hannah. It was also used as a location in the classic film noirs *Double Indemnity*, *D.O.A.*, and *Chinatown*.

ABOVE RIGHT
The magnificent Victorian lobby of the Bradbury Building, as famously featured in the classic 1982 sci-fi film, *Blade Runner*.

OPPOSITE
Hop Louie's is a classic stop for chop suey and a stiff mai tai.

CHINATOWN

Chinatown's Central Plaza has been around since the early 1930s and in 1938 was dubbed "new Chinatown." It's now known as "old Chinatown," which is great because we like old things even better! Aside from once being a supremely glamorous tourist destination, this wonderfully shabby courtyard includes the location where the Hong Kong Café once stood (it's now a souvenir shop), which was one of L.A.'s most legendary punk rock clubs. In the '70s and '80s, it showcased groundbreaking bands like X, The Motels, The Knack, Black Flag, and The Germs. It was also featured in the seminal 1981 L.A. punk documentary, *The Decline of Western Civilization.*

Built by the Chinese, this colorful neighborhood is not only one of modern America's first "Chinatowns," but also one of the first malls. Here faded red paper lanterns are strung from the tops of rickety pagoda roofs, swinging overhead as the gentle sound of wind chimes haunt the air. It's a great place to stroll during the weekend, and new art galleries and boutiques are popping up constantly on Chung King Road. Old Chinese restaurants, like Hop Louie, are also constantly being rediscovered and appreciated for their intricate Asian details. Chinatown's main walkway, Gin Ling Way, was named after a famous street in Beijing, and it translates to "street of golden treasures." The street is lined with mysterious souvenir shops, stocked to the rafters with antique curios next to touristy plastic fans and dragon-embroidered satin slippers. Here you can spend all day discovering places like the Empress Pavilion, which is a giant Hong Kong-style dim sum dining hall, or the kitschy booze joint with the unlikely name Quon Bros. Grand Star Jazz Club. There is also a famous good-luck wishing well, where you toss coins into cans marked Love, Wisdom, or Vacation.

900 N. Broadway, Los Angeles
chinatownla.com

Clifton's Brookdale - 648 So. Broadway
Los Angeles, Cal.

CICADA

This magnificent restaurant is located in the historic Oviatt Building, and is one of the most pristine and elegant Art Deco buildings in the the world, let alone Los Angeles. Originally built in 1928 as a fashionable men's haberdashery called Alexander & Oviatt, it dressed the likes of John Barrymore, Clark Gable, and Adolph Menjou, and it still has its original inlaid walnut display cases. For Art Deco enthusiasts, this is Xanadu. It resembles an old ocean liner, furnished with priceless René Lalique glass, an illuminated ceiling, and a dance floor worthy of Fred and Ginger. If you can't afford the restaurant (it's not cheap), put on some elegant attire and have a cocktail in their second-floor lounge for the full swanky experience. Reservations required.

617 S. Olive St., Los Angeles
(213) 488-9488
oviatt.com or cicadarestaurant.com

CLIFTON'S BROOKDALE CAFETERIA

Founded by Clifford E. Clinton, this cafeteria and "soupeasy" has been a Downtown landmark since 1931. It resembles a mountain ski lodge, with a famous mosaic-tile entry and an indoor waterfall. Its kitschy décor also features faux forest dioramas, animatronic taxidermy, and a miniature chapel topped with a neon cross. It has a historic time-warp atmosphere—and it's favored by kitsch-adoring hipsters, fashionistas on their lunch breaks from the nearby garment district, and senior citizens who adore Jell-O with whipped cream. It is extremely affordable, and it's credited with saving the lives of many hungry people during the Great Depression, with its "pay what you wish" policy. The meal checks used to say, "Regardless of the amount on this check, our cashier will cheerfully accept whatever you wish to pay—or you dine free." Can you imagine a modern restaurant sharing that same philosophy? There are enough tables here to seat what seems like a billion people, so bring the whole family!

648 S. Broadway, Los Angeles
(213) 627-1673
cliftonscafeteria.com

OPPOSITE
Vintage postcard of Clifton's wonderfully, woodsy, and wacky Brookdale Cafeteria.

RIGHT
The Golden Gopher's interior has recently been revamped, but still looks from the outside like someplace Harrison Ford's character would've gone for a whiskey in the classic sci-fi film Blade Runner, which was actually set in this neighborhood.

FIGUEROA HOTEL

This Moroccan-themed hotel is perfect for nighttime cocktails. There is beautiful atmosphere and the vibe is lovely. Relax on one of the leather poofs on the floor or on the kilims inside the private tents. Straight out of *Casablanca*, there are metallic sari pillows, drapes, and beautiful antique fixtures. There is also a pool that many Eastside rock 'n' roll kids love to sneak into on steamy summer nights. It reminds me of where The Rolling Stones would've hung out after filming their *Rock 'n' Roll Circus*.

939 S. Figueroa St., Los Angeles
(213) 627-8971
figueroahotel.com

GOLDEN GOPHER

Once strictly a joint for scumbags, it's recently been revamped, and is rock 'n' rolled into chicdom. Try to avoid eye contact with the crackheads outside, and once you're safely through the door, you'll realize this is a rockin' watering hole with a sultry ambience, adorned with twinkly chandeliers, velvety wallpaper, cushy wraparound couches, and yes, actual glowing golden gophers!

The Golden Gopher was originally a speakeasy, and it's the owner of one of the oldest liquor licenses in L.A. Hanging out here after work is a hoot, with The Yeah Yeah Yeahs, Ol' Blue Eyes, and James Brown coming out of the jukebox. While the bar is too touristy on the weekends, there is a fun crowd on weeknights. Because it's surrounded by L.A.'s fashion, financial, and jewelry districts, it's become an after-work hang for suits, models, Downtown loft dwellers, and artists—all drinking everything from Pabst to fine scotch. There are no eats here, but they'll let you have pizza delivered. Check out the cute hatcheck booth—now an in-house liquor take-out store with booze, gum, and disposable cameras. They also have an outdoor smoking patio and vintage video games like Ms. Pac-Man, Centipede, and Asteroids.

417 W. 8th St., Los Angeles
(213) 614-8001
goldengopherbar.com

LOS ANGELES PUBLIC LIBRARY

The Los Angeles Public Library's Central Library is perhaps the city's most beloved architectural monument. Based on a singular design by Bertram Goodhue and built in the mid-twenties, the library incorporates Byzantine, Spanish, and Egyptian styles with bold, modern geometric shapes. The pyramidal tower, with its torch symbolizing "The Light of Learning," ties together the many contributions to the library from sculptors, muralists, and engravers. Be sure to check out the second floor, with its mind-blowing zodiac chandelier representing the solar system, and elaborate murals by Dean Cornwall. Another site worth a detour is Albert Herter's 1929 mural of a fiesta with beautiful flamenco dancers, located in the children's literature department.

630 W. 5th St., Los Angeles
(213) 228-7000

LOWENBRAU KELLER

This is an ornate Bavarian bar and restaurant where your waitress is probably named Helga. This place is kitsch heaven—there is a taxidermy petting zoo (deer, boar, stuffed owls), gold cupids, a knight in shining armor, antler chandeliers, and cushy leather booths. You can turn your evening into a Fassbinder film, art directed by Walt Disney. The original owner (sadly deceased) was said to be one of Billy Wilder's set designers, so there's much attention to detail. The food is of the heavy 1950s wiener schnitzel variety, so I'd stick to the drinks if you're at all health conscious. There are beer steins to clank, keg barrels, and a piano that anyone can play, if they ask permission first (remember, this is a pretty senior citizen scene, so skip the Black Sabbath). It's a small joint, so reservations are suggested if you want to sit down and eat.

**3211 Beverly Blvd., Los Angeles
(213) 382-5723**

MUSEUM OF NEON ART (MONA)

The Museum of Neon Art displays exhibits honoring many forms of electric media and historic illuminated signage. MONA also funds the LUMENS project (Living Urban Museum of Electric and Neon Signs), which has raised funds and organized the restoration of more than 100 vintage neon signs in Los Angeles (with many more to go). The organization says that the first neon sign in the United States was lit in 1923 at a Los Angeles Packard dealership.

MONA is independently funded, so if you get misty-eyed at a good Art Deco movie marquee like I do, then be sure to make a donation while you're at the museum—or just make all your friends

visit when in town. That way they can relight many more of the hundreds of dormant Art Deco neon signs around the city—I actually spot new ones daily, wishing I could see how they dazzle when all lit up. Though lately, as I've been exploring Hollywood, I've spotted several newly lit vintage signs (thanks to LUMENS) and felt absolutely elated at how easily a little neon can change an entire landscape for the better. After all, what would L.A. be without all the flashy "liquor" signs and glowing movie theater marquees to complete its jazzy noir setting?

**501 W. Olympic Blvd., Suite 101, Los Angeles
(213) 489-9918
neonmona.org**

LA-19 TYPICAL OF EARLY LOS ANGELES—OLVERA STREET, LOS ANGELES, CALIFORNIA

OLVERA STREET

Built by L.A.'s first settlers in 1781, Olvera Street is its oldest thoroughfare, and one of the most fun. It's a total tourist trap—but definitely wonderful and worth a trip. Visit the authentic Mexican outdoor marketplace with crooked cobblestone, taquitos to die for, and great margaritas at every turn.

The shops blast you with shades of Technicolor merchandise—from hand-painted, pink flamenco guitars to personalized tooled leather belts, to handmade marionettes with curly mustaches wearing ponchos, to plastic woven Frida Kahlo tote bags for $5, and perfect dyed leather flamenco shoes for only $30 (take that, Marc Jacobs!). Make sure to stop by the great souvenir shop Casa Bernal, which sells sexy senorita dresses, velvet sombreros, and turquoise jewelry. And do not leave without tasting the fantastic mole tacos at Olvera Street's most famous (and most crowded) eatery, La Golondrina Café, which was built in 1850. You can also walk through the Avila Adobe, L.A.'s oldest house, built in 1818. It's a romantic date place on weeknights, but the weekends are a blast, so come down on a Saturday and experience a true Mexican fiesta.

Tip: *Take a cab or choose a designated driver.*

845 N. Alameda St., Los Angeles
(213) 680-2525
olvera-street.com

ABOVE AND LEFT
Olvera Street has some of
the most vibrantly fun and
festive souvenir shopping in
all of Los Angeles.

Q&A
Vintage

The Leading Lady

SAMANTHA SHELTON

VINTAGE L.A. LOCATION
OLVERA STREET, DOWNTOWN

Samantha Shelton is a native Angeleno—and a classic blond bombshell with a set of wicked mezzo-soprano pipes. She's an accomplished actress who has appeared in many TV shows, including *Charmed*, *CSI Miami*, *Freaks and Geeks*, and *Gilmore Girls*. She has also appeared in the films *Shopgirl*, *White Oleander*, *Ellie Parker* (costarring Naomi Watts), and *Rise* (with Lucy Liu). She is also part of the cabaret duo If All the Stars Were Pretty Babies alongside actress/singer Zooey Deschanel. In dazzling vintage gowns, they croon to a variety of 1920s standards, and they are currently recording tunes for their debut LP!

JENNIFER BRANDT TAYLOR: What do you love about this place?

SAMANTHA SHELTON: Downtown is the heart of Los Angeles... rich in history, culture, glamour, and excitement. I love the architecture of the old buildings and how it gives you the feeling you are in another era. When I was a kid, my family would go Downtown, exploring, seeing concerts, and eating at places like Philippe's French Dip, which is where my folks got engaged!

JBT: What do you love about living in L.A.?

SS: The possibility to be in such vastly different landscapes in such a short period of time—to go to the desert, the mountains, the beach, and then have a cosmopolitan city at your fingertips is amazing. I love the dusty sunsets, the scent of orange blossoms at night. L.A has always been a place where artists, regular folks, and nut jobs alike have come to find their pot of gold, to re-create their destiny.

JBT: What are your favorite L.A. haunts?

SS: Casa Bianca Pizza Pie [Eagle Rock], Buster's Coffee [S. Pasadena], H.M.S. Bounty [Wilshire District], Griffith Park [Los Feliz], Decades [Melrose Heights], New Beverly Cinema [Beverly Blvd.], The Farmers Market [Fairfax District], Vista Movie Theatre [Los Feliz], the Central Library [Downtown], Hidden Treasures [Topanga Canyon], and the Hotel Café [Hollywood].

JBT: What are the quintessential L.A. films?

SS: *Chinatown*, *The Big Sleep*, and *L.A. Story*.

JB: What are you favorite books about L.A.?

SS: *Ask the Dust* by John Fante and *Red Wind* by Raymond Chandler.

JBT: What is your L.A. theme song?

SS: "California Here I Come!"

ORIGINAL PANTRY CAFÉ

Around since 1924, this is a popular Downtown greasy spoon. It's open 24 hours a day, every day of the year (there isn't even a lock on the door!). It's perfect for a simple tuna sandwich, butterfly steak, or eggs and hash browns after attending the opera or an art opening in Chinatown. Just don't go after a Lakers game at the nearby Staples Center, or you'll be waiting all night for a table.

877 S. Figueroa St., Los Angeles
(213) 972-9279

PACIFIC DINING CAR

Since 1921, this old-fashioned grill has been located in an antique railroad car. This is a classic steak house, with fabulous hearty American food, and masculine, Southern-inspired décor (think hunter green walls, dark wood paneling, and burgundy leather seats). It's the perfect place to pretend you're a character in *Gone with the Wind* while eating your delectable steak. It's open 24 hours, so the crowd is always a wacky mix of stockbrokers who stayed late at the office, fashion photographers who just wrapped a shoot, teens with deep pockets munching after the prom, and night owls.

1310 W. 6th St., Los Angeles
(213) 483-6000
pacificdiningcar.com

PHILIPPE THE ORIGINAL

Whenever the word original is in the name of a restaurant, you know it's old. This one dates back to 1908, where they claim the French dip sandwich was invented. Supposedly, a bun accidentally fell into a roasting pan and soaked up some of the yummy juices. After one bite, you'll wholeheartedly believe them. Philippe's is kind of a freak show, with a mixed-up crowd of fashionistas, lawyers, baseball fans, judges, vagabonds, tourists, and vintage lovers, all queueing up for the perfect sandwich. There's a big, cafeteria-style dining room with communal picnic tables and sawdust on the floor. A French-dip beef, lamb, or pork sandwich will set you back between $3.85 and $4.15. They also have a delicious coconut custard cake and a great list of wines by the glass. Every time I'm there, somebody gets kicked out for losing their marbles, but hey, it's Downtown, kid.

1001 N. Alameda St., Los Angeles
(213) 628-3781
philippes.com

SHAREEN DOWNTOWN

"Vintage & eclectic clothing for the urban gypsy" is how fashion stylist/actress Shareen Mitchell describes her boutique. This is a secret (well, not anymore) warehouse of dreamy vintage apparel, catering to a trend-conscious celebrity clientele, but any secondhand fan can afford to buy her glam garb because her prices are quite fair, ranging from $1 to $150, for truly fabulous garments. And if that's not enough of a steal, Shareen holds major sales every third Saturday of the month.

3294 E. 26th St., Los Angeles
(323) 264-3294
shareendowntown.com

THE STARLIGHT STUDIO

Mark A. Vieira, Hollywood historian and author of *Greta Garbo: A Cinematic Legacy*, runs his own little movie house in a historic Downtown building, where he screens high-quality 16mm prints from his personal collection of classic black-and-white '30s and '40s films, many of which are pre-code rarities (reservations required).

672 S. Lafayette Park Pl., Suite 48, Los Angeles
(213) 383-2448
thestarlightstudio.com

UNION STATION

Built in 1939, Union Station, located on the eastern edge of Downtown Los Angeles, is quite an impressive sight, to say the least, especially if you are one of those people who dreams of hopping a train to an unknown destination, changing your name, and starting a new life. Well, that may be a little dramatic, but so is this place. The structure fuses Spanish Colonial, Art Deco, and modern architecture into one mind-bendingly beautiful landmark, with ceilings four stories high. It's where the romance of the past and the spirit of the future seamlessly merge. You can just picture Jean Harlow arriving here after a press tour, secretaries trailing behind her jotting down notes, and chauffeurs carrying her hatboxes. Sit in the walkway to Union Station concourse and take in the most gorgeous wood and marble Art Deco motifs (possibly) in all of L.A. Or relax on the secret outdoor patio in back. Have a Downtown lunch or a fancy dinner date at the station's Traxx restaurant (located in the lobby)—a great place for fish, steak, and wine. Union Station represents the dream of the golden age—of glamorous travel, when the elite had Louis Vuitton steamer trunks with monogrammed pajamas inside. This is where countless stars of the golden era arrived when called upon to Hollywood, either by themselves or by the studios. Greta Garbo first arrived here when summoned from Sweden by studio chief Louis B. Mayer. It was used as a location for the 1972 Barbra Streisand film, *The Way We Were*, and as a police station in the 1982 sci-fi classic *Blade Runner*.

800 N. Alameda St., Los Angeles
(213) 625-1999

MY BARBARIAN

ALEX SEGADE, JADE GORDON, MALIK GAINES

VINTAGE L.A. LOCATION:
BOB BAKER'S MARIONETTE THEATER (DOWNTOWN)

My Barbarian is an L.A.-based performance art collective comprised of three individuals whose talents include singing, acting, writing, filmmaking, dancing, and composing. Their shows are dazzling, Dada-esque exhibitions of costumes, music, mythology, pop culture, and hot Fosse-esque choreography. They have the unique ability to deliver important social critique, to a disco dance beat. They recently debuted *Double Future*, an inventive, politically minded rock opera, at Disney's REDCAT Theater. They also perform in museums, biennials, and at art galleries around the world. Their first full-length album, *Cloven Softshoe*, was released in 2005.

mybarbarian.com

JENNIFER BRANDT TAYLOR: What do you love about this place?

ALEX: The enchanted Marionette Theater is an example of a personal fantasy made real, by hand, with love.

JBT: What about L.A. do you find most inspiring?

ALEX: I have been able to reinvent myself here. The fact that we have the space to disappear and reappear means that we are free to change.

JADE: I moved to Hollywood when I was 8. I remember singing "Hooray for Hollywood" as my mom and I got off the Greyhound bus. I now live in Highland Park in a big wooden house, circa 1905. In L.A., it's easy to live in your own fantasy world and create work based on that alternate reality.

MALIK: The combinations of the urban and the natural, the confounding proximity to the image-world's leading industry, the enchiladas, and the fact that we live in a megalopolis but our cats can go outside.

JBT: What are some of your favorite L.A. haunts?

JADE: The Gamble House in Pasadena, Elysian Park, Inn of the Seventh Ray and Hidden Treasures in Topanga Canyon, Carroll Street in Angeleno Hts., Mission Street in S. Pasadena, Brand Park in Glendale with the gorgeous mini-Taj Mahal art library, and Little Tokyo.

JBT: What are some of your most treasured vintage finds?

ALEX: Martin Gottfried's '70s coffee-table book, *Broadway Musicals*, an out-of-print masterpiece of performance photos. I got it at the St. Vincent de Paul for $10.

JADE: Vintage items given to me by my mom. I have a pair of black platform boots from 1976 that I treasure.

MALIK: I recently bought a quilt of beautiful African-print textiles at Minette's antiques shop on Sunset (Silver Lake). That store is great!

JBT: What films are quintessentially L.A.?

ALEX: *Blade Runner*.

JADE: *Day of the Locust*, *The Last Tycoon*.

MALIK: *Sweet Sweetback's Baadasssss Song*, Melvin van Peebles, 1971.

JBT: What is the quintessential L.A. read?

ALEX: *Play It As It Lays* by Joan Didion (I'm a sucker for screwy blondes with big glasses).

JADE: *Hollywood* by Charles Bukowski.

MALIK: *Helter Skelter*, Vincent Bugliosi, 1974.

JBT: What is the quintessential L.A. soundtrack?

ALEX: *Barefoot in Beverly Hills*, Grace Jones.

JADE: *Unicorns L.A.!*, My Barbarian.

MALIK: *Can I Speak to You Before You Go to Hollywood?* LaBelle (1973).

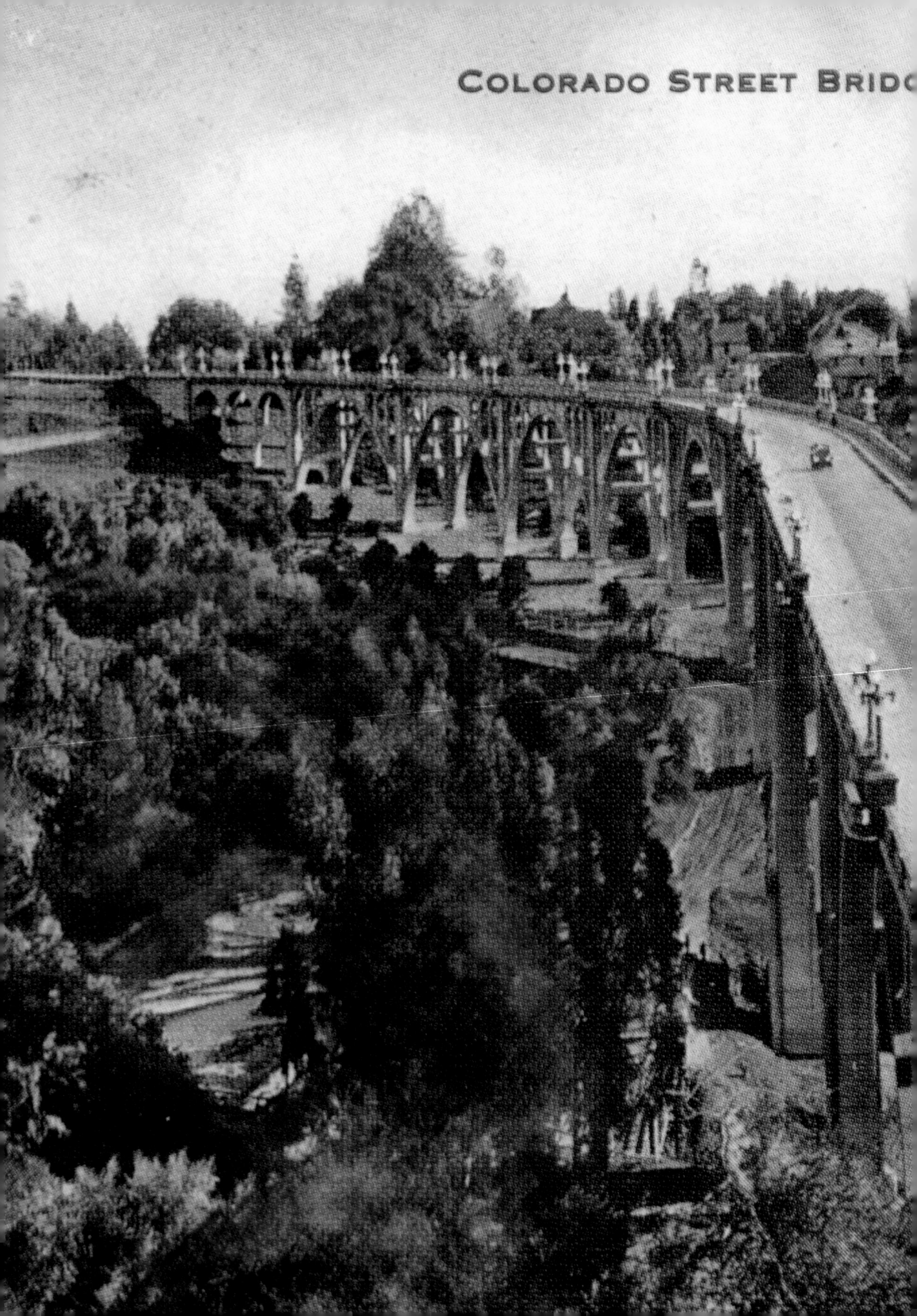
COLORADO STREET BRID

ASADENA, CALIF.

OLD PASADENA

Eagle Rock ✦ Glendale ✦ Pasadena ✦ South Pasadena

Old Pasadena, and the neighborhoods that surround it (which include Eagle Rock, Glendale, and South Pasadena), all date back to the late 1800s, and feature great pockets of legendary architecture from that era, most of which have been perfectly restored. Though only a short ride from Hollywood, Pasadena is worlds away, in look and lifestyle. It's more cultured and conservative than rock 'n' roll, but that shouldn't stop you from coming here to view the lush gardens, and stunning landmark homes built during the groundbreaking Mission and Arts and Crafts design movements of the early 1900s. There are also tons of great antique and vintage shopping.

pasadenaheritage.org

ALL STAR LANES

The décor is straight out of the 1950s, and it's full of old-school character to prove it. It sports a killer arcade for all you pinball wizards, perfectly shabby retro décor, and a karaoke bar where there always seem to be rockabilly couples dancing slow. This has always been one of my favorite places for birthday parties. It's cheap, and they even have themed Bowl-A-Rama nights with live swing bands. On any given night, you'll find serious metalheads, local teens, and beehive-coifed gals bearing tattooed sleeves. It's all part of the charm of this fabulously dingy bowling dive. There's also a pro shop, pool tables, a fully stocked bar (naturally), and fantastic candy machines filled with plastic jewelry and glitter cholita stickers.

4459 Eagle Rock Blvd., Los Angeles
(323) 254-2579

CASA BIANCA PIZZA PIE

The neighborhood's favorite old-time pizza parlor since 1955. Just look for the great original neon sign. They serve traditional garlicky thin-crust pizza, sweet marinara sauce, and Coca-Cola. Sit with your friends at the checkered tablecloths, and come with cash—it's all they take, but dirt cheap! It's the perfect spot for struggling guitarists who want to take their muses on a sweet date.

1650 Colorado Blvd., Los Angeles
(323) 256-9617

THE CHALET

Pretend you're in Aspen circa 1967. The Chalet was once Toppers Tavern, but it has recently undergone a wintry renovation. It's now a sexy Alpine ski lodge-style pub for Swiss misses and misters, with a cozy vibe. It's extremely intimate, with vintage woodsy paintings, plaid carpeting, a '70s fireplace, and deep, cushy red leather booths with mod throw pillows. Sing along to the killer late-80s-filled jukebox that plays Iggy Pop, Radiohead, Stone Roses, and The Smiths. It's the perfect setting for pretending you've just hit the slopes, while sipping White Russians, malt scotches, and ale.

1630 Colorado Blvd., Los Angeles
(323) 258-8800

DESCANSO GARDENS

I once interviewed a hip-hop group from NYC who, when I asked what they wanted to see while visiting L.A, answered "foliage." So I sent them here, and they were totally awestruck. Descanso is a naturally gorgeous 160-acre public garden, filling a natural "bowl" in hills once inhabited by Indians. It houses a grand mansion dubbed the The Boddy House, which houses an art gallery, 25 acres of live oak forest, camellias, and thousands of other gorgeous natural specimens to astonish any concrete-jungle dweller.

1418 Descanso Dr., Los Angeles
(818) 949-4200
descanso.com

FATTY'S & CO.

Don't let the name fool you—this restaurant is for the health-conscious. Housed in a great 1930s Art Deco building, this organic cafe features mostly vegetarian dishes, yet traditional diner food (i.e., it's really delicious for everybody). They're known for their brunch omelets, veggie fondue, and meatless sloppy joes.

5110 Vincent Ave., Los Angeles
(323) 254-8804

LUCY FINCH

Lucy Finch is Eagle Rock's most fabulous vintage boutique, curated by a seasoned L.A. vintage buyer, who has a terrific eye for future trends (I used to buy gothic velvet baby-doll dresses from her in high school). Due to being well-connected in the vintage-buying world, she always has a killer selection of diaphanous '70s dresses, men's mod suits, rock tees, '80s secretary dresses, angora Valley girls sweaters, and leather go-go boots.

5054 Eagle Rock Blvd., Los Angeles
(323) 255-2565
lucyfinch.com

JANET KLEIN

Please allow me to introduce you to the lovely Janet Klein. She is seen here playing her beloved vintage ukulele, in her 1908 Craftsman cottage south of Pasadena. She lives every day as if it were 1929, and is the vocalist for the popular vaudeville-inspired L.A. band, Janet Klein and Her Parlour Boys, who play whimsical, naughty, and obscure ditties from the 1910s to the 1930s. Janet and her sweet husband, Robert, live on a historic block in Alhambra, which she loves because right next door live "collectors of old Model T cars and rusty milk cans, and one of the ladies in the neighborhood was a ragtime musician." Needless to say, she feels right at home. When visiting L.A., a Janet Klein performance is a must-see, as she's simply the bee's knees!

janetklein.com

MARK RYDEN AND MARION PECK

VINTAGE L.A. LOCATION
THEIR HOME, THE ROCK HOUSE (EAGLE ROCK)

Mark and Marion are each accomplished painters whose highly detailed techniques recall the old masters, by way of modern pop culture and Victoriana. Their emotionally charged works are set in an imaginary land of fluffy bunnies, whimsical 1940s children's books, surrealism, and the macabre. Think classical French formalists meets rock 'n' roll. While they may paint on separate canvases, they work alongside each other in their historic home, among their beloved vintage Colonel Saunders statues, Abraham Lincoln paintings, skeletons, and antique toys. Fans of their work include Marilyn Manson, Ringo Starr, Leonardo DiCaprio, Long Gone John, Danny Elfman, and Christina Ricci. They have been exhibited at art galleries and museums worldwide.
markryden.com; marionpeck.com

JENNIFER BRANDT TAYLOR: What do you love about this place?

MARK and MARION: It was our destiny to find it, just like it was our destiny to find each other. It was handmade during the 1920s with rocks picked out of the Arroyo Seco by a doctor whose family lived in this house until the 1980s. This house has great soul. Old things have always been more interesting to us. They have so much more juju.

JBT: What do you love most about living in L.A.?

M and M: Los Angeles has an open spirit. Everybody is welcome and anything goes. We love the open-minded people.

JBT: What are your favorite L.A. haunts?

MARION: The Rose Bowl Swap Meet, the Natural History Museum, Forest Lawn Cemetery, and the Formosa Café.

MARK: The La Brea Tar Pits. I had a very big museum retrospective show in Pasadena, called "Wondertoonel."

JBT: What are some of your starstruck moments?

M and M: Christina Ricci came to visit our studio and we think she is a classic Hollywood star.

JBT: What are the quintessential L.A. films?

M and M: *Mullholland Drive* and *Sunset Boulevard*.

JBT: What is your favorite book about L.A.?

M and M: *Alice in Wonderland*.

JBT: What is the quintessential L.A. soundtrack?

M and M: "Do You Know the Way to San Jose?" by Dionne Warwick.

RIGHT
Painters Marion Peck and Mark Ryden in the living room of their historic Eagle Rock home, surrounded by many of their beloved vintage collectibles, which inspire their art.

ALEX THEATRE

Built in 1925, the Alexander Theatre, as it was originally known, first opened its doors as a vaudeville and silent-movie house. Featuring Greek and Egyptian motifs, the Alex is an important example of the movie palaces of the early twentieth century. From the late 1920s through the 1950s, the Alex Theatre served as a preview house for major Hollywood movies and was visited by hundreds of glamorous stars, including Elizabeth Taylor and Judy Garland. In 1940, architect S. Charles Lee, who designed over 400 movie theaters during his career, created a 100-foot-tall neon Art Deco tower with a sparkling starburst at the top, as well as a three-dimensional marquee, ticketing kiosk, and a decorative terrazzo floor pieced of vibrant tropical colors.

It was restored to its original gleaming splendor in 1992 and is now host to the Alex Film Society, which frequently shows classic movies, preceded by vintage cartoons, newsreels, and shorts. Recent screenings have included *A Hard Day's Night*, *The Music Man*, *The Bride of Frankenstein*, and Hitchcock's *Notorious*. They also throw an annual Vaudeville Extravaganza, which sometimes features a performance by popular L.A. musical act Janet Klein and Her Parlour Boys.

216 N. Brand Blvd., Glendale
(818) 243-ALEX
alexfilmsociety.org

BRAND CASTLE

This dramatic castle was built in 1904, after California real estate developer Leslie C. Brand attended the 1893 World's Fair in Chicago and became transfixed by the East Indian Pavilion. As a result, he began construction on this unique Glendale "castle," which he officially named "El Miradero" ("Grandview"). He hired architect Nathaniel Dryden to translate his dream into reality, adding Indian arches, minarets, and huge bulbous Moorish domes. Ornately carved, Victorian-style woodwork and Tiffany leaded-glass windows were also added, as well as a solarium and music salon. On the hillside, there is also a Brand family cemetery (where Leslie C. Brand now rests), as well as a groovy art gallery and recital hall that was added in 1969. When Mr. Brand died in the castle in 1925 (can you say, haunted?), he bequeathed it to the city of Glendale. It was converted into a library in 1956, and the entire 488 acres is now a public park.

1601 W. Mountain St., Glendale
(818) 548-2051

FOREST LAWN MEMORIAL PARK

In 1917, Dr. Hubert Eaton set out to build the world's most beautiful cemetery, one that would inspire the living as well as the ghosts. He had a flair for the dramatic, banning all traditional tombstones, and naming areas things like Slumberland, Lullabyland, and Everlasting Love. People can even get married here, like Ronald Reagan and his first wife, Jane Wyman, did. It's also great for art exhibits, long walks, and haunted picnics. They have a great gift shop, for those with a morbid sense of humor, where they sell kitschy things like Forest Lawn viewmasters. Their on-site museum recently hosted an exhibit called Revolutions, which displayed famous rock album cover art, including Pink Floyd and Led Zeppelin. They also have "the world's largest painting" of the Resurrection. They present the painting with a light show and cheeseball sci-fi effects. As for the cemetery itself, these are no regular plots! There is music piped in through the trees, a swan lake, and more celebrities than an Oscar ceremony. Irving Thalberg (MGM's "boy wonder") is buried here, along with original blond bombshell Jean Harlow, who tragically passed away at age 26. She is entombed in a French pink marble room designed by her then beau, actor William Powell. The original silent-screen vamp Theda Bara is also buried here, and Carole Lombard and Clark Gable reside next to each other. Other famous residents include

Humphrey Bogart, Bette Davis (whose epitaph reads "She did it the hard way"), Mary Pickford, Sid Grauman, Lucille Ball, Chico Marx, Dorothy Dandridge, Buster Keaton, Jimmy Stewart, Nat King Cole, vaudeville stars The Dolly Sisters, "It Girl" Clara Bow, as well as Sammy Davis Jr. and Walt Disney, making this essentially death's Disneyland. The cult 1965 film *The Loved One*, starring Liberace (who also happens to be buried here), was inspired by this cemetery.

1712 S. Glendale Blvd., Glendale
(800) 204-3131
forestlawn.com

MOONLIGHT ROLLERWAY

A funny little old-school roller rink, where the DJ spins "couples only" skates, the hokey-pokey, "The Hustle," and "Jam on It," so you can pretend you're in *Fame*. If you're yearning to show off your moves, they'll even let you have a "solo skate" in the spotlight if it's your birthday. It has an incredible Art Deco neon sign, a giant sparkly disco ball, and an occasional organ player (I'm still trying to figure out what the occasion has to be to get him to play). Take a groovy time machine back to 1976.

5110 San Fernando Rd., Glendale
(818) 241-3630
moonlightrollerway.com

INSET
A 1930s booklet for the "little churches of Forest Lawn," where aside from funerals, many glamorous Hollywood celebrities have actually gotten hitched.

INSIDE SCOOP

During the 1920s, a very young John Wayne worked behind the popcorn counter at the Alex Theatre.

ADESSO ECLECTIC IMPORTS

Come here for alluring eighteenth- and nineteenth-century antiques, midcentury pieces, and modern art. The items are romantic, dramatic, avant-garde, and exquisite with unusual flair. The warm and inviting owner, Selma Cisic, is an architect and designer with old-world sophistication. She sells Italian, French, Spanish, and Argentinian antiques from varied eras, to help create an air of deep-rooted history in your home. Nearly every piece in Cisic's inventory is museum worthy (i.e., not for those on a budget).

38 Holly St., Pasadena
(626) 683-3511
adessoimports.com

CASTLE GREEN

Built in 1898 by architect Frederick I. Roehrig as the annex for what was then the Hotel Green, the Castle Green is a seven-story Moorish, Colonial, and Spanish-style building sitting next to Old Pasadena's Central Park. It has an ornate, Victorian design with domes, arches, pillars, balconies, and verandas, and has been meticulously restored in recent years. Once a lavish resort for the well-to-do who wanted to escape the harsh eastern winters, the Hotel Green became the social center of Pasadena, playing host to vacationing tycoons, actors, artists, and presidents. No longer a hotel, the Central Annex has been divided into 50 individually owned units, and I dream of one day living in one (the waiting list is many years long). The sitting rooms contain their original 1898 furniture, the sunroom is filled with historic wicker, and the grand lobby retains its stunning mosaic tile floor. Of course, like any great hotel, there is a Palm Terrace Ballroom, which breathes opulence. Many motion pictures have been filmed here, including Rudolph Valentino's *Out of Luck* in 1919 and 1973's *The Sting*, starring Paul Newman and Robert Redford. It is listed on the National Register of Historic Places, and twice a year the nonprofit organization, Friends of Castle Green, give special tours of the property.

99 S. Raymond Ave., Pasadena
(626) 793-0359
castlegreen.com

THE HUNTINGTON GARDENS

The Huntington Library, Art Collections, and Botanical Gardens is a research and educational center set among 120 acres of breathtaking gardens. Three art galleries and a library showcase magnificent collections of paintings, sculptures, rare books, manuscripts, and decorative arts. The botanical collection features over 14,000 different species of plants. It was founded in 1919 by railroad and real estate developer Henry Edwards Huntington, who had a deep, lifelong interest in books, art, and gardens. He first opened the gardens to the public in 1928. The spectacular library is full of books amassed by Huntington over his lifetime, during which he collected rare manuscripts in the fields of British and American literature. The library holds about six million items. Among these treasures, you will see an original manuscript of Chaucer's *Canterbury Tales* (c. 1410), a vellum Gutenberg Bible (c. 1455), a rare edition of Audubon's *Birds of America*, and early editions of Shakespeare's works. In the art galleries you will find Gainsborough's masterpiece *The Blue Boy* (c. 1770), Edward Hopper's *The Long Leg*, Rogier van der Weyden's *Madonna and Child* (15th century), and American paintings from the 1730s to the 1930s, including works by John Singer Sargent and Mary Cassatt. There is also a permanent exhibit devoted to the work of early Arts and Crafts pioneers, Pasadena architects Charles and Henry Greene. Other galleries feature Renaissance paintings and eighteenth-century French sculpture, tapestries, porcelain, and furniture. The Botanical Gardens cover 150 acres, and there are 12 themed gardens arranged within a parklike landscape of rolling lawns. Among the most remarkable are the Desert Garden and the Japanese Garden. The camellia collection is one of the largest in the country. Have English tea in the Rose Garden Tea Room after you've stopped to smell the flowers.

1151 Oxford Rd., San Marino
(626) 405-2100
huntington.org

THE GAMBLE HOUSE

Siblings Charles and Henry Greene were two of the most important and groundbreaking architects of the early twentieth century. They were responsible for starting the wildly popular Arts and Crafts design movement, which incorporated detailed workmanship, clean Asian lines, and nature-inspired elements, stepping away from the Victorian foufyness that had infected exterior design for many years. The most important examples of this movement are on the West Coast, specifically in Pasadena. In 1908, Greene & Greene built the Gamble House (as in Procter & Gamble), for a wealthy Ohio family to live in. They designed every beautiful detail, down to the teak furniture. It is a historic landmark that has been phenomenally restored. Tours are given Thursday through Sunday.

4 Westmoreland Pl., Pasadena
(626) 793-3334
gamblehouse.org

NORTON SIMON MUSEUM

Norton Simon, who passed away in 1993, was one of the greatest American-art collectors of the twentieth century. He was an industrialist who once owned the Canada Dry soda company and Max Factor cosmetics; henceforth, he was loaded. His collecting obsession began in the '50s, and by the '70s he had amassed hundreds of original pieces from the old masters, Impressionists, modern art stars, and masterpieces from India and Southeast Asia. The museum contains oil paintings by Raphael and Botticelli, masterworks from the Italian, Spanish, and French (Fragonard) schools, Rembrandts and Rubenes, and important Impressionist and Postimpressionist works by Monet, Renoir, van Gogh, and Cézanne. From the twentieth century, there are wonderful works by Modigliani (my favorite), Picasso, Matisse, Klée, Kandinsky, and over 100 works of Degas. Marcel Duchamp had a star-studded opening here in '63 where everyone did the twist, including Andy Warhol. It's ripe with artsy-fartsy fabulous history and visions of rare beauty.

411 W. Colorado Blvd., Pasadena
(626) 449-6840
nortonsimon.org

OLD FOCALS

This is every Hollywood costume designer's best-kept-secret resource for vintage eyeglasses. They have a fashionably fabulous selection of dead-stock sunglasses and prescription frames for both guys and dolls. Styles include Jackie O styles, Blues Brothers Ray-Bans, Elvis Costello nerd specs, '70s aviators, huge plastic '80s girly shades, and glam, rhinestoned cat eyes. Check out the photos scattered around the store, showing Old Focals' specs adorning actors like Tom Hanks and Johnny Depp.

45 W. Green St., Pasadena
(626) 793-7073

PASADENA CITY COLLEGE FLEA MARKET

This fun flea market at the "PCC" has more than 450 vendors who sell cool collectible toys from the '40s through the '70s. You'll find endless arrays of atomic-age kitchenware, psychedelic home décor, midcentury furniture, crystal chandeliers, rare '60s rock records, and even '70s Toot-a-Loop radios that double as bangle bracelets. It's for both serious hunters and those seeking a visually stimulating Sunday stroll. It's more organized and less overwhelming than the nearby Rose Bowl flea market (p. 188), so I prefer this market for a more mellow junking experience. The PCC is held on the first Sunday of every month (and it's free)!

1570 E. Colorado Blvd., Pasadena
(626) 585-7123
pasadena.edu/fleamarket

REBECCA'S DREAM

Visiting this vintage clothing and accessories boutique feels like shopping in a wacky yet saucy 1940s grandma's closet. I found a pair of violet alligator leather '50s slingback kitten heels for $45.00. They were designed for the historic Madonna Inn motel's gift shop in San Luis Obispo (p. 218) in the early '60s, and they're unbelievably rare and gorgeous. The racks here are toppling over with swanky treasures to be discovered.

16 S. Fair Oaks Ave., Pasadena
(626) 796-1200

ROSE BOWL FLEA MARKET

Bring your sunscreen, parasol, and rolling cart, because for vintage hunters, this is a haggler's paradise. This is the world's largest flea market; they claim there are over 2,000,000 antique and vintage items to be discovered here. It's been known as "America's Marketplace of Unusual Items" for over 30 years. It's divided into two enormous sections of new stuff (who needs that?), and of course, old stuff. No use listing what you'll find here, since the anwer would be "everything on eBay." From antique furniture, to vintage

INSIDE SCOOP

If you want to arrive before the hoards arrive, there's a special early bird admission price of $20 to enter from 5 a.m. to 7 a.m. This is when the professional decorators and serious collectors go to snag all the best stuff. Admission gets $5 cheaper by the hour, starting after 7 a.m. If you do go before sunrise, remember to bring a flashlight!

clothing, to tables of knickknacks that you can browse until your eyes fall out. My favorite finds are the antique wind-up Victrolas, the vintage postcards, and the dazzling costume jewelry. For vintage fiends, this feels like Christmas morning. You'll feel like a little kid. It's a favorite Sunday out for the stars; I have spotted Debi Mazar, Patricia Arquette, Rebecca Romijn, Sofia Coppola and her dad, Francis Ford Coppola. It's held the second Sunday of every month, rain or shine, at the world-famous Rose Bowl from 9 a.m. to 3 p.m.

1001 Rose Bowl Dr., Pasadena
(323) 560-SHOW
rgcshows.com

BAHOOKA RIBS

This is the last remaining original Polynesian restaurant in the Southland. Someone will have to explain to me why there aren't tiki bars like this on every corner, like Starbucks. This world would be much better off, and we'd all know how to hula dance. There are Disneyland-worthy mazes of booths, surrounded by walls collaged with Hawaiian kitsch, and jail cell doors that make it seem like it's been submerged in an underwater pirate ship since the psychedelic '60s. It's superdark and dare I say, romantic? If your heart flutters at the sight of bubbling, fluorescent aquariums, then this is your place! It's decked out in nautical-themed props—décor so insane you won't need a flaming cocktail in a coconut to see double. It's a wild place and so worth the 40-minute drive from Hollywood. Aloha!

4501 N. Rosemead Blvd., Rosemead
(626) 285-1241

CLEARMAN'S NORTH WOODS INN

Located in Clearman's Village, this "Steak and Stein" belongs in Disneyland; the kitsch level is off the charts! Let me set the scene...it's housed in a giant log cabin in an artificially snowy forest, in the middle of a suburban parking lot. It's surrounded by a faux-Western outdoor mall where everything has been painted barnyard red, and there's also a gun shop, and a square-dancing supply store. Also plopped in the middle of the parking lot is a giant riverboat that contains a buffet and video game arcade, but the North Woods Inn is where the real action is. There are wagon wheels, taxidermy, faux-Matterhorn icicles, large Nouveau paintings for that faux-fancy effect, bearskin rugs, fireplaces, flocked velvet wallpaper, and peanut shells on the floor (of course)! Order the huge, meaty four-course meals that arrive with two side salads, a baked potato, and cheese toast). I'd highly recommend dragging all your wackiest friends here for an impromptu dinner party, which will surely result in some very fun and raucous behavior.

7247 N. Rosemead Blvd., San Gabriel
(818) 286-8284

FAIR OAKS PHARMACY AND SODA FOUNTAIN

Since 1915, this old-fashioned ice cream parlor has been located on California's historic Route 66, in historic South Pasadena. It functions as a popular neighborhood corner pharmacy, but they are most famous for their authentic fountain, where soda jerks whip you up perfect hand-dipped milkshakes, chocolate malts, fancy sundaes, old-fashioned phosphates, lime rickies, and egg creams. It features a long counter with swivel stools that has been restored to its original turn-of-the-century splendor. There are authentic tin ceilings, and they also have a great selection of hard-to-find vintage candies.

1526 Mission St., South Pasadena
(626) 799-1414
fairoakspharmacy.net

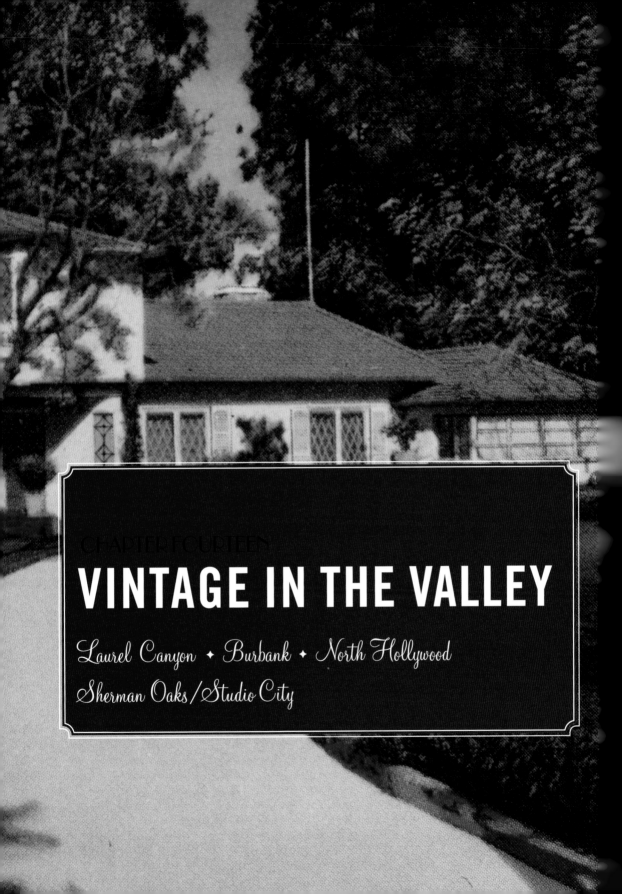

CHAPTER FOURTEEN

VINTAGE IN THE VALLEY

Laurel Canyon ✦ *Burbank* ✦ *North Hollywood*
Sherman Oaks/Studio City

While the Valley is surrounded by a negative stigma of being thought of as uncool by closed-minded Angelenos, it's not fair to judge it until you really understand it. Wander down the never-ending Ventura Blvd., and you're bound to come across great hidden boutiques, antiques, used-bookstores, secondhand clothing shops, and weird old architecture.

The Valley is the perfect place to hunt for vintage finds that are much less picked over than the shops and markets in L.A.'s major metropolis. You just need a real Valley Girl to show you its secrets—and I happen to be one, born and bred. These spots will always remain secrets because (fortunately for us) many Hollywood hipsters are too closed-minded to explore this part of the world. Too many people love to jump on the Valley hater bandwagon. So we are very careful about dispelling our secondhand secrets. That said, I'm throwing caution to the wind! I'm about to make my secrets known, a lifetime of exploring from beautiful downtown Burbank (as Johnny Carson used to say) to the hardcore West Valley. "The Val," as some locals call it, is the perfect spot to visit when you are seeking refuge from the nonstop hipness of Hollywood. Venture "over the hill"—I promise it will be a rewarding experience.

Aside from giving birth to the "Valley Girl" phenom of the 1980s, the San Fernando Valley also boasts some of the most important Hollywood history, outside of Hollywood itself. In fact, more movies and TV shows are filmed in the Valley than anywhere else in the world on a daily basis. When movie industry pioneer Carl Laemmle came to California from the East Coast in 1914, he set out to turn a chicken ranch on Lankershim Blvd. into what he called Universal City, which needless to say, became known as Universal Studios. Other major studios located in the Valley are Disney, Warner Bros., CBS, and NBC, to name a few! In the 1940s, it became a very fashionable thing for the movie stars and moguls to build ranch houses in the Valley, where they could horseback ride and get away from the city for the weekend. Bette Davis, Gene Autry, Clark Gable and his wife, Carolle Lombard, all lived here, and even Marilyn Monroe was a Valley girl. She lived here from childhood into her twenties and graduated from Van Nuys High, where incidentally, the classic teen film *Fast Times at Ridgemont High* was filmed in 1982.

INSIDE SCOOP

To fully understand the Valley aesthetic watch the classic 1983 film *Valley Girl*, starring Nicolas Cage and Deborah Forman, and the 1980 drama *Foxes*, starring Jodie Foster, Scott Baio, and Cherie Currie (of the great '70s all-girl band, The Runaways). Both of these films display the beauty of cruising Ventura Blvd. late at night.

Laurel Canyon

The most historic and scenic path from Hollywood to the San Fernando Valley is to drive over Laurel Canyon. First used as a road in the early '20s, it's the path that leads the Valley to civilization over on the other side of the hill. Laurel Canyon holds a mythology and mystique, which is what first lured my mom to L.A. in the '60s, when she heard the psychedelic girl group the GTOs, sing about its secret charms. Laurel Canyon has always represented an ideal, dreamy lifestyle with the hippie-pop monarchy. It's like a magical hippie forest, with sunshine peeking through the eucalyptus trees, which is why its country/city duality lends itself so perfectly to being the enclave of choice for rock stars who want to live in treehouses yet still need to be close to the action.

Decorating the canyon's twists and turns are woodsy, romantic bungalows with stained-glass windows, creaky oak floors, antiques, fireplaces, and embroidered gypsy shawls draped over pianos. Laurel has a very colorful history. In the 1920s, magician Harry Houdini lived here in what is now a dilapidated mansion that is rumored to be haunted. Other famous residents included Errol Flynn, Keith Richards, Mary Astor, and Orson Welles.

Its golden era started around 1968, when its rock 'n' roll residents included Jim Morrison, James Taylor, Frank Zappa, The Eagles, Jackson Browne, Eric Burdon, Keith Moon, Carole King, Love, Crosby, Stills and Nash, and Joni Mitchell. Laurel Canyon's most famous couple was Graham Nash and Joni Mitchell, who lived together in a cottage on Lookout Mountain. Joni has always been like the poet laureate of Laurel Canyon, and she even painted their beloved cottage on the cover of her folk masterpiece, *Ladies of the Canyon*. That same house was also the inspiration for Graham Nash's hit CSN&Y tune, "Our House." Be sure to stop by the legendary Canyon Country Store, located in the center of the canyon, where every musician previously mentioned stocked their liquor cabinets.

INSIDE SCOOP

To get a visual feel for what Laurel Canyon looks like today, as well as a sampling of the lifestyle, rent Lisa Cholodenko's great 2002 film, *Laurel Canyon*, starring Frances McDormand and Christian Bale.

PREVIOUS SPREAD
Legendary silver-screen cowboy Gene Autry lived in this ranch-style home in North Hollywood throughout the 1940s.

ABOVE
The author, playing her vintage guitar in Laurel Canyon in homage to Joni Mitchell's classic 1970 LP, *Ladies of the Canyon*.

The Lady of the Canyon

THEADORA VAN RUNKLE

VINTAGE L.A. LOCATION
HER WHITE COTTAGE IN WOODSY LAUREL CANYON

Visionary costume designer and L.A. native Theadora Van Runkle's Laurel Canyon 1920s cottage is filled with things she adores—art, antiques, plants, seashells, and books. She has designed daring and inspired costumes for some of my favorite films, including *I Love You, Alice B. Toklas!,* starring Leigh Taylor-Young (1968), *Bullitt,* starring Steve McQueen (1968), *New York, New York,* starring Liza Minnelli (1977), and *The Jerk,* starring Bernadette Peters (1979); not to mention her three costuming Oscar noms for the films *Bonnie and Clyde* (1967), *The Godfather, Part II* (1974), and *Peggy Sue Got Married* (1986). She is also a brilliant painter who is currently writing and illustrating a book titled *Little Lost Cat,* about her late, beloved kitty Hazel.

JENNIFER BRANDT TAYLOR: What do you love about this place?

THEADORA VAN RUNKLE: I bought this house in the '60s. It was my refuge from the "coup de vie," as the French say. There's a force center in Laurel Canyon that's very mystical, a very spiritual place.

JBT: What do you love most about living in L.A.?

TVR: I don't think there is anything like Hollywood on a rainy afternoon. My kid took me to Musso's (Musso & Frank's) for my birthday. It was raining and we were the only people there. We sat at the Charlie Chaplin table and I had two gin martinis. It was fabulous. There's energy emanating from the marvelous architecture here. People have been coming here forever hoping to be stars. There's a narcotic quality to this business...maybe this creative project will be the one!

JBT: Have you ever had a starstruck moment?

TVR: When I was working at Warner Bros. on *Bonnie and Clyde*, Cecil Beaton was there working on *My Fair Lady*. He was wonderful to me. All of his art and photography was what inspired my entire life of visual experience. Another beloved is Marlene Dietrich. I met her when I was working on *The Thomas Crown Affair* (1968). She was about 78 and was wearing a skin-tight little Levi's outfit, and a newsboy cap. I also got to meet Vincent Minnelli. He kissed me full on the mouth and said I was a genius. He was the sweetest man that ever lived!

JBT: What are the quintessential L.A. films?

TVR: *Souls for Sale* (1923), and *Mata Hari* and *Camille* (both starring Greta Garbo), for my favorite costuming that I *didn't* do.

LEFT
Antiques, flowers, and seashells fill the idyllic Laurel Canyon cottage of legendary costumer Theadora Van Runkle, as well as her own paintings and costume sketches for films like *Bonnie and Clyde*.

JUNK FOR JOY

The proprietors of Junk For Joy describe their merchandise as "silly and ugly clothing of good and bad taste." This has been my favorite secret vintage jackpot since the ninth grade, so you can imagine how hard this secret is for me to give up. Since I adore the owners so much, I want everyone to go there so I can get discounts for sending so many new customers. There, now you know my secret scheme. This shop is like Cyndi Lauper's closet circa 1984. Tons of new/old stock, wacky '60s and '70s fashions, and a ceiling covered in the frilliest petticoats you've ever seen. You can find sequined tube dresses, hippie caftans, hipster belts, military apparel and mod gear for guys (the necktie selection is truly godhead), and the most fun (and largest) selection of new/old stock vintage costume jewelry I've ever laid overaccessorized eyes on. They have racks of owl necklaces, wooden beads, '70s glass heart-shaped sunglasses, '80s band pins, E.T. stickers, leg warmers, thousands of original '70s T-shirt iron-ons, sequined berets, platform shoes, and lots more—all never-worn vintage. They have everything to make a killer costume, which is why movie costumers love it. If you love to make people laugh with your ensembles, set aside a few hours for this festival of forgotten-fashion trends.

3314 W. Magnolia Blvd., Burbank
(818) 569-4903
junkforjoy.com

SAFARI INN

I've never actually stayed here, but the neon sign is so fantastic, I may need to try it soon. This motel truly evokes another era. There is a pool in front of the hotel where you can picture girls in leopard print bikinis listening to Bobby Darin on their transistor radios while they bake in the sun with cat-eye sunglasses and reflectors shining on their faces. It's a retro, surf-inspired roadside motor lodge with slick 1950s style in the heart of beautiful downtown Burbank. It's surrounded by palm trees swaying in the breeze; giant spears decorate the rock walls, and all the ironwork features banana leaves. It's best to arrive in a pink Cadillac convertible, like Patricia Arquette and Christian Slater did in *True Romance*, which was filmed here.

1911 W. Olive Ave., Burbank
(818) 845-8586

TEXTILE, COSTUME & CLOTHING SHOW

You can get designer finds from overpriced to perfect steals here. They sell all primo vintage—clothing, accessories, fabrics, findings, buttons and beads, lace and linens, and Victorian garb. The selection is always gorgeous, sold by California's best dealers, and I've never left empty-handed. Be sure to check out the neighboring ice-skating rink and bowling alley while you're there. Make an old-fashioned day of it! Call for schedule of future dates.

The Pickwick Gardens, 1001 Riverside Dr., Burbank
(310) 455-2886
caskeylees.com

UNIVERSAL STUDIOS TOUR

It's obviously touristy beyond comprehension, but sometimes cheeseball things are the most fun. They tore down the *E.T.* ride, which I loved, but they have an *I Love Lucy* museum, and the tram tour is a rip-roaring howl of a time for classic movie fans. See the original *Psycho* house and Bates motel where Janet Leigh took her famous last shower, Harrison Ford's car from *Blade Runner*; the village from *The Hunchback of Notre Dame*; *The Munsters* house at 1313 Mockingbird Lane; the clock tower from *Back to the Future*; a rusty ol' *Jaws* that pops out of the water but has seen better days; K.I.T, the obnoxious talking car from the '80s TV show *Knight Rider*; and a giant *King Kong* that shakes the tram while the air is scented with banana breath. It is still Hollywood's largest film studio and has been at this hilltop location since 1914.

100 Universal City Plaza, Universal City
universalstudios.com

WARNER BROS. VIP STUDIO TOUR

Visit the world's most famous motion picture studio! Take the two-hour-long V.I.P. tour of this dream factory that has been turning out movies since 1918. It is more intimate than the Universal Studios Tour, being that they never allow more than 12 people at a time. You'll get to see locations on the legendary lot where stars filmed tearjerkers, Buster Keaton filmed comedies, Doris Day filmed musicals, James Dean filmed dramas, Warren Beatty and Faye Dunaway filmed *Bonnie and Clyde*, Judy Garland filmed *A Star Is Born*, and Audrey Hepburn filmed *My Fair Lady*. There's really no end to the cinematic history to learn about here. Take a glimpse at old and new hit TV show sound stages, the prop house, and costume house, which is my favorite part! They have so many costumes not yet archived, and every day they find new items with the stars' name tags still in them. The last time I took the tour they had just discovered one of Joan Crawford's 1930s dresses in the archives that they had never noticed. The tour concludes with a walk through the Warner Bros. memorabilia museum. There's also a chance of seeing today's stars as the cart cruises through the lot. Our tour group happened upon Jennifer Aniston, Courtney Cox, and Lisa Kudrow hanging out in front of the commissary, where in fact, Humphrey Bogart signed his contract for *Casablanca* on one of the tables.

3400 Riverside Dr., Burbank
(818) 972-8687
studio-tour.com

SMOKE HOUSE

After you've gone on the Warner Bros. tour, come here for a whiskey sour. It's across the street from NBC and Warner Bros., and it's a favorite of moguls and stars. The Smoke House was founded in 1946 and has been adored by regulars like Sinatra, Judy Garland, Milton Berle, Robert Redford, Bob Hope, and Bing Crosby. Originally built in 1947 by Danny Kaye, it was renovated in 1955 by the famous Southern California architect Wayne McAllister, to appear more modern. At that time, McAllister was also working on the Sands Hotel in Las Vegas. He brought an unusual flair to every project he touched, including Bob's Big Boy in Toluca Lake.

It's a great American grill where you can get good steaks, cocktails, and their world-famous garlic bread. It's also been the home to *Laugh-In*, which used to rent the restaurant for parties, and Jack Parr hosted the *Tonight Show* from the Smoke

House in 1956. Also cool is that in 1975 the Captain & Tennille performed in the lounge and were discovered by Wink Martindale when he heard them singing their future-infectious Grammy-winning hit "Love Will Keep Us Together." Today, it's still a favorite with stars like George Clooney.

4420 W. Lakeside Dr., Burbank
(818) 845-3731
smokehouserestaurant.net

HOLLYWOOD FANCY FEATHER CO.

Hollywood Fancy Feather Co. started in 1944 with an idea to take chicken feathers, dye them, and turn them into boutonnieres. It's a family-owned business, and the walls are covered in photos of the owner with glamour girls, like Marilyn Monroe (whom he made boas for), Jane Russell, Betty Grable, Zsa Zsa Gabor, and '20s cabaret star Josephine Baker. They've also made pieces for Vegas showgirls for decades, for popular shows like the Casino de Paris at the Dunes, Lido at the Stardust, and the Folies Bergère at the Tropicana. I love going to their huge warehouse and playing in the giant bins of marabou boas, ostrich plumes, and peacock feathers.

12140 Sherman Way, North Hollywood
(818) 982-2929
hollywoodfancyfeather.com

WESTERN COSTUME

One of the oldest motion picture businesses in Hollywood is Western Costume Co. Since 1912, Western Costume has dressed many, if not most, of the greatest films ever made, including *The Sound of Music*, *West Side Story*, *The Godfather*, Buster Keaton's *The General*, and Al Jolson's *The Jazz Singer* (which was the first film to feature sound), and they even created Judy Garland's iconic ruby slippers for *The Wizard of Oz*. In Western's archives of over three million garments, they possess some of the world's most historic movie costumes, including Rita Hayworth's famous black gown from her "Put the Blame on Mame" number in *Gilda*, Vivien Leigh's green "Scarlett O'Hara" curtain gown, and Clark Gable's suits from *Gone with the Wind*. Welcome to wardrobe heaven! (By appointment only.)

11041 Vanowen St., North Hollywood
(818) 760-0900
westerncostume.com

Sherman Oaks / Studio City

AROMA CAFÉ

If you're wondering where to nosh during your Valley vintage excursion, this is the most comfy coffeehouse in all of L.A. They serve great lattes, salads, sandwiches, and decadent desserts (the apple pie is a must). There are romantic patios surrounding the cottage, but my favorite place to sip hot chocolate and chat is the secret back patio where there is a bird bath that has a constant stream of feathered friends and friendly squirrels. The cafe is always littered with actresses memorizing their lines, and screenwriters typing away. In the back room of the cottage is a great little antique books and collectibles shop called Portrait of a Bookstore. It's filled with the best new fiction and photography books, as well as antique British tomes with gorgeous gilded bindings, and delicate Victorian tea sets.

4360 Tujunga Ave., Studio City
(818) 769-3853
portraitofabookstore.com

INSIDE SCOOP

The classic "Here's looking at you, kid" scene in 1942's *Casablanca*, where Bogie says a final farewell to Ingrid Bergman, was filmed at Van Nuys Airport.

CARTER SEXTON

Carter Sexton has been offering fine art materials since 1944. This is a real old-fashioned mom-and-pop art supply store. They sell new/old stock brushes and sketch books, and even the new items seem vintage. It smells like erasers and No. 2 pencil shavings, and the walls are covered in the greatest 1940s imitation Rockwell portraits and WWII pinups. It's pristine and organized, like you've entered the art supply shop in *Pleasantville*. Check out the fab array of easels, out of print clip art and "how to draw nudes" instruction books. It's so beatnicky cool, that you'd expect Jackson Pollock to walk in any moment for paints.

5308 Laurel Canyon Blvd., North Hollywood
(323) 763-505
cartersexton.com

CASA VEGA

Opened circa 1958, this old-school Mexican joint is so dark, it takes about 10 minutes for your eyes to adjust. You can then be dazzled by a kitsch display of year-round Christmas lights, red leather banquettes, ghastly (in a good way) bullfighting paintings, faux-Tiffany lamps, waitresses in shoulder-aring senorita dresses, and cranky waiters in red waistcoats. It's one of the most popular margarita joints in the Valley, so unless your want to wait at least 45 minutes for a table, try to arrive before 5:30 p.m. or after 10 p.m. There is no nouveau Mexi-cuisine here—just the classics like their delicious crispy, drippy beef tacos. The margaritas are so good that even after a small earthquake, no one moved a muscle. Also try their famous dessert drink the Tequila Rosa—it's dangerously yummy. The bar is a total scene, and they won't break capacity rules so you may be relegated to the Disneyland-esque tiled waiting area until some people leave. It's worth the wait just for the chips and salsa.

13301 Ventura Blvd., Sherman Oaks
(818) 788-4868

DU~PAR'S

Since 1948, this restaurant and bakery has been a star attraction in Studio City, due to its classic pies and old-school character. It's full of overstuffed vinyl Naugahyde swivel chairs, 80-year-old waitresses with violet-tinted beehives and attitudes to match, and the coffee is so strong it hails from another era. The large selection of pies is especially perfect after a movie date. Du-Par's was immortalized in the classic '80s teen romance *Valley Girl*.

12036 Ventura Blvd., Studio City
(818) 766-4437
dupars.com

GRETA GARBAGE

Being that I'm a Garbo fanatic, the name first caught my eye. This is one of the Valley's best-kept vintage secrets, and one of my all-time favorite boutiques, ever. You can find fine vintage clothing and accessories at very reasonable prices. It's primarily women's, but they do stock a small selection of men's rock 'n' roll-worthy gear. I picked up a pair of killer YSL green velvet and gold platforms with Carmen Miranda fruit shoe clips for only $200! Unlike many other high-end L.A. vintage boutiques, Greta Garbage is not just about designer labels. They stock pieces that are unique or special, even if they're label-less. They have fabulous designer disco dresses, beaded '50s pinup girl sweaters, antique bohemian blouses, cinch belts, and a mind-boggling selection of original '70s platforms. You must stop and chat with the owner, Kenya, because his enthusiasm and fashion knowledge are refreshingly infectious. He's not only one of the best collectors on the scene, but the sweetest. Greta Garbage is also a celeb favorite. Private appointments with Kenya are highly recommended.

14106 Ventura Blvd., Suite 103
Sherman Oaks
(818) 783-4430

RIGHT
The author is greeted by Kenya, the always exuber-antly sweet proprietor of the fabulous Greta Garbage boutique, which stocks the most fun bohemian, decadent rock 'n' roll wares in the city.

ABOVE
If you are a vintage collecting girl, then you should probably be wishing right now that life was like an episode of *Star Trek*, and you could have Scottie beam you straight into this boutique. It's that good.

HOLLYWOOD AVIATOR

How Katharine Hepburn/Howard Hughes–style glamorous would it be to learn to fly? Well here you can like many other Hollywood legends have in the past. If you're too fearful to take off, you can always watch the planes fly away into the sky from the windows at their kooky restaurant facing the runway, 94th Aero Squadron. The restaurant has been open for over 40 years and is filled with WWII flying memorabilia and pipes big-band tunes through the speakers (although the food is pretty much cafeteria caliber). Hold on to your coffee cup when the rumble of the engine shakes the table.

7535 Valjean Ave., #2, Van Nuys
(818) 994-2004
hollywoodaviators.com

ILIAD BOOKSHOP

This has been one of L.A.'s largest used-book stores for almost 20 years, specializing in literature and the arts. I always wind up spending an entire day browsing their packed shelves of rare and reasonably priced tomes on music, film history, photography, design, and counterculture, not to mention a staggering selection of fiction, poetry, and out-of-print classics. They've made shopping here like going to a really hip library, with antique chairs, jazz on the turntable, and kitty cats walking around. If you're a New Yorker who misses the Strand Book Store, then the Iliad will put a smile on your face.

5400 Cahuenga Blvd., North Hollywood
(818) 509-BOOK
iliadbooks.com

THE IVY

Located in the antiques and design center of Studio City, this is not your average antiques store. It's an antiques superstore! This is an upscale maze of private booths curated by individual dealers, with over 55 glass showcases that display exquisite fine antique and Art Deco furniture, signed designer costume jewels, Czech glass, antique china, Venetian mirrors, and knickknacks of every era. They have two stories of great finds—antique lace-embroidered Irish linens and Victorian cameos from the 1800s, '60s purses, collectible dolls, and Bakelite to die for. They also have a spectacular selection of antique engagement and wedding rings.

12318 Ventura Blvd., Studio City
(818) 762-9844

KIT KRAFT, INC.

As a little Valley girl, instead of taking us to Toys "R" Us, my parents would take us here and allow us to pick out projects that kept our creative minds dreaming. They have a huge selection of vintage car and sci-fi creature model kits and an unparalleled selection of dead-stock jewelry findings, rhinestones, feathers, paints, beads, and anything else you would ever need to ace a school diorama or science project. This is where I was taught about the joys of decoupage and Mod Podge and glitter puffy paint. There's always a helpful staff of art students (you'll usually hear The Smiths as you roam the aisles) and cool art devotees. Kit Kraft has been a family-run business since 1946, when the owners, Joe and Gussie, discovered their love for leather crafting in the USO.

12109 Ventura Pl., Studio City
(818) 509-9739
kitkraft.biz

LA FONDUE BOURGUIGNONNE

This is the 1970s on a stick, literally. It's a faux-fancy French fondue restaurant that has had patrons dunking baguettes into melty Gruyère since the disco era. It's straight out of *Three's Company*. It's reminiscent of a medieval auberge as designed by Walt Disney, with lots of copper accents and dark diagonal wood paneling. To complete La Fondue's pseudo-romantic vibe, there are amber votives flickering on every table; they've got Muzak versions of classical tunes playing on a repetitive tape loop, and the whole place smells a bit like cherry brandy. Everyone is served California burgundy in giant carafes, and a feast of melted cheese with veggies and various meats is presented in giant copper pots. I prefer the dessert fondue, which is a bubbling pot of Swiss chocolate with strawberries, marshmallows, and fruit to dip. *Vive la fondue!*

13359 Ventura Blvd., Sherman Oaks
(818) 788-8680

The Legend BOB MACKIE

One could say that Bob Mackie invented Hollywood red-carpet glamour as we know it. He's been designing glitzy Oscar goddess gowns out of his secret Studio City HQ since the 1960s, after starting out under the tutelage of legendary costumers Edith Head, and Jean Louis, who happenedto be costuming Marilyn Monroe at the time. Mackie was responsible for sketching Marilyn's infamous "Happy Birthday, Mr. President" gown. He's received three Oscar nominations, for *Lady Sings the Blues* (1972), *Funny Lady* (1975), and *Pennies from Heaven* (1981), and eight Emmys for his costuming of Sonny and Cher, and the *Carol Burnett Show*. Mackie is currently writing a book about his colorful career, titled "The Bob Mackie Follies."

JENNIFER BRANDT TAYLOR: When have you had a starstruck moment?

BOB MACKIE: When I first started with the *Carol Burnett Show* in 1963 we had Betty Grable on as a guest star. She'll always be my favorite because what you loved as a kid you never stop loving. Rita Hayworth also came on, and Gloria Swanson. I worked on the Judy Garland show when I was 23 years old, and one of Barbra Streisand's first TV specials…The most incredible people!

JBT: What are your favorite L.A. haunts?

BM: Musso & Frank's, the Downtown theaters…one of the things I did as a kid was go to Olvera Street during the war and I loved it! In *Anchors Away*, Gene Kelly dances with a little girl on Olvera Street (of course, it was really a sound stage) and that cemented it.

JBT: What are your favorite films for a healthy dose of vintage L.A. glamour?

BM: *Anchors Away*, *The Dolly Sisters* (with Betty Grable and June Haver), *A Star Is Born*, and *Chinatown*.

LEFT
The author achieves her lifelong dream of being draped in a dazzling feather boa (just like the ones he used to make for Cher and Diana Ross!) by the legendary god of glam himself: Bob Mackie.

Vintage

Q&A

ABOVE
The author admiring a pristine pair of 1970s Diane von Furstenberg sunglasses, at Playclothes, in Studio City, which she's been frequenting religiously since high school.

LEFT
The author tries on a delicately veiled 1930s hat at Playclothes, surrounded by the boutique's always dazzling selection of baubles, beads, and pretty things.

PLAYCLOTHES

Owner Wanda Soileau calls Playclothes a "vintage living store," and that's precisely what it is. It's a 3,500-sq.-ft. vintage apparel and home décor boutique, located in what was once the historic Moorpark Pharmacy, from which it still features all the original 1940s neon pharmacy signs and fixtures. Soileau has brilliantly curated the space like a mini department store, stocked to the rafters with primo vintage steals, like women's and men's apparel from the Victorian era to the 1980s, shoes, hats, jewelry, collectibles, antique textiles, and twentieth-century home furnishings. Everything is in stellar condition, a large portion of it dead stock, and the prices are fab, rarely if ever exceeding $250. Basically, you can make over your entire life in one stop! Because there is so much wonderful merchandise, shopping at Playclothes is like an adventure, where old steamer trunks are filled with hundreds of silk scarves, dressing rooms are decorated like French boudoirs, and there is sparkly costume jewelry strewn everywhere. With something dazzling to be found around every corner, Playclothes is a favorite shopping spot for serious collectors, as well as TV and film costumers. This is where Kim Basinger's '40s gowns for the film *L.A. Confidential* came from, as well as Nicole Kidman's '50s dresses for the film version of *Bewitched*. There is even an adorable children's section and an incredibly swank men's department, which is so handsomely displayed that it actually makes me wish I were a dude. They've got dead-stock, snap-button Western shirts, '40s film noir-worthy suits, fedora hats, mod mohair skinny pants, alligator shoes, Beatle boots, James Dean-style '50s windbreakers, hand-painted ties, and all sorts of hep cat rockabilly wear. And if you've ever wondered where Bob Dylan buys his cool gabardine jackets, or Kid Rock gets his rhinestoned Western Nudie suits, now you know.

1422 Moorpark St., Studio City
(818) 755-9559
vintageplayclothes.com

SCAVENGERS PARADISE

Located in a magnificent old church, they sell an awesome array of salvaged architectural elements, antiques, religious statues, and carved wooden doors. In the past, I've even seen actual antique confessionals on sale here and giant hand-painted wall murals of nude Art Nouveau women rescued from a dilapidated burlesque house. Their items run a bit on the bizarre side, but that's what I love about it. Whenever I'm in need of an original 1920s claw-foot bathtub, a large wooden bar saved from a demolished '50s restaurant depicting the Roman Empire, or a large-scale replica of a pirate ship, I come here.

5453 Satsuma Ave., North Hollywood
(818) 761-5257
scavengersparadise.com

SHERMAN OAKS ANTIQUE MALL

Get lost in a maze of over 100 individually curated booths filled with wacky vintage finds and tchotchkes. This is the perfect place for a day of digging, where you can find great designer costume jewelry, vintage Hollywood memorabillia, records, jadeite and milk glass kitchenware, kitschy toys like Howdy Doody dolls, Bakelite radios, and tin lunch boxes. They also have a great selection of books on collecting specific vintage items.

14034 Ventura Blvd., Sherman Oaks
(818) 906-0338
soantiquemall.com

SHERMAN OAKS CASTLE PARK

A funky 1970s miniature golf course with candyland and gingerbread houses, huge fountains, wacky boathouses, giant tulip lamps, and pastel painted kitsch as far as the eye can see. It's the perfect setting for a funny birthday party, or an old-fashioned date. Pretend you don't know how to swing and let him put his arms around you. It may sound cheesy, but anything goes in this hokey fantasyland designed to look like the grounds of a medieval castle. There's a classic '80s-style video game arcade with skee-ball and the heavenly scent of churros wafting through the air. They even sport batting cages if you feel like hitting something. Wanna go back to high school in an instant? I've got your time machine right here.

4989 Sepulveda Blvd., Sherman Oaks
(818) 756-9459
laparks.org/shermanoaks_castlepk

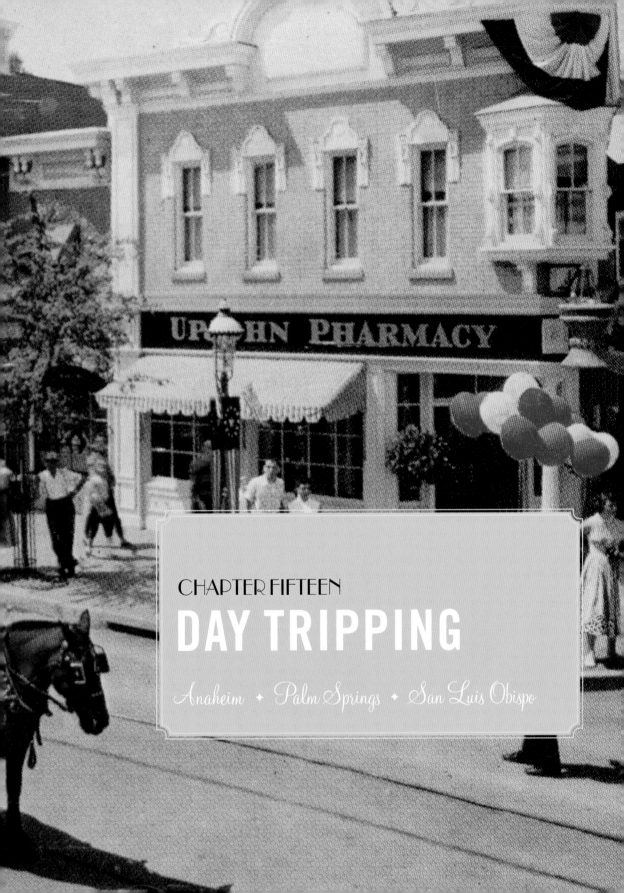

CHAPTER FIFTEEN

DAY TRIPPING

Anaheim ✦ *Palm Springs* ✦ *San Luis Obispo*

Let's split L.A. for a day or two, shall we? I mean, I know it's positively beaming with endless glamour and charm, but there are a few nearby respites that are much too marvelously vintagey and fun to pass up. All the following locales are reachable by automobile within four hours, and each is perfect for a one- to two-day vacay.

Located in the O.C. (yes, the same one from the show), it's only about 45 minutes south of L.A. and is a theme park wonderland of kitschy motels, and, as everybody knows by now, it's Gwen Stefani's hometown.

DISNEYLAND

For many cultured adults, the idea of visiting the "Happiest Place on Earth" creates horrible images in your mind of gluttonous tourists consuming tacky souvenirs while wearing potato-sack-sized logo T-shirts. Yes, while that's all true, if you have the power to block out the bratty kids and pushy parents, you can have one of the most magical days ever! D-Land has recently hit its 50th golden anniversary, so it's the perfect time for vintage style fanatics to pay homage to this visual "Fantasyland" of mod design. It's full of '50s pastel dreaminess, fabulous faux-Victoriana, medieval madness, and Day-Glo psychedelia (which is why you'll frequently see ravers and hippie kids strolling around wide-eyed on hallucinogenics here). And though Disneyland is sadly into updating, hundreds of Walt's original concepts remain perfectly preserved, as if it were an outdoor museum of kitsch. Since 1955, Disneyland's imagineers have flourished with groovy architectural ideas, and more astute aesthetes will notice that these well-schooled designers took inspiration from not only classical and Baroque painters, but from the surrealists (hello, Dalí!). In Disneyland's

INSIDE SCOOP

No need to feel overwhelmed at the enormity of the park; detailed maps are given as you enter. If you want to skip the nouveau stuff and experience all the best vintage Disney in a day, don't pass up the following rides and attractions
(in order of my favorites).
See page 207–209.

formative years, Walt would accompany his artists around the globe in search of inspiration for the park, resulting in rides that are culturally and historically researched and meticulously detailed. These memorable and beloved attractions are actually capable of taking you to another world, which is the intent of any great architect. Many icons have played in the magic kingdom, including Sofia Loren, Muhammad Ali, and Elizabeth Taylor. (Taylor even had her 60th birthday party here, with a display of lavender fireworks to match her eyes.) Andy Warhol also spent the day here in 1963, insisting he couldn't return to N.Y. without experiencing it.

IT'S A SMALL WORLD

Follow the magical tick-tock of the happy face grandfather clock that echoes throughout Fantasyland, and you'll find an extraordinary pastel castle with unicorn topiaries and a blue moat that takes you on a musical, multicultural tour of the world in a tiny fiberglass boat. The ride has a facade that is reminiscent of a castle in Candyland as painted by Piet Mondrian. It was designed in 1966 by Disney's most brilliant animator and conceptual artist, Mary Blair. She designed the ride as an idealistic view of a peaceful planet of friendly, big-eyed children, all coming together to sing the song "It's a Small World After All." (I apologize in advance about the fact that this song will be stuck in your head for the rest of the day. Please don't let this dissuade you from taking this whimsical ride.) The "Mary Blair kids," as Disney called them, from each country are represented here in different vignettes of animatronic puppets, from cowboys in America to miniature Cleopatras in Egypt. It displays a glorious, Day-Glo naïveté that is often sadly lacking in the real world in which we live.

PIRATES OF THE CARIBBEAN

This is a dark and spooky underground boat ride through vignettes of lifelike pirates pillaging through villages, wenches being auctioned off to the highest bidder, and battles on the sea—there's even an animatronic Captain Jack Sparrow, and all the while the characters sing the catchy theme song, "Yo Ho, Yo Ho, a pirate's life for me!" There is also a treasure room scene which so inspired me as a little girl that I recently designed a jewelry collection based on its dazzling beauty, after experiencing the joy of the ride where "dead men tell no tales."

New Orleans Square

HAUNTED MANSION

Experience death, Disney-style. Queue up in a make-believe cemetery with witty epitaphs, and let Victorian-garbed morticians lead you to tour inside a legendary and lively haunted house. Hop into a cozy "Doom Buggy" and encounter a "moon hanging over a dead oak tree as swinging spooks arrive for a midnight spree," as the groovy theme song suggests. There are also "grim grinning ghosts who come out to socialize"—right before your very eyes! If you were ever a goth in high school, a fan of Vincent Price movies, or relished reading Edgar Allan Poe stories, this is the perfect ghoulish ride for you.

New Orleans Square

SLEEPING BEAUTY'S CASTLE

When I was a little girl, my parents would torture us by taking their sweet time walking down Main Street while snacking and shopping, but at the end, we would get our first glimpse of glorious Sleeping Beauty's Castle. It was the sign in our hearts that we had finally arrived at the Fantasyland gates, and that endless fun awaited us in all the surrounding lands. To this day I still get that same excited feeling. Besides that, architecturally it's überbrilliant. The castle's facade was inspired by Walt's obsession with the eccentric King Ludwig II of Bavaria's neo-Romanesque "Neuschwanstein," which is straight out of a surreal, real-life fairy tale.

Fantasyland

PREVIOUS SPREAD
Disneyland's cotton candy-colored attraction, Main Street, U.S.A., which first debuted in 1955.

LEFT
The whimsical facade to Disneyland's "It's a Small World" ride, designed by the brilliant artist and animator, Mary Blair, in 1966.

TIP
Throw a coin into the wishing well to the right of the castle entrance and hear it echo the 1930s tune "I'm Wishing" from *Snow White*.

MATTERHORN BOBSLEDS

Built in 1959 and based on the Matterhorn of the Swiss Alps, this was the world's very first steel multicar roller coaster. This coaster swooshes you in circles around hairpin turns hugging a mammoth ice-covered faux-Alpine mountain, at racing toboggan-style speeds. You sit tandem-style in the bobsleds, and are assaulted by a funny yodeling soundtrack, happy engineers in lederhosen and a finale of a screaming abominable animatronic yeti with red glowing eyes.

Fantasyland

SPACE MOUNTAIN

Disneyland's fastest roller coaster that shoots you in stomach-twisting circles around outer space in total darkness—except for trippy astral projections of the planets all around you. My only gripe is that the geeky surf-inspired music the Space Mountain provides doesn't fit the spacey mood. So I suggest bringing your iPod along and giving the ride your own futuristic '80s soundtrack, like Kraftwerk's "It's More Fun to Compute" or Giorgio Moroder's "Faster Than the Speed of Love." Those perfectly accompany the otherworldly electro-ride you're in for.

Tomorrowland

20TH CENTURY MUSIC COMPANY

For music geeks, Disneyland even has a tiny record shop where you can order custom CDs and make your own compilations of rare vintage tunes from Disney rides and film scores. Much of the music in this store is hard to find, with limited pressings, and unavailable anywhere outside the park.

Main Street, U.S.A.

MAIN STREET CINEMA

I vote this as cutest vintage location in all of Disneyland. It's a tiny, old-fashioned movie house that screens 1920s Mickey Mouse cartoons, incuding Mickey and Minnie's debut in the 1928 cartoon *Steamboat Willie*. This cartoon was the first ever to feature synchronized sound. There's never anyone in here, so if on a date, it's the perfect place to kiss without freaking out any kids.

Main Street, U.S.A.

SILHOUETTE STUDIO

Located on Main Street, you can have an artist perfectly cut your profile in only minutes—eyelashes, eyeglasses, and all. They then add it to filigree-adorned white paper and place it neatly in a Victorian-style oval-shaped black frame. Et voilà... hipster wall art! Just be sure to let the artist know how much you admire his work and he'll sometimes take requests to add any accessory you want. I have asked for everything from Jackie O sunglasses to '70s floppy hats, but when I last asked what the most unusual request anyone has ever made was, the artist said, "a man came to Disneyland once just to get a silhouette of himself holding a toaster." They're never judgmental and I love that.

Main Street, U.S.A.

THE CANDY PALACE

Since 1955, this original confectionery on Main Street has been selling a Technicolor array of retro sweets, like saltwater taffy, foil-wrapped chocolates, and giant rainbow lollipops, to make you feel like you just stepped into Willy Wonka's sugar-dusted playground. They also have demonstrations on the artistry of making fudge, caramel apples, truffles, and other cavity-causing delectables.

Main Street, U.S.A.

THE DISNEY GALLERY

Disneyland even has an art scene. It's housed above the Pirates of the Caribbean ride, and this gorgeous gallery displays priceless archival paintings, original models, and exhibits of original Disney concept art, as well as limited-edition prints of the original '50s and '60s posters for the rides, that you can purchase.

New Orleans Square

ALSO BE SURE TO VISIT:

PETER PAN'S FLIGHT

Soar high over Neverland while viewing magical detailed miniature dioramas below you to the film's dreamy "I Can Fly" soundtrack.

Fantasyland

ALICE IN WONDERLAND

Ride a clumsy Day-Glo caterpillar through a hookah smoke haze with the singing daisies, the perennially late March Hare, and of course, the Queen of Hearts (all courtesy of the brilliant vision of Disney's '60s animator, Mary Blair).

Fantasyland

MAD HATTER TEA PARTY

Take a spin in a psychedelically painted teacup—but make sure you visit before you eat to avoid any nasty queasiness.

Fantasyland

CASEY JR. CIRCUS TRAIN

Choo-choo through miniature towns while riding in a closed monkey cage, while Casey toots "I think I can, I think I can."

Fantasyland

THE GIBSON GIRL ICE CREAM PARLOUR

It features great faux-Art Nouveau art everywhere, a giant jade glass elephant, the heavenly scent of waffle cones in the air, and the best damn ice cream sundaes ever.

Main Street, U.S.A.

THE PENNY ARCADE

They have a vintage fortune-telling machine that features the gypsy, Esmeralda, as well as original silent comedies you can watch through Mutoscopes (flip-book viewing devices developed in the late 1800s).

Main Street, U.S.A.

Palm Springs

If you're looking for the midcentury mothership, you'll find it has landed in the middle of the California desert. Palm Springs, located in the Coachella Valley, is only about two hours from L.A. (or much quicker, depending on how you drive), and has always been my favorite weekend getaway, where I can put on banana-scented Coppertone, soak in the natural hot springs, smell the desert flowers that scent the warm air, and of course...vintage shop like there's no tomorrow.

During Hollywood's golden age, P.S. became the playground for the rich and infamous (they even have their own "walk of stars"). Howard Hughes was one of the first moguls to keep his mistresses hidden away here, as did certain enigmatic American presidents. Stars have always loved to come here to relax, and early residents include Lucy and Desi, Carmen Miranda, Elvis, Sinatra, Sammy Davis Jr., Bob Hope, Lana Turner, Marilyn Monroe, Ann Miller, and Liberace (which is probably why all the thrift stores here are filled with so many scores)!

This is also where the architectural style known as Desert Modernism was born. And you'll spot primo examples of it as soon as you enter town, whether by air (Donald Wexler designed the Palm Springs Airport) or by road (Albert Frey's winglike Tramway Lift Station is now P.S.'s visitor center). The Aerial Tramway, a popular P.S. attraction, is located behind the visitor center, and lifts you high above San Jacinto, providing incredible desert views from the observation deck. P.S., I love you!

PALM SPRINGS MODERN ARCHITECTURAL TOURS

P.S. has one of the largest concentrations of modern architecture in the United States. Mod architecture enthusiasts should most definitely attend one of Robert Imber's highly informed 3-hour, 35-mile chauffeured tours of these famous structures. He explains in delicious detail the stark beauty of architects Albert Frey's and Richard Neutra's work, as well as the importance of Bob Alexander, who brought mod architecture to the masses in the '60s and designed over 2,200 of these desert homes. Many of the homes have swanky sunken rooms (made of real desert rocks) and retractable glass walls. Imber provides you with an instant, in-depth vintage education, and you can also view homes impossible to see on your own, like the 1968 Arthur Elrod house, built by architect John Lautner, which was used in the James Bond film *Diamonds Are Forever*.

(760) 318-6118
psmoderntours@aol.com

ANTIQUE MALL

The Antique Mall has hundreds of individually curated booths showcasing both extraordinary midcentury furniture and funny '70s pieces of kitsch. They sell designer and non, funky junk and real jewels, tiki mugs, and clear lucite swag lamps straight out of *Boogie Nights*. There are kooky surprises around every corner. There's a huge assortment of '60s pop knickknacks as well as more serious collectibles, like an Eero Saarinen table and a mauve leather wraparound couch (which would go for over $2,000 in L.A. but was listed here at a steal for $1,600). There are two locations—both are fabulous.

2500 N. Palm Canyon Drive #B1
(760) 864-9390 (Palm Springs)
68-401 E. Pal Canyon Dr.
(760) 202-0215 (Cathedral City)

TIP

If you're a modern-design fanatic, visit during Palm Springs Modernism Week in February.
palmspringsmodernism.com

They sell vintage decorative accessories for the modern home with a fanciful twist. A great place to find pottery from the 1930s to the 1980s, glass vases in a rainbow of colors, figurines, Bjorn Wiinblad ceramics, Rosenthal porcelain, midcentury sculptures, metal works of art, hard-to-find enameled copperware by Annemarie Davidson, and a fun selection of '70s owl necklaces. Proprietors James Elliot-Bishop and Patrick Barry have created the most wonderfully whimsical home décor shopping experience in Palm Springs. This is where décor wunderkind Jonathan Adler found many fabulous pieces for his eye-popping Parker Hotel (p. 216). All items are priced very reasonably, so you can actually afford to take home something you adore. Items here are so warmly curated that it becomes hard to decide what I can leave behind without being heartbroken. Forget the sunshine and clean air; this shop will keep me coming back to P.S. always. Located in the Galleria.

457 N. Palm Canyon Dr. #3, Palm Springs
gmcb.com/shop

MELVYN'S RESTAURANT & LOUNGE

Melvyn's is located at the historic Ingelside Inn where the guest book includes signatures from Greta Garbo, Salvador Dalí, Liza Minnelli, and John Travolta. This swanky boîte was also a favorite of Cher, Marlon Brando, Goldie Hawn, and Sinatra. Try the clams casino and a dry martini—the bartenders make the best in town. Originally built in 1935, the tuxedo-clad waiters, white tablecloths, and ornate chandeliers recall another glitzy era gone by, and it's a blast!

200 W. Ramon Rd., Palm Springs
(760) 325-0046
inglesideinn.com

ANGEL VIEW THRIFT SHOPS

With 10 locations all over the desert, this is the mama of all resale shops. The chain consistently delivers a mix of flash gear and wearable garb—and everything is at dirt-cheap prices. I spotted a sequin-covered poncho for only $8, piles of ladylike vintage leather clutch purses, and perfect '80s Valley Girl heels for $15. Vintaging at these locations does involve a little digging—so they're not for the prima donna with a case of OCD.

462 N. Indian Canyon Dr., Palm Springs
(760) 323-8771

DAZZLES

Dazzles sells Art Deco and retro home décor—and a "dazzling" selection of vintage costume jewelry. Owner Mike Sauls has been collecting since the first retro boom in the '80s, and I've been buying fun accoutrements from him since my formative vintage years when he had an awesome boutique in Studio City. When arriving in town, this is always the first shop that causes me to slam on the brakes. For a serious costume jewelry collector (like me), his selection makes you feel as if you've died and gone to Bakelite heaven! I last picked up a surrealist-style black and gold ceramic horse pin for $45. My sister found another pony pin—this one also from the '40s but handcrafted of stuffed and stitched brown leather with a ribbon tail and tiny brass details for $38. His prices are quite fair, running from $20 to very expensive, and everything is curated in collections (rhinestones, metal enamel floral brooches, plastics, copper) so it's not too overwhelming to the eye. Mike says of his shop: "I always think that if this store would've been here when Carmen Miranda had her house in Palm Springs, she would've loved it!" He also specializes in vintage retro patio furniture, box purses, Hawaiian shirts, cocktail caddies, and anything to help further "dazzle" your vintage home. If baubles are your bag, this boutique is a must-visit!

1035 N. Palm Canyon Dr., Palm Springs
(760) 327-1446

INSIDE SCOOP

P.S. is supercasual about punctuality, and many of the following locations have seasonal hours, so I suggest calling before you visit.

THE FRIPPERY

Owner Chander Erickson has thankfully opened Palm Springs' first real designer-vintage boutique, filled with select vintage clothing and accessories for men and women. The décor alone makes this boutique a total shopping experience. The shop is designed with Deco-inspired silver '70s Pop Art wallpaper, hand-painted '60s dollybird hat stands, and glowing white lacquer paneling. Find Pucci dresses, big Jackie O sunglasses for $75, stretchy cinch belts, Enid Collins box purses, '70s men's attire, leisure styles, and sexy mod velvet suits—perfect to wear for summery nighttime cocktails at the Parker. Located in the Galleria.

The Frippery at the 111 Antique Mall
2005 N. Palm Canyon Dr. #11, Palm Springs
(760) 864-9390
thefrippery.com

INSET
The Frippery's whimsical logo was taken from the pattern on the store's groovy 1970s silver foil wallpaper.

KORAKIA PENSIONE

If a seductive sheik, or better yet, Rudolph Valentino lured you to his exotic casbah, it probably wouldn't look much different than Korakia. It's a historic Moroccan breakfast inn built in 1924 by Scottish painter Gordon Coutts, inspired by his travels to Tangier. It is set against the stunning backdrop of the San Jacinto mountains, and over the years it has welcomed guests as eclectic as Sir Winston Churchill, Joel Grey, and Jennifer Jason Leigh. Stay in their glamorous bohemian bungalows that were at the heart of Palm Springs' literary and art community. I've had many magical summer nights here, floating in the black-bottom pool as I was served sangria under the stars. For guests, they also screen classic movies at night against one of the villa walls, like *How to Marry a Millionaire*, where you sit on charmingly rickety old chairs on what doubles as a boccie ball court.

257 Patencio Rd., Palm Springs
(760) 864-6411
korakia.com

LA QUINTA RESORT & CLUB

Originally built in 1926, it's a popular desert resort that has been remodeled over the years, but there are still many original Spanish bungalows you can stay in for the vintage La Quinta experience. Diane Keaton is a fan, and so was film director Frank Capra, who wrote most of his classic scripts in his "lucky" bungalow here, including *It Happened One Night* (which won the Academy Award in 1934), *Mr. Smith Goes to Washington*, *You Can't Take It with You*, and *It's a Wonderful Life*.

49-499 Eisenhower Dr., La Quinta
(800) 598-3828
laquintaresort.com

INSIDE SCOOP

Even if you happen to be a starving artiste, like every good vintage boho should be, even the chicest Palm Springs hotels slash their prices during the scorching summer months, when the town becomes a ghostlike oasis.

LAS CASUELAS TERRAZA

At the center of the Palm Canyon strip sits this bright, colorful, and slightly tacky landmark. Originally opened in 1958, it's gone from a pequito joint to a huge rowdy Spanish "MexiCantina." They serve authentic food in huge portions and waitresses wear shoulder-baring embroidered senorita dresses. The outside bar is nearly 100 years old with a crazy thatched roof. You can sometimes catch great mariachi music and unfortunately, bad bar rock. Despite its touristy crowd, I've had many fun, sunburnt, sloshy evenings on the patio. Great for too many margaritas and yummy, crispy tacos. Reservations recommended.

222 S. Palm Canyon Dr., Palm Springs
(760) 325-2794
lascasuelasterraza.com

MODERN WAY

This shop carries furniture from the '50s to the '70s, unique mushroom-shaped lamps, abstract flokati and Danish rugs, fab objets d'art, leather cocoon chairs designed by Joe Colombo, and a '60s Pierre Cardin bedroom set ($6,500) that was straight out of *Beyond the Valley of the Dolls*. There's also a great selection of Hollywood Regency-style furnishings culled from celebrity Palm Springs estates, like Danny Thomas' dreamy pink tufted bed ($1,200). They also have a mod acid-green Arthur Elrod-designed couch ($2,200) and huge Regency-style country club doors, and fab iron patio sets. Things I was personally drooling over were the spectacularly sexy clear lucite stereo cabinet ($975), and the amazing original Igor Pantuhoff painting of a nude, big-eyed blonde ($1,500).

2755 N. Palm Canyon Dr., Palm Springs
(760) 320-5455
psmodernway.com

MOVIE COLONY HOTEL

A streamlined, modern masterpiece of a small hotel, with silver screen set-worthy décor. Designed by famed modernist architect Albert Frey in 1935, it resembles a swanky ocean liner stranded in the middle of the desert. It's been gorgeously restored, making it as fit for today's Hollywood elite as it was for yesterday's. This is the kind of classy joint where you can imagine Joan Crawford doing laps in the pool or Cary Grant waiting for his date in the lobby in a white dinner jacket. Even Jim Morrison loved it in the '60s. Don't forget to go at happy hour when the Movie Colony's bar serves their signature "Dean Martinis."

726 N. Indian Canyon Dr., Palm Springs
(888) 953-5700
moviecolonyhotel.com

PALM CANYON GALLERIA

Located in the best little vintage-filled courtyard in P.S., this serious vintage collectors' emporium is housed in a historic 1941 building as exquisite as its contents. The shop is filled with objets d'art, out-of-print design books, sophisticated Art Deco and modern furniture, antique steamer trunks, killer lamps, and home accessories like apothecary jars, seashells, and jazzy authentic '50s Jackson Pollock-inspired oil paintings.

457 N. Palm Canyon Dr., Palm Springs
(760) 323-4576

PALM SPRINGS DESERT MUSEUM

This is an awesome collection of contemporary art housed in a stark yet earthy space designed in 1976 by famed modern architect E. Stewart Williams. They've recently had wonderful retrospectives on potter Beatrice Wood, and landscape photographer Ansel Adams.

101 Museum Dr., Palm Springs
(760) 325-7186
psmuseum.org

PALM SPRINGS FOLLIES

A P.S. tradition, it is classic vaudeville, with a kick line of long-legged vintage lovelies, performing Sally Rand-style fan dances and geriatric Busby Berkeley routines. By "vintage" I mean senior, and they are totally amazing! The costumes for the "pretty girl" number are bedazzled and feathered Bob Mackie-esque creations with 10-foot-high feather headdresses that not even I could balance. My favorite part is when they are introduced onstage with their show biz résumés, climaxing, in a drum roll, with their age (all of them are over 60!). This is high MGM-style camp, fully loaded with a guy who spins plates and a ventriloquist act involving a Hispanic parrot named Francisco.

128 S. Palm Canyon Dr., Palm Springs
(760) 327-0225
psfollies.com

THE PARKER

Originally opened in 1959 as one of California's first Holiday Inns, it was under the ownership of movie cowboy Gene Autry in the '60s as his Melody Ranch, and in the '80s TV personality Merv Griffin turned it into the Givenchy Resort. Now the groovy Parker Meridien hotel has been blissfully redesigned in what my sister Lizzie calls "perfect high-brow hodgepodge," by ceramist and interior décor wunderkind Jonathan Adler. It's a visual delight from the moment

you enter. From the Roxy Music soundtrack piped through the speakers, to the rare Guy Bourdin books stacked around the lobby, to the mod kids canoodling on the wicker swing chairs. Pop Art icon Tom Wesselmann's giant Lucite wall art from his '70s Smoker series hangs above the main staircase, the perfect statement: giant, lush red lips with a smoky cigarette hanging out of them Bette Davis-style. Not that I'm saying you should take up smoking while staying at the Parker, but indulge a bit. Have three crème brûlées, have one too many White Russians, get too much sun, charge really pricey beauty treatments to your room and deal with the bill later. Have some decadent fun for a change! It's a 13-acre resort designed in mod Moroccan-inspired, Technicolorful '60s style, catering to an eclectic clientele of hipsters, rock 'n' rollers, fashionistas, and the country club set. Every detail here has been brilliantly designed by Adler, including the copper conversational fire pit in the lobby, the poolside lemonade stand, the pétanque and croquet courts, the silver disco wall-papered gift shop, and the striped and tassled pool umbrellas. I also adore that on a map of the grounds they actually refer to a part of the garden as a "hookah chill-out zone."

As for the dining experience, you simply *can't* leave Palm Springs without trying Mister Parker's for dinner, dessert, or a sexy nightcap. Enter through the Day-Glo psychedelic painted door with the hand pointing you inside, push aside the black velvet curtains, and say hello to the wonderful and elegant maître d' Michael Crawford, who is so handsome, he's straight out of an early '60s *Esquire* advertisement for expensive gin. Not only is the food to die for, but it has positively the best interior ambience of any place I've ever dined. The chairs and carpets are upholstered with mismatching vintage Pop Art fabrics, and the dark-wood-paneled walls are adorned with pricey Pop Art,

Ava in the poolhouse. It was also wonderful to see young people drinking martinis around Frankie's piano-shaped pool. It is said that in the afternoons, Sinatra would raise a Jack Daniel's flag on top of the house to signal neighbors that it was cocktail time. Such rituals continued until 1957, when he divorced Gardner and moved to Rancho Mirage. When Sinatra first arrived in P.S., he heralded in the town's most swingin' years, and was responsible for luring more talent to the desert than you can shake a shish kebab at; which is why all over town you will see so many landmarks bearing his name, including Frank Sinatra Dr.

1145 E. Via Colusa, Palm Springs

TWO BUNCH PALMS

Palm Springs got its name from the towering palms and natural hot springs, and the desert's most famous samplings of these natural wonders are here at this resort. Two Bunch Palms is a classic spa hotel with an Old Hollywood allure, a rich hippie vibe, and a seductively sinister history. It was originally built in the 1920s by gangster Al Capone as a hideout for him and his girlfriend, silent-film actress Gladys Walton. When Capone's Hollywood friends, like Charlie Chaplin, Theda Bara, and Marion Davies, wanted to relax in the hot springs and drink illegal hooch during Prohibition, they came here—far away from the cameras and the cops. What is now Two Bunch's dining room was once Capone's private casino and sometime brothel for visiting stars and politicians. It features faux-Tiffany swag lamps and a great collection of original Hurrell movie star portraits. Even the bulletproof Deusenberg coupe Capone had custom built for Gladys is on display in front of the hotel. Gladys' son John Walton acts as tour guide, always happy to tell new guests about the joint's wild jazz-age history. This retreat is like a sleepaway camp for grown-ups, offering organic dining and cozy lodging in bungalows that feature Art Nouveau stained-glass windows. It's most known for its healing mineral hot spring grottos, which are beneficial for your skin and countless ailments. You can also hike the nature trails, get an underwater Watsu massage, Egyptian-clay body wrap, or take a detoxifying mud bath (as seen in Robert Altman's *The Player*). Nicholson and Streisand are fans. It's much more private and Zen than other hotels (they play quiet Indian sitar music everywhere); signs encourage you to whisper while bunnies hop around the grass, and actual roadrunners sprint by your feet on the pathways.

67425 Two Bunch Palms Trail, Desert Hot Springs
(800) 472-4334
twobunchpalms.com

like David Bailey's portraits of The Beatles, mixed in with humorously bad garage sale finds. There are '70s Lucite chandeliers and a white grand piano. It's where Peter Sellers and Leigh Taylor-Young would go for a casserole while stoned in the 1968 film *I Love You, Alice B. Toklas!* It also reminds me of the groovy nightclub where Natalie Wood dances the pony in the 1969 film *Bob & Carol & Ted & Alice*. This is essentially the desert's Disneyland.

Le Parker Meridien Palm Springs
4200 E. Palm Canyon Dr., Palm Springs
(866) 559-3821
(760) 770-5000
theparkerpalmsprings.com

SINATRA'S TWIN PALMS ESTATE

Dubbed "Twin Palms" for two trees that still stand in the yard, architect and "Desert Modern" master E. Stewart Williams custom built this killer domain in 1947 for Ol' Blue Eyes himself and his second wife, the glamorous Ava Gardner. Lana Turner and Garbo were house guests at Twin Palms, and I was lucky to be invited once to a party at this legendary home, where I was beyond delighted when touching up my lipstick in the very same mirror Frank had added for

VICEROY

This is an old Hollywood hideaway, with a refreshing, '40s-style color palette of white, yellow, and black. Interior designer Kelly Wearstler revamped the interior of the hotel and the style evokes the days when Hollywood and Palm Springs basked in their own glamour. First opened in 1933, the hotel was a favorite film industry haunt for stars like Tyrone Power, Errol Flynn, Joan Crawford, Lucille Ball, Bing Crosby, and Orson Welles. Today, anyone would be easily attracted to the overgrown gardens, the abundance of orange and lemon trees. white roses, and bright bougainvillea. The hotel was renovated in a modern Hollywood Regency-style (the style of glitzy décor popularized in the 1960s), where designers took modest boxy bungalows and gave them a more important pedigree by adding whimsical and inventive French-style facades. All of the furniture has been custom designed by Kelly, along with the black-and-white curtains that envelop the bungalows. And the black-and-white leaf wallpaper and white lacquer cabinets evoke the spirit of Kelly's design idols, Tony Duquette and David Hicks. Cast-iron whippets stand guard at the entrance of every villa to keep the guests safe.

415 South Belardo Rd., Palm Springs
(760) 320-4117
viceroypalmsprings.com

BEAT HOTEL

This cool 1957 motel with eight rooms and a pool has been restored to its original Beatnik-style glory by Steven Lowe, a one-time writing collaborator and friend of William Burroughs (author of *Naked Lunch*). Lowe has made this cool Desert Hot Springs getaway into not only a hotel, but a mini-museum of rare Beat-generation artifacts. His collection, which he's always happy to share with those interested to learn, includes many of Burroughs' original paintings and first editions, drawings by Allen Ginsberg, art by Robert Rauschenberg and Keith Haring. The Beat even boasts a mini library where you can borrow books by writers like Kerouac during your stay, and a vintage typewriter in every room for when inspiration calls.

67840 Hacienda Ave., Desert Hot Springs
(760) 288-2280
dhsbeathotel.com

INSIDE SCOOP

On the way to the Madonna Inn, you will pass the legendary Hearst Castle, built by newspaper magnate William Randolph Hearst for him and his longtime love, actress Marion Davies, to play king and queen. This house is stunning and ornate—and still filled with his lifetime collection of mind-boggling priceless antiques and architectural details.

San Luis Obispo

MADONNA INN

Having nothing at all to do with the Material Girl, it's a giant roadside motel—one that must be seen to be believed, where each of the 109 rooms has been decorated in a different off-the-wall theme and psychedelic color scheme. Though it's about a four-hour drive from Los Angeles along the Pacific Coast Highway, if you're to ask any in-the-know L.A. vintage lover where to find the most tripped-out, gaudy-as-all-get-out, wild weekend destination, they will inevitably send you to the Madonna Inn. Built in 1958 by a highway contractor, Alex Madonna, who assigned his wife Phyllis decorating duties with no prior experience, this is a palace of kitsch never to be outdone. She knew how to mix leopard fur with polka dots, with panache, and that's talent! Every inch of this place has been tricked-out, from the patterned carpets in the rooms, to the rock waterfall loo in the men's room, to the pink sugar on the coffee shop tables. Even deciding which room you will stay in is a blast. You'll have to choose between the "Caveman Room" and "Krazy Dazy," or between "Gypsy Rock" and "Sir Walter Raleigh." They have two restaurants, the Copper Café, which is an old-school coffee shop (take a slice of apple pie back to your room!), and the Gold Rush Steak House, which is a froufrou fantasyland of fuchsia tufted-leather booths, heart-shaped chairs, cotton candy-pink flocked velvet wallpaper, and giant gold cherub chandeliers.

100 Madonna Rd., San Luis Obispo
(805) 543-3000
madonnainn.com

TOP
Anyone with a yen for whacked-out, kitschy vintage décor simply must experience the décor of the Madonna Inn's Gold Rush Steak House at least once in their lifetime (you'll never look at colors the same way again).

BOTTOM
This is a view of "The Madonna Suite," Room 141, at the gloriously gaudy Madonna Inn Hotel in San Louis Obispo.

CHAPTER SIXTEEN

FADE OUT

A love letter to L.A.'s lost landmarks

We have visited some divine shopping spots and landmark locales, both hidden and well-known, but sadly, many of the places I'd love to have sent you to are no longer gracing the Los Angeles landscape. One mission I had by writing this book was to bring awareness and appreciation of this city's gorgeous structures that are, or may one day be, in danger of a beastly bulldozer.

There have been countless landmarks tragically destroyed in recent years. Joni Mitchell so eloquently sang, "they paved paradise and put up a parking lot," about the destruction of silent-film actress Alla Nazimova's Garden of Allah Hotel. Here is a list of locations I would have been delighted to have sent you to, or to have visited myself, but was born too late. To paraphrase a line from *Blade Runner*, a film darkly depicting the future of Our City of Angels, while these lost structures may have disappeared "like tears in rain," they will not be

ABOVE
Pickfair, the lavish home of silent-screen legends Mary Pickford and Doublas Fairbanks, was the closest thing that Hollywood had to a royal fairy-tale castle (it was even surrounded by a moat). Sadly, it was demolished when Mary relocated to heaven in 1979.

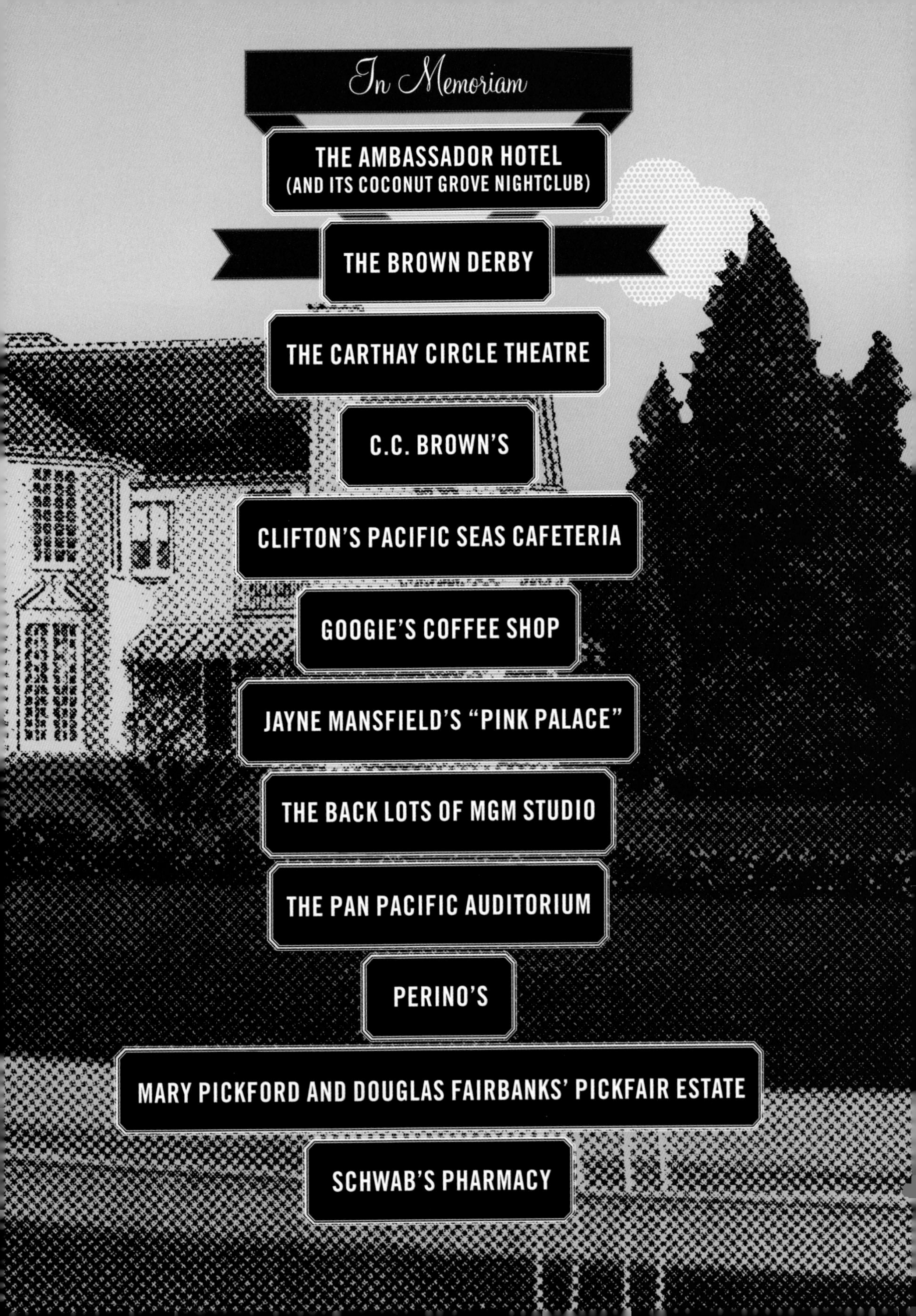

In Memoriam

THE AMBASSADOR HOTEL
(AND ITS COCONUT GROVE NIGHTCLUB)

THE BROWN DERBY

THE CARTHAY CIRCLE THEATRE

C.C. BROWN'S

CLIFTON'S PACIFIC SEAS CAFETERIA

GOOGIE'S COFFEE SHOP

JAYNE MANSFIELD'S "PINK PALACE"

THE BACK LOTS OF MGM STUDIO

THE PAN PACIFIC AUDITORIUM

PERINO'S

MARY PICKFORD AND DOUGLAS FAIRBANKS' PICKFAIR ESTATE

SCHWAB'S PHARMACY

Index

Page numbers in italics refer to illustrations